MYTHS AND LEGENDS SERIES

SPAIN
LEWIS SPENCE

THE CID BIDS FAREWELL TO HIS WIFE

Fr.

MYTHS AND LEGENDS SERIES

SPAIN

LEWIS SPENCE

WITH ILLUSTRATIONS FROM DRAWINGS AND FAMOUS PAINTINGS

STUDIO EDITIONS
LONDON

Previously published by George G Harrap & Co
This edition published 1993 by Studio Editions Ltd
Princess House, 50 Eastcastle Street
London W1N 7AP, England

ISBN 1 85891 042 0

Printed and bound in Great Britain
by The Bath Press

PREFACE

SINCE the days of Southey the romantic literature of Spain has not received from English writers and critics the amount of study and attention it undoubtedly deserves. In no European country did the seeds of Romance take root so readily or blossom so speedily and luxuriantly as in Spain, which perhaps left the imprint of its national character more deeply upon the literature of chivalry than did France or England. When we think of chivalry, do we not think first of Spain, of her age-long struggle against the pagan invaders of Europe, her sensitiveness to all that concerned personal and national honour, of the names of the Cid Campeador, Gayferos, and Gonzalvo de Cordova, gigantic shadows in harness, a pantheon of heroes, which the martial legends of few lands can equal and none surpass. The epic of our British Arthur, the French *chansons de gestes*, are indebted almost as much to folklore as to the imagination of the singers who first gave them literary shape. But in the romances of Spain we find that folklore plays an inconsiderable part, and that her chivalric fictions are either the offspring of historic happenings or of that brilliant and glowing imagination which illumines the whole expanse of Peninsular literature.

I have given more space to the proofs of connexion between the French *chansons de gestes* and the Spanish *cantares de gesta* than most of my predecessors who have written of Castilian romantic story. Indeed, with the exception of Mr Fitzmaurice Kelly, whose admirable work in the field of Spanish letters forms so happy an exception to our national neglect of a great literature,

5

Legends & Romances of Spain

I am aware of no English writer who has concerned himself with this subject. My own opinion regarding the almost total lack of Moorish influence upon the Spanish *romanceros* is in consonance with that of critics much better qualified to pass judgment upon such a question. But for my classification of the ballad I am indebted to no one, and this a long devotion to the study of ballad literature perhaps entitles me to make. I can claim, too, that my translations are not mere paraphrases, but provide renderings of tolerable accuracy.

I have made an earnest endeavour to provide English readers with a conspectus of Spanish romantic literature as expressed in its *cantares de gesta*, its chivalric novels, its *romanceros* or ballads, and some of its lighter aspects. The reader will find full accounts and summaries of all the more important works under each of these heads, many of which have never before been described in English.

If the perusal of this book leads to the more general study of the noble and useful Castilian tongue on the part of but a handful of those who read it, its making will have been justified. The real brilliance and beauty of these tales lie behind the curtains of a language unknown to most British people, and can only be liberated by the spell of study. This book contains merely the poor shadows and reflected wonders of screened and hidden marvels.

L. S.

EDINBURGH
June 1920

6

CONTENTS

ILLUSTRATIONS

CHAPTER I: THE SOURCES OF SPANISH ROMANCE

Romance, Romance, the songs of France,
The gestes of fair Britaine,
The legends of the sword and lance
That grew in Alemaine,
Pale at thy rich inheritance,
Thou splendour of old Spain!
Anon.

IF, spent with journeying, a stranger should seat himself in some garden in old Granada, and from beneath a tenting of citron and mulberry leaves open his ears to the melody of the waters of the City of Pomegranates and his spirit to the sorcery of its atmosphere, he will gladly believe that in the days when its colours were less mellow and its delicious air perhaps less reposeful the harps of its poets were the looms upon which the webs of romance were woven. Almost instinctively he will form the impression that the Spaniard, having regained this paradise after centuries of exile, and stirred by the enchanted echoes of Moorish music which still lingered there, was roused into passionate song in praise of those heroes of his race who had warred so ceaselessly and sacrificed so much to redeem it. But if he should climb the Sierra del Sol and pass through the enchanted chambers of the Alhambra as a child passes through the courts of dream, he will say in his heart that the men who builded these rooms from the rainbow and painted these walls from the palette of the sunset raised also the invisible but not less gorgeous palace of Spanish Romance.

Or if one, walking in the carven shadows of Cordova,

think on the mosque Maqsura, whose doors of Anda-
lusian brass opened to generations of poets and
astrologers, or on the palace of Azzahra, built of rose
and sea-coloured marbles rifled from the Byzantine
churches of Ifrikia, will he not believe that in this
city of shattered splendours and irretrievable spells
the passion-flower of Romance burst forth full-blown?

But we cannot trace the first notes of the forgotten
musics nor piece together the mosaic of broken har-
monies in the warm and sounding cities of the Saracens,
neither in "that mine of silk and silver," old Granada,
nor among the marble memories of Cordova, whose
market-place overflowed with the painted parchments
of Moorish song and science. We must turn our backs
on the scarlet southern land and ascend to the bare
heights of Castile and Asturias, where Christian Spain,
prisoned for half a thousand years upon a harsh and
arid plateau, and wrought to a high passion of sacrifice
and patriotism, burst into a glory of martial song, the
echoes of which resound among its mountains like
ghostly clarions on a field of old encounter.

Isolation and devotion to a national cause are more
powerful as incentives to the making of romance than
an atmosphere of Eastern luxuriance. The breasts of
these stern sierras were to give forth milk sweeter than
the wine of Almohaden, and song more moving if less
fantastic arose in Burgos and Carrión than ever inspired
the guitars of Granada. But the unending conflict of
Arab and Spaniard brought with it many interchanges
between the sensuous spirit of the South and the more
rugged manliness of the North, so that at last Saracen
gold damascened the steel of Spanish song, and the
nets of Eastern phantasy wound themselves about the

The Cradle of Spanish Song

Spanish soul. In a later day an openly avowed admiration for the art and culture of the Moslem leavened the ancient hate, and the Moorish cavalier imitated the chivalry, if not the verse, of the Castilian knight.[1]

The Cradle of Spanish Song

The homeland of Spanish tradition was indeed a fitting nursery for the race which for centuries contested every acre of the Peninsula with an enemy greatly more advanced in the art of warfare, if inferior in resolution and the spirit of unity. Among the flinty wastes of the north of Spain, which are now regarded as rich in mineral resources, are situated at intervals luxuriant and fertile valleys sunk deep between the knees of volcanic ridges, the lower slopes of which are covered with thick forests of oak, chestnut, and pine. These depressions, sheltered from the sword-like winds which sweep down from the Pyrenees, reproduce in a measure the pleasant conditions of the southern land. Although their distance one from another tended to isolation, it was in these valleys that Christian Spain received the respite which enabled her to collect her strength and school her spirit for the great struggle against the Saracen.

In this age-long contest she was undoubtedly inspired by that subtle sense of nationhood and the possession of a common tongue which have proved the salvation of many races no less desperately situated, and perhaps her determination to redeem the lost Eden of the South is the best measure of the theory that, prior to the era of Saracen conquest, the Castilian tongue was a mere

[1] The *moro latinado*, or Spanish-speaking Moor, is a prominent figure in later Spanish story.

jargon, composed of the elements of the Roman *lingua rustica* and the rude Gothic, and, according to some authorities, still lacking in grammatical arrangement and fixity of idiom.[1] It is certainly clear that the final phases in the evolution of Castilian took place subsequently to the Arabic invasion, but it is a straining of such scanty evidence as we possess to impute to the form of Castilian speech current immediately before that time the character of an undisciplined *patois*.

Roman and Visigoth

When in the early part of the fifth century the Visigoths, following in the wake of the Vandal folk, entered Romanized Spain, they did not build upon the ruins of its civilization, but retained the habits of their northern homeland and for some generations seem to have been little impressed with Roman culture. Nor did the Latin speech of the people they had conquered at first find favour among them, although, dwelling as they had done on the very flanks of the Empire, they were certainly not ignorant of it. They found the people of the Peninsula as little inclined to relinquish the cultivated language in which their compatriots Martial, Lucan, and Seneca had contributed to the triumphs of Roman letters. A military autocracy is not usually successful in imposing its language upon a subject people unless it possesses the dual advantages

---

[1] Bishop Odoor's will (747) shows the break-up of Hispanic Latin, and Charles the Bald in an edict of 844 alludes to the *usitato vocabulo* of the Spaniards—their "customary speech." On the Gothic period see Père Jules Tailham, in the fourth volume of Cahier and Martin's *Nouveaux Mélanges d'Archéologie, d'Histoire, et de Littérature sur le Moyen Age* (1877).

Roman and Visigoth

of an ascendancy in arms and literary capacity, and the Visigoths, unable to compete in this latter respect with the highly civilized colonists of Hispania, fell, with the passing of the generations, into the easy acceptance of the Roman tongue. Their illiteracy, however, was not the sole reason for their partial defeat in the give-and-take of linguistic strife, for, though powerful in military combination, they were greatly outmatched in numbers. As invaders they had brought few women with them, and had perforce to intermarry with native wives, who taught their children the Roman tongue. The necessary intercourse between conqueror and conquered in time produced a sort of pidgin-Latin, which stood in much the same relation to the classic speech of Rome as the trade languages of the Pacific did to English.[1]

The use of Latin as a literary tongue in that part of Spain where the Castilian speech was evolved considerably retarded its development from the condition of a *patois* to a language proper. Nevertheless it continued to advance. The processes by which it did so are surprisingly obscure, but the circumstance of its literary fixity in the early eleventh century is proof that it must have achieved colloquial perfection at least before the era of the Moorish invasion. The Saracen conquest, by forcing it into the bleak north-west, did it small disservice, for there it had to contend with other dialects of the Roman tongue, which enriched its vocabulary, and over which, ultimately, it gained almost complete ascendancy as a literary language.

[1] This jargon owed much more to the *lingua rustica* than to Gothic, which has left its mark more deeply upon the pronunciation and syntax of Spanish than on its vocabulary.

Legends & Romances of Spain

The Romance Tongues of Spain

Three Romance or Roman languages were spoken in that portion of Spain which remained in Christian hands : in Catalonia and Aragon the Provençal, Catalan, or Limousin ; in Asturias, Old Castile, and Leon the Castilian ; and in Galicia the Gallego, whence the Portuguese had its origin. The Catalan was almost entirely similar to the Provençal or *langue d'oc* of Southern France, and the accession of Raymond Berenger, Count of Barcelona, to the throne of Provence in 1092 united the Catalonian and Provençal peoples under one common rule. Provençal, the language of the Troubadours, was of French origin, and bears evidence of its evolution from the Latin of Provincial Gaul. It appears to have been brought into Catalonia by those Hispani who had fled to Provence from Moorish rule, and who gradually drifted southward again as the more northerly portions of Spain were freed from Arab aggression. The political connexion of Catalonia with Provence naturally brought about a similarity of custom as well as of speech, and indeed we find the people of the Catalan coast and the province of Aragon deeply imbued with the chivalry and gallantry of the more northerly home of the *Gai Saber*.

Throughout the whole Provençal-Catalan[1] tract were held those romantic courts of love in which the erotic subtleties of its men and women of song were debated with a seriousness which shows that the art of love had entered into competition with the forces of law and

[1] Catalan differed slightly in a dialectic sense from Provençal. It was divided into *plá Catalá* and *Lemosé*, the common speech and the literary tongue.

A GLIMPSE OF OLD SPAIN

A TROVADOR OF OLD SPAIN

religion, and had, indeed, become the real business of life with the upper classes of the country. Out of this glorification of the relations of the sexes arose the allied science of chivalry, no less punctilious or extravagant in its code and spirit. This spirit of Provençal chivalry gradually found its way into Castile, heightened and quickened the imagination of its people, and prepared the Spanish mind for the acceptance and appreciation of Romantic literature. But at no time was Castilian imagination passively receptive. It subjected every literary force which invaded it to such a powerful alchemy of transmutation that in time all foreign elements lost their alien character and emerged from the crucible of Spanish thought as things almost wholly Castilian.

The perfection of rhyming verse was undoubtedly accomplished by the Troubadour poets of Provence and Catalonia, and opened the way for a lyric poetry which, if it never attained any loftiness of flight or marked originality of expression, has seldom been surpassed in melody and finish. But it is remarkable that this extensive body of verse, if a few political satires be excepted, has but one constant theme—the exaltation of love. A perusal of the poetry of the pleasant Provençal tongue pleases the ear and appeals to the musical sense. The melody is never at fault, and we can count upon the constancy of a pavane-like stateliness, which proceeds, perhaps, as much from the genius of the language as from the metrical excellences of its singers. But the monotonous repetition of amatory sentiment, for the expression of which the same conceptions and even the same phrases are again and again compelled to do duty, the artificial spirit which inspires these uniform cadences, and the lack of real human warmth soon weary and disappoint the reader, who will gladly resign the entire poetical kingdom of Provence to the specialist in prosody or the literary antiquary in exchange for the freer and less formal beauties of a music better suited to human needs and less obviously designed for the uses of a literary caste. The poetry of Provence reminds us of those tapestries in which the scheme is wholly decorative, where stiff, brocaded flowers occupy regular intervals in the pattern and a monotonous sameness of colour is the distinctive note. No episode of the chase nor pastoral scene charms us by its liveliness or reality, nor do we find the silken hues distributed in a natural and pleasing manner.[1]

The Provençal and Catalan troubadours had, indeed, a certain influence upon the fortunes of Castilian poetry and romance, and proofs of their early intercourse with Castile are numerous. The thirteenth-century *Book of Apollonius*, an anonymous poem, is full of Provençalisms, as is the rather later *History of the Crusades*. During the persecution they suffered at the period of the Albigensian wars numbers of them fled into Spain, where they found a refuge from their intolerant enemies. Thus Aimeric de Bellinai fled to the Court of Alfonso IX,[2] and was later at the Court of Alfonso X, as were Montagnagunt and Folquet de Lunel, as well as Raimond de Tours and Bertrand Carbunel, who, with

[1] "On the whole," says Professor Saintsbury, "the ease, accomplishment, and, within certain strict limits, variety of the form, are more remarkable than any intensity or volume of passion or of thought" (*Flourishing of Romance and Rise of Allegory*, pp. 368–369). He further remarks that the Provençal rule "is a rule of 'minor poetry,' accomplished, scholarly, agreeable, but rarely rising out of minority."
[2] *D.* 1214.

Riquier, either dedicated their works to that monarch
or composed elegies on the occasion of his death.
King Alfonso himself wrote verses of a decidedly
Provençal cast, and even as late as 1433 the Marquis
de Villena, a kinsman of the famous Marquis de Santillana, whom we shall encounter later, wrote a treatise
upon the art of the Troubadours,[1] which, following the
instincts of a pedant, he desired to see resuscitated in
Castile.[2]

The Galician, a Romance language which sprang from
the same root as the Portuguese, is nearly allied to the
Castilian. But it is not so rich in guttural sounds, from
which we may be correct in surmising that it has less
of the Teutonic in its composition than the sister
tongue. Like Portuguese, it possesses an abundance
of hissing sounds, and a nasal pronunciation not unlike
the French, which was in all probability introduced
by the early establishment of a Burgundian dynasty
upon the throne. But Galician influence upon Castilian
literature ceased at an early period, although the reverse
was by no means the case.

The Rise of Castilian

The evolution of Castilian from the original Latin
spoken by the Roman colonists in Spain was complicated
by many local circumstances. Thus in contracting the
vocables of the Roman tongue it did not omit the same
syllables as the Italian, nor did it give such brevity to

---

[1] It was entitled *El Arte de Trobar*, and is badly abridged in Mayan's
Orígenes de la Lengua Española (Madrid, 1737).

[2] On Provençal influence upon Castilian literature see Manuel Milá y
Fontanal, *Trovadores en España* (Barcelona, 1887); and E. Baret,
Espagne et Provence (1857), on a lesser scale.

them as Provençal or Galician. Probably because of the greater admixture of Gothic blood among those who spoke it, it is rich in aspirates, and has a stronger framework than almost any of the Romance tongues. Thus the Latin *f* is in Castilian frequently altered to *h*, as *hablar = fabulari*, 'to speak.' The letter *j*, which is strongly aspirated, is frequently substituted for the liquid *l*, so that *filius*, 'a son,' becomes *hijo*. Liquid *ll* in its turn takes the place of Latin *pl*, and we find Latin *planus*, 'smooth,' appearing in Castilian as *llano* (*pron.* lyáh-no). The Spanish *ch* supplies the place of the Latin *ct*, as *facto = hecho*, *dictu = dicho*, and so on. Other proofs of Teutonic association are not lacking. Thus the *g* before *c* and *i*, which in Gothic and German is a guttural, has the same character in Castilian. The Spanish conversion of *o* into *ue* also resembles the similar change in German, if, for example, we compare Castilian *cuerpo* and *pueblo* with the German *Körper* and *Pöbel*.

Southward Spread of Castilian

The rise of Castilian as a colloquial and literary tongue was achieved by the ceaseless struggle of the hardy race who spoke it against the Saracen occupation of their native land. As the Castilian warriors by genera-tions of hard fighting gradually regained city after city and district by district rather than province by province, their language encroached by degrees upon the area of that of their Arab enemies,[1] until at length the last stronghold of the Moors fell and left them not a foot-hold in the Peninsula. "It was indeed a rude training

[1] Still they found many Spanish-speaking people in that area; and it was the Romance speech of these which finally prevailed in Spain.

which our forefathers, mighty and hardy, had as a prelude
to so many glories and to the conquest of the world,"
says Martinez in his novel *Isabel de Solis*.[1] "Weighed
down by their harness and with sword in hand, they
slept at ease no single night for eight centuries."

From the period of the defeat of Roderic, "last of the
Visigoths," at the battle of Xerez de la Frontera in
711 until the fall of Granada in 1492, Spain was indeed
a land of battles. Almost immediately after their first
defeat by Arab arms the armies of the Visigoths were
pursued to the north-western limits of the Peninsula,
where they found a rallying-place in the mountains of
Biscay and Asturias. There, like the Welsh after the
Saxon invasion of Britain, they might have become
reconciled to the comparatively narrow area left to
them, but the circumstances of their virtual imprisonment served only to unite them more closely in a
common nationality and a common resolve to win back
their original possessions.

For many generations their efforts were confined to
border forays and guerrilla fighting, in which they were
by no means uniformly successful, for the fiery courage
of the Saracens would permit of no mere defensive
policy, and nearly every victory of which the Castilians
could boast was counterbalanced by reverses and losses
which their inferior numbers could ill sustain. But by
degrees their valorous obstinacy was rewarded, and ere
a century had passed they had regained the greater
part of Old Castile. The very name of this province,
meaning as it does 'the Land of Castles,' shows that
even when regained it was held only by fortifying its
every hill-top with strongholds, so that at last this

[1] Madrid, 1839.

castellated tract gave its name to the race which held it so dearly. Before another twenty years had passed the Castilian warriors had established a footing in New Castile, and from this time onward seem to have been assured of ultimate success.

The fall of Toledo in 1085, after three centuries and a half of Saracen occupation, marked a further epoch in the southern advance of the Castilians, and by the taking of Saragossa in 1118 the tables were turned upon the Arab invaders, who were now driven into a more confined part of the country, to the south and south-west. This circumstance, however, seems to have consolidated rather than crippled their resisting powers, and they had yet to be reckoned with for nearly four centuries ere, with the fall of Granada, Boabdil, or Abu-Abdallah, the last of the Moorish kings, gave up its keys to Ferdinand of Castile, looked his last upon the city, and crossed to Africa to fling away his life in battle.

In these circumstances of constant strife and unrest the Romantic literature of Spain was born. It is by no means remarkable that its development coincided with the clash of arms. Trumpets re-echo in its every close. As it expresses the spirit of a martial race, it was also the nursling of necessity, for from the songs and fables of mighty heroes the knights of Castile drew a new courage and experienced an emulous exhilaration which nerved them on the day of battle. Well might the wandering knight of Castile chant, as in the old ballad :

> Oh, harness is my only wear,
> The battle is my play :
> My pallet is the desert bare,
> My lamp yon planet's ray. [1]

---

[1] In the *Cancionero de Romances* (Antwerp, 1555).

The Literary Development of Castilian

Border warfare, with its frequent change of scene and constant alarms, was a fitting introduction to errantry.

The Literary Development of Castilian

Castilian, although more than one alien influence impinged upon it, evolved a literary shape peculiarly its own, especially as regards its verse, as will be seen when we come to deal separately with its several Romantic forms. Thus it owed nothing to the literary methods of Provençal or Catalan, though much to their spirit and outward manners. When the courtly and rather pedantic poetic system of the Troubadours encountered the grave and vigorous Castilian, it was ill fitted to make any prolonged resistance. As political causes had hastened their encounter, so they quickened the victory of the Castilian. The ruling power in Aragon had from an early period been connected with Castilian royalty, and Ferdinand the Just, who came to the throne of Aragon in 1412, was a Castilian prince. The Courts of Valencia and Burgos were, therefore, practically open to the same political influences. If our conclusions are correct, it was during the reigns of Ferdinand the Just and Alfonso V (1412–58) that the influence of Castilian first invaded the sphere of Catalan. We find it definitely recognized as a poetic tongue on the occasion of a contest of song in honour of the Madonna held at Valencia in 1474, the forty poems sung at which were afterward collected in the first book printed in Spain. Four of these are in the Castilian tongue, which was thus evidently regarded as a literary medium sufficiently developed to be represented at such a contest. Valencia, indeed, at first wholly Catalan in speech and art, seems to have possessed a school of Castilian poets of its own from 1470 to 1550, who did much to popularize their adopted tongue. But the Catalonians were not minded that their language should lose the literary hegemony of Spain so easily, and they made every endeavour to sustain it by instituting colleges of professional troubadours and vaunting its beauties at their great public contests of song. It was in vain. They had encountered a language more vigorous, more ample in vocabulary, more rich in idiomatic construction, and backed by a stronger political power than their own.

The Poetical Courts of Castile

The evolution of Castilian as a literary language was also assiduously fostered by the scholarly character of many of the rulers of Castile. Alfonso the Wise was himself a poet, and cultivated his native tongue with judiciousness and care, affording it purity and precision of expression. Under his supervision the Scriptures were translated into Castilian, and a *General Chronicle of Spain* as well as a history of the First Crusade were undertaken at his instance. He made it the language of the law-courts, and attempted to infuse into its verse a more exact spirit and poetical phraseology by the imitation of Provençal models.

Alfonso XI composed a *General Chronicle* in the easy, flowing rhyme of the native *redondillas*, instead of the stiff, monkish Alexandrines then current in literary circles, and caused books to be written in Castilian prose on the art of hunting and the genealogy of the nobility.[1] His relative Don Juan Manuel did much to discipline Spanish imagination and give fixity to Spanish prose in

[1] See the article on Alfonso XI in N. Antonio, *Bibliotheca Hispana Vetus*.

his *Conde Lucanor*,[1] a volume of ethical and political maxims, the morals of which are well pointed by tales and fables drawn from history and classical literature. Juan II,[2] although a weak and idle monarch, was a great patron of letters, wrote verses, associated with poets, and caused a large collection of the best existing Spanish verse to be made in 1449. But the spirit of his Court was a pedantic one; it strayed after Italian models, and he himself affected the Provençal manner. Despite such artificial barriers, however, Castilian speech continued to advance upon its conquering way. It had definitely become the language of Romance, and Romance, within a generation of this period, was to become the most powerful literary form in the Peninsula.

The Rise of Romance

The development of Romance in Spain, its evolution and the phases through which it passed, has not, as a theme, met with that painstaking treatment at the hands of English writers on Spanish literature that might have been expected at this late day, when the literary specialist has to search diligently into the remotest corners of the earth if he seek new treasures to assay. Its several phases are rather hinted at than definitely laid down, not because of the poverty or dubiety of the evidential material so much as through the laxity and want of thoroughness which characterize most Britannic efforts at epochal fixation or attempts to elucidate the connexion between successive literary phases. I can scarcely hope to succeed in a task which other and better equipped authorities have neglected, perhaps for sound reasons. But I had rather fail in an attempt to reduce the details

---

[1] English translation by James York.   [2] Reigned 1407-54.

of the evolution of Spanish Romance to orderly sequence than place before the reader an array of unrelated facts and isolated tags of evidence which, however interesting, present no definite picture, permit of no reasonable deduction, and are usually accompanied by a theoretical peradventure or so by way of dubious enlightenment.

If we regard the literary map of Europe from the eleventh to the thirteenth century we behold the light shining from two quarters—Jewish-Arabic Spain and France. With the first we have, at the moment, no concern. Its literature was at the time alien and inimical to Christian Spain, which, as we shall see later, did not regard anything Saracen with complacence until its sword crossed no longer with the scimetar. But in France Castile had an illustrious exemplar, whose lessons it construed in its own peculiar manner—a manner dictated both by national pride and political necessity.

With the influence of Southern France we have already dealt. At the era alluded to, Northern France, the country of the *langue d'oïl*, although in a measure disturbed by unrest, was yet in a much better case to produce great literature than Castile, whose constant vendetta with the Moslem left her best minds only a margin of leisure for the production of pure literature— a margin, however, of which the fullest advantage was taken. The rise of a caste of itinerary poets in France supplied the popular demand for story-telling, and the *trouvères* of the twelfth century recognized in the glorious era of Charlemagne a fitting and abundant source for heroic fiction such as would appeal to medieval audiences. The poems, or rather epics, which they based upon the history of the Carlovingian period were known as *chansons de gestes*, 'songs of the deeds' of the great Frankish emperor and his invincible paladins, or, to the *trouvères* themselves, as *matière de France*, as the Arthurian tales were designated *matière de Bretagne*, and those based upon classical history *matière de Rome*.

Until comparatively recent times these immense works, many of which comprise six or seven thousand lines of verse, were practically unknown, even to the generality of literary authorities.[1] As we now possess them they are comparatively late in form, and have undergone much revision, probably for the worse. But they are the oldest examples of elaborate verse in any modern language, with the exception of English and Norse, and undoubtedly stand in an ancestral relation to all modern European literature.

These *chansons* were intended to be sung in the common halls of feudal dwellings by the itinerant *trouvères*, who composed or passed them on to one another. Their subject-matter deals more with the clash of arms than the human emotions, though these are at intervals depicted in a masterly manner. The older examples among them are written in batches of lines, varying from one to several score, each of which derives unity from an assonant vowel-rhyme, and known as *laisses* or *tirades*. Later, however, rhyme crept into the *chansons*, the entire *laisse*, or batch, ending in a single rhyme-sound.

[1] Gaston Paris, *La Littérature Française au Moyen Age* (Paris, 1888), and Léon Gautier, *Les Épopées Française* (Paris, 1878–92), are the leading authorities upon the *chansons de gestes*. Accounts of these in English can be found in Ludlow's *Popular Epics of the Middle Ages* (1865) and in my *Dictionary of Medieval Romance* (1913).

Legends & Romances of Spain

Castilian Opposition to the Chansons de Gestes

In these poems, which probably originated in the north of France, the *genre* spreading southward as time progressed, Charlemagne is represented as the great bulwark of Christianity against the Saracens of Spain. Surrounded by his peers, Roland, Oliver, Naymes, Ogier, and William of Orange, he wages constant warfare against the Moors or the 'Saracens' (pagans) of Saxony. Of these poems Gautier has published a list of one hundred and ten, a moiety of which date from the twelfth century. A number of the later *chansons* are in Provençal, but all attempts to refer the entire cycle in its original condition to that literature have signally failed.

That this immense body of romantic material found its way into Castile is positively certain. Whether it did so by way of Provence and Catalonia is not clear, but it is not impossible that such was the case. It might be thought that Christian Spain, in the throes of her struggle with the Moors, took kindly to a literature so constant in its reference to the discomfiture of her hereditary foes. At first she did so, and certainly accepted the *chanson* form. But two barriers to her undivided appreciation of it presently appeared. In the first place, the Castilian of the twelfth century seems to have been aware that if Charlemagne invaded Spain at all, he encountered not only the Moor but the Spaniard as well. This is not borne out, as some authorities imply, by a piece in the popular poetry of the Basques known as the *Altobiskarko Cantar*, or *Song of Altobiskar*, which tacitly asserts that the defeat of Charlemagne's rearguard at Roncesvalles was due not to Saracens, but to Basques, who resented the passage of the Frankish army through their mountain passes. The whole piece is an effusion written in Basque by a Basque student named Duhalde, who translated it from the French of François Garay de Montglave (c. 1833).[1] A second battle of Roncesvalles took place in the reign of Louis le Debonair in 824, when two Frankish counts returning from Spain were again surprised and defeated by the Pyrenean mountaineers. But there appears to have been a still earlier battle between Franks and Basques in the Pyrenees in the reign of Dagobert I (631–638). The folk-memory of these contests seems to have been kept alive, so that the Spaniard felt that the Frank was somewhat of a traditional enemy. Archbishop Roderic of Toledo inveighed against those Spanish *juglares* who sang the battles of Charlemagne in Spain, and Alfonso the Learned belittles the mythical successes of the Frankish emperor.

But this was not all. The idea that Charlemagne had entered Spain as a conqueror, carrying all before him, was offensive to the highly wrought pride and patriotism of the Castilians, who chose to interpret the spirit of the *chansons de gestes* in their own way, and, instead of copying them slavishly, raised an opposing body of song to their detriment. Accepting as the national hero of the Carlovingian era an imaginary knight, Bernaldo de Carpio, they hailed him as the champion of Castile, and invented songs of their own in which he is spoken of as slaying and defeating Roland at Roncesvalles at the head of a victorious army composed not of Arabs or Basques, but Castilians.

[1] See W. Wentworth Webster, in the *Boletin* of the Academia de Historia for 1883.

Legends & Romances of Spain

The Cantares de Gesta

But if the Castilians did not accept the matter of the *chansons*, they assuredly adopted their form. Their literary revolt against the alien spirit and politics of the *chansons* seems to have taken place at some time soon after the diffusion of these throughout Spain. A Spanish priest of the early twelfth century wrote the fabulous chronicle of Archbishop Turpin of Rheims, which purported to be the work of that warlike cleric, but in reality was intended to popularize the pilgrimage to Compostella to which it had reference. Many Franks travelled to the shrine, among them *trouvères*, who in all likelihood passed on to the native Castilian singers the spirit and metrical system of the *chansons*, so that later we hear of Spanish *cantares de gesta*, most of which, however, unlike their French models, are lost to us. The famous *Poema del Cid*, dealing with the exploits of a great Castilian hero, is nothing but a *cantar de gesta* in form and spirit, and we possess good evidence that many of the late *romanceros* or ballads upon such heroes as Bernaldo de Carpio, Gonzalvo de Cordova, and Gayferos are but ancient *cantares* 'rubbed down,' or in a state of attrition.

As in France, so in Spain, degeneration overtook the *cantares de gesta*. In course of time they were forced into the market-place and the scullions' hall. Many of them were worked into the substance of chronicles and histories ; but the *juglares* who now sang them altered them, when they passed out of fashion, into corrupt abridgments, or broke them up into ballads to suit the taste of a more popular audience.[1]

[1] See Manuel Milá y Fontanal, *Poesía heróico-popular Castellana* (Barcelona, 1874).

The Chronicles—The Ballads

The Chronicles

But if the majority of the *cantares de gesta* are irreplaceable as regards their original form, we find fragments of them in the ancient chronicles of Spain. Thus the *General Chronicle of Spain* (c. 1252), which, according to the latest research, is believed to have undergone at least three specific alterations or rearrangements of its text, tells the stories of Bernaldo de Carpio, Fernán González, and the seven Children of Lara, and provides sketches of Charlemagne, while its latter portion recounts the history of the Cid, and at times even appeals to the *cantares* as its authority for such and such an episode. Many of the passages in the chronicles, too, are obviously copied in their entirety from certain *cantares*. So strongly, indeed, do they retain the assonant verse-formation typical of the *cantares* that many of the later balladeers seem easily to have cast them into verse again, especially those relating to Bernaldo de Carpio and the Infantes de Lara, and in this manner they appeared once more in the *cancioneros*, or collections of folk-songs.

The Ballads

The immortal ballads of Spain have been the subject of the sharpest controversy, and their importance as Romantic material demands special treatment in a separate chapter. Regarding the period to which they belong and their relations to the larger narrative poems and chronicles, we must deal briefly with them here. Some authorities ascribe them to an early age and insist upon their priority to such poems as the *Poema del Cid* and such chronicles as that of Alfonso the Learned, while others are equally assured of the late date of the greater number. It seems to me that the truth resides in both hypotheses, and that in this case, as frequently in literary navigation, it is wise to steer a middle course. In my view the ballads of Spain are of four fundamental types : those which arose spontaneously in Northern Spain at some time subsequent to the formation of the Castilian language, and which, if we possess any remnants of them at all, have probably come down to us in such a form as would render them unrecognizable to those who first sang them ; ballads which are based on passages in *cantares de gesta* as chronicles ; folk-ballads of a later date, more or less altered ; and, lastly, the more modern productions of conscious art.

I also believe that the ballads or *romanceros* are again of two broad classes : those of spontaneous folk-origin, owing nothing to literary sources, and those which are mainly *cantares de gesta*, or chronicle passages in a lyric state of attrition. With the great body of authorities upon ancient Spanish literature I do not believe that the *cantares* or chronicles owe anything to the ballads of any age, which seem to me wholly of popular origin. Of course the two classes lastly indicated do not include the more 'poetic' or sophisticated ballads written after the ballad became an accepted form for experiments in conscious versification, and it is plain that such efforts could belong to neither category.

No definite proof exists as to the degree of sophistication and alteration which the ballads underwent before their ultimate collection and publication. It would be strange, however, if no ballads of relatively early date had reached us, altered or otherwise, and it seems to me merely a piece of critical affectation to deny antiquity

to a song solely because it found its way into print at
a late period, or because it is not encountered in ancient
MSS., just as it would be to throw doubt upon the
antiquity of a legend or folk-custom current in our own
day—unless, indeed, such should display obvious marks
of recent manufacture. At the same time few of these
ballads seem to me to bear the stamp of an antiquity more
hoary than, for example, those of Scotland or Denmark.

Few of the ballad systems of Europe are better worthy
of study than that of Spain. But in this place we are
considering it merely from the point of view of its
bearings upon Romance. That it has a close affinity
with the Romantic literature of the Peninsula is evident
from the name given to these poems by the Spaniards,
who call them *romanceros*.[1] Some of them are, indeed,
romances or *cantares de gesta* in little, and in fact they
deal with all the great subjects sung of in the *cantares*
or prosed upon in the chronicles, such as the Cid,
Bernaldo de Carpio, Count Alarcos, and so forth. But
they seem to have little in common with the later
romances proper, such as *Amadis*, *Palmerin*, or *Felixmarte*, for the good reason that by the time these were
in fashion the ballad had become the sole property of
the common people. As the Marquis de Santillana
(1398–1458), himself a poet of note, remarks in a letter
famous for the light it throws on the condition of
Spanish literature in his day : " There are contemptible
poets who, without order, rule, or rhythm, make those
songs and romances in which vulgar folk and menials

---

[1] The term, first employed by Count William of Poitiers, the earliest
troubadour, at first implied any work written in the vernacular Romance
languages. Later in Spain it was used as an equivalent for *cantar*,
and finally indicated a lyrico-narrative poem in octosyllabic assonants.

take delight." So might Lovelace or Drummond of Hawthornden have written of our own balladeers.

The ballads thus relegated to the peasantry and lower classes, those of the upper classes who found time for reading were accordingly thrown back upon the chronicles and the few *cantares de gesta* which had been reduced to writing. But on the destruction of the Moorish states in Spain the increase in wealth and leisure among the upper classes, and the introduction of printing, aroused a demand for books which would provide amusement. A great spirit of invention was abroad. At first it resuscitated the Romantic matter lying embedded and almost fossilized in the chronicles. It is, indeed, but a step from some of these to the romances proper. But Spain hungrily craved novelty, and the eyes of romance-makers were turned once more to France, whose fictional wealth began to be exploited by Spanish writers about the beginning of the fifteenth century.

The Heyday of Romance

Perhaps the first literary notice that we possess of the romance proper in Spain is that by Ayala, Chancellor of Castile (*d.* 1407), who, in his *Rimado de Palacio*, deplores the time he has wasted in reading such "lying stuff" as *Amadis de Gaul*. He might have been much worse occupied, but, be that as it may, in his dictum we scarcely have a forecast of the manner in which this especial type of romance was to seize so mightily upon the Castilian imagination, which, instead of being content with mere servile copying from French models, was to re-endow them with a spirit and genius peculiarly Spanish. Perhaps in no other European country did

The Heyday of Romance

the seed of Romance find a soil so fitting for its germination and fruition, and certainly nowhere did it blossom and burgeon in such an almost tropical luxuriance of fruit and flower.

Amadis had for sequel a long line of similar tales, all of which the reader will encounter later in these pages. By general consent of critics, from Cervantes onward, it is the best and most distinctive of the Spanish romances, and was translated into French, Italian, and indeed into most European languages,[1] a special translation, it is said, even being made for Jewish readers. At a stroke Peninsular romanticism had beaten French chivalric fiction upon its own ground. But *Amadis* was not, as Cervantes seems to think, the first book of chivalry printed in Spain, for this distinction belongs to *Tirante the White* (1490) which, according to Southey, is lacking in the spirit of chivalry.[2] Among other figures it introduces that of Warwick the King-maker, who successfully withstands an invasion of England by the King of the Canary Islands, and ultimately slays the invader single-handed and routs his forces. But if Cervantes errs in his bibliography, his barber's summing-up of *Amadis* as "the best of all books of its kind that has been written" is not far from the truth.[3] Tasso thought it "the most beautiful and perhaps the most profitable story of its kind that can be read." Did he merely follow the tonsorial critic's opinion, as his language would tempt one to believe?

[1] In German it was known from 1583, and in English from 1619. Southey's translation (London, 1803) is (happily) an abridgment, and has been reprinted in the "Library of Old Authors" (1872). I provide full bibliographical details when dealing with the romance more fully.

[2] *Omniana*, t. ii, p. 219 (London, 1812).

[3] *Don Quixote*, Part I, chap. vi.

Amadis was followed by a host of imitations. Its enormous success, from a popular point of view, brought into being a whole literature of similar stamp and intention, if not of equal quality. The first of such efforts, in consequence if not in chronology, is that of *Palmerin de Oliva*, the earliest known edition of which appeared at Seville in 1525, and was followed, like the *Amadis*, by similar continuations, *Primaleón*, *Platir*, and *Palmerin of England*, perhaps the best of the series.[1] Regarding the alleged Portuguese origin of *Amadis* and *Palmerin* I have more to say elsewhere, and will content myself here by observing that no Portuguese original, printed or manuscript, exists, although the priority of such seems undoubted. But these romances became as Castilian as the Arthurian series became English, despite the latter's Brythonic or other origin, and Spanish they have remained in the belief and imagination of all Europe, popular as well as critical.

The *Palmerin* series only fed and increased the passion for romantic fiction, so hungry was Spain for a literary diet which seemed so natural and acceptable to her appetite that those who sought to provide her with romantic reading could scarce cope with the call for it. The natural result ensued. A perfect torrent of hastily written and inferior fiction descended upon the public. Invention, at first bold, became shameless, and in such absurdities of distorted imagination as *Belianis of Greece*, *Olivante de Laura*, and *Felixmarte of Hyrcania* the summit of romantic extravagance was reached. But ridiculous and insulting to human intelligence and decent taste as most of these productions were, still they found countless thousands of readers, and there is

[1] English translation by Southey, 4 vols. (London, 1807).

The Heyday of Romance

every indication that publishing in the Spain of the late sixteenth and the seventeenth centuries must have been extremely lucrative. These preposterous and chimerical tales, lacking the beauty and true imaginative skill and simplicity of the older romances, stood in much the same relation to them as a host of imitative novels published in the early years of the nineteenth century did to the romances of Scott. Mexia, the sarcastic historian of Charles V, writing of romance in 1545, deplores the public credulity which battened on such feeble stuff. "For," he says, "there be men who think all these things really happened, just as they read or hear them, though the greater part of the things themselves are absurd." So might a critic of our own day descant upon the popular predilection for the cheap novel, or the whole desert of sensation-fodder which pours from the all too rapid machines of the Fiction Trusts.

Still another extravagant and more unpleasant manifestation of the popular craze for romance arose in such religious tales as *The Celestial Chivalry*, *The Knight of the Bright Star*, and others of little worth, in which Biblical characters are endowed with the attributes of chivalry and go on adventure bound. The time occupied by the appearance of these varying types, and indeed in the whole latter-day evolution of Spanish romance, was strikingly brief. But half a century elapsed between the publication of *Amadis* and the most extreme of its worthless imitations. But it is not difficult to account for the rapid manufacture and dissemination of such a mass of literature, good and bad, when we recall that Spain had been for ages the land of active knighthood, that her imagination had been wrought to a high pitch of fervour in her long struggle with her pagan enemies, and that in the tales of chivalry she now gazed upon with such admiration she saw the reflection of her own courtly and heroic spirit—the most sensitive and most fantastically chivalrous in Europe.

Possible Moorish Influence on Spanish Romance

There is indeed evidence—pressed down and flowing over—that the age-long death-grapple with the Saracen powerfully affected Spanish romantic fiction. But was this influence a direct one, arising out of the contiguity and constant perusal of the body of Moorish fiction, or did it proceed from the atmosphere of wonder which the Saracen left behind him in Spain, the illusions of which were mightily assisted by the marvels of his architecture and his art? One can scarcely find a Spanish romance that is not rich in reference to the Moor, who is usually alluded to as a *caballero* and a worthy foe. But is it the real Moor whom we encounter in these tall folios, which beside our modern volumes seem as stately galleons might in the company of ocean-going tramps, or is it the Saracen of romance, an Oriental of fiction, like the Turk of Byronic literature? The question of the influence of Moorish literature upon Spanish romance has been shrouded by the most unfortunate popular misconceptions. Let us briefly examine the spirit of Arabic literary invention, and see in how far it was capable of influencing Castilian art and imagination.

The history of the development of the Arabic language from the dialect of a wandering desert people to a tongue the poetic possibilities and colloquial uses of which are perhaps unrivalled is in itself sufficient to

Arabic Poetry

furnish a whole volume of romantic episode. The form in which it was introduced into Spain in the early eighth century can scarcely fail to arouse the admiration of the lover of literary perfection. As a literary medium its development was rapid and effective. It is, indeed, as if the tones of a harsh trumpet had by degrees become merged into those of a silver clarion whose notes ring out ever more clearly, until at length they arrive at a keenness so intense as to become almost intolerably piercing. This eloquent language, the true speech of the literary aristocrat, has through the difficulty of its acquirement and the bewildering nature of its written characters remained almost unknown to the great mass of Europeans—unknown, too, because the process of translation is inadequate to the proper conveyance of its finer shades and subtler intimations. Even to the greater number of the Arabs of Spain the highly polished verse in which their literature was so rich was unknown. How much more, then, was it a force removed from the Castilian or the Catalan?

Arabic Poetry

The desert life of the Arabs while they were yet an uncultured people, although it did not permit of the development of a high standard of literary achievement, fostered the growth of a spirit of observation so keen as to result in the creation of a wealth of synonyms, by means of which the language became greatly enriched. Synonymous meaning and the discovery of beautiful and striking comparisons are the very pillars of poetry, and within a century of the era of Moslem ascendancy in the East we find the brilliant dynasty of

39

the Abbassides (*c.* A.D. 750) the generous patrons of a poetic literature which the language was so well prepared to express. Story-telling had been a favourite amusement among the Arabs of the desert, and they now found the time-honoured, spontaneous exercise of the imaginative faculty stand them in good stead. The rapidity of the progress of Arabic literature at this period is, indeed, difficult of realization. Poetry, which we are now assured has 'no market value,' was to the truly enlightened upper classes of this people an art of the first importance, more precious than those bales of the silks of Damascus, those gems of Samarkand, or those perfumes of Syria the frequent allusion to which in their legends encrusts them, like the walls of the cavern of Ala-ed-din, with fairy jewels. But words were jewels to the Arab. When Al-Mamoun, the son of Haroun-al-Raschid, dictated terms of peace to the Greek emperor Michael the Stammerer, the tribute which he demanded from his conquered enemy was a collection of manuscripts of the most famous Greek authors. A fitting indemnity to be demanded by the prince of a nation of poets!

But conquered Spain was more especially the seat and centre of Arabian literature and learning. Cordova, Granada, Seville—indeed, all the cities of the Peninsula occupied by the Saracens—rivalled one another in the celebrity of their schools and colleges, their libraries, and other places of resort for the scholar and man of letters. The seventy libraries of Moorish Spain which flourished in the twelfth century put to shame the dark ignorance of Europe, which in time rather from the Arab than from fallen Rome won back its enlightenment. Arabic became not only the literary but the

Arabic Poetry

colloquial tongue of thousands of Spaniards who dwelt in the south under Moorish rule. Even the canons of the Church were translated into Arabic, about the middle of the eighth century, for the use of those numerous Christians who knew no other language. The colleges and universities founded by Abderahman and his successors were frequented by crowds of European scholars. Thus the learning and the philosophy if not the poetry of the Saracens were enabled to lay their imprint deeply upon plastic Europe. If, however, we inquire more closely into the local origins of this surprising enlightenment, we shall find it owing even more to the native Jews of Spain than to the Moors themselves.

The phase of Arabian culture with which we are most nearly concerned is its poetic achievement, and the ultimate influence which it brought to bear upon Spanish literary composition. The poetry of this richly endowed and imaginative people had at the period of their entrance into Spain arrived, perhaps, at the apogee of splendour. Its warm and luxuriant genius was wholly antagonistic to the more restrained and disciplined verse of Greece and Rome, which it regarded as cold, formal, and quite unworthy of translation. It surpassed in bold and extravagant hyperbole, fantastic imagery, and emotional appeal. The Arab poet heaped metaphor upon metaphor. He was incapable of seeing that that which was intrinsically beautiful in itself might appear superfluous and lacking in taste when combined with equally graceful but discordant elements. Many critics hasten to reassure us regarding his judgment and discrimination. But even a slight acquaintance with Arabic literature will show that they have been carried away by their prejudice in favour of the subject on which they wrote. In the garden of the Arabian poet every flower is a jewel, every plot is a silken carpet, tapestried with the intricate patterns of the weavers of Persia, and every maiden is a houri, each of whose physical attributes becomes in turn the subject of a glowing quatrain. The constant employment of synonym and superlative, the extravagance of amorous emotion, and the frequent absence of all message, of that large utterance in which the poets of the West have indicated to the generation they served how it might best grapple with problems of mind and soul—these were the weaknesses of the Arab singers. They made apophthegm take the place of message. They were unaware that the fabric of poetry is not only a palace of pleasure, but a great academy of the soul.

The true love of nature, too, seems to have been as much lacking in the Arab as in the Greek and the Roman. He enamelled his theme with the meticulous care of a jeweller. Not content with painting the lily, he burnished it until it seemed a product of the goldsmith's art. To him nature was a thing not only to be improved upon, but to be surpassed, a mine of gems in the rough, to be patiently polished.

But it would be wrong to refuse to the imaginative literature of the Arabs a high place among the world's achievements, and we must regret that, for causes into which we cannot enter here, opportunities for development and discipline were not vouchsafed it. As we read the history of the Arabian states with their highly developed civilization, their thronged academies, and their far-flung dominions, reaching from Central Asia to the western gates of the Mediterranean, and turn to-day to the scenes where such things flourished, we must indeed be unimaginative if we fail to be impressed by the universal wreck and ruin to which these regions have been exposed. The great, emulous, and spirited race which conquered and governed them gathered the world to its doors, and the rude peoples of Europe clustered about its knees to listen to the magical tales of unfolding science which fell from its lips. From the desert it came, and to the desert it has returned.

> Djamshîd, the palace is a lions' lair
> Where ye held festival with houris fair ;
> The desert ass bounds upon Barlaam's tomb :
> Where are the pomps of yesterday, ah, where ?

Moorish ' Fashion ' in Spanish Romance

Of Moorish grandeur of thought and luxuriance of emotion we find little in Spanish literature, at least until the beginning of the fifteenth century. Its note is distinctively, nay almost aggressively, *European*, as will be readily understood from the circumstances of its origin.[1] But it would seem that with the Castilian occupation of the Moorish parts of Spain the atmosphere which the Saracen had left behind him powerfully affected the Spaniard, who appears to have cast a halo of romance round the character of his ancient foe, with whose civilization, as expressed in its outward manifestations of architecture and artifact, he could scarcely have failed to be deeply impressed. If our conclusions are well founded it would appear that about the era alluded to a Moorish

---

[1] In the chapter entitled " Moorish Romances of Spain " the reader will find specimens of the romantic fictions of that people, from which he can judge for himself of their affinity or otherwise with the Spanish romances.

'fashion' set in in Spanish literature, just as did an Oriental craze in the England of Byron and Moore, when English people began to travel in the Levantine countries. But this fashion was in great measure pseudo-Saracenic, unaffected by literary models and derived indirectly more from atmosphere and art than directly from men or books. Long before the fifteenth century, however, with its rather artificial mania for everything Moresque, the Arab spirit had been at work upon Spanish literature, although in a feeble and unconscious manner. Spanish literary *forms*, whether in verse or prose, owe absolutely nothing to it, and especially is this the case in regard to the assonance which characterizes Castilian poetry, a prosodic device found in the verse of all Romance tongues at an early period. The Moors, however, seem to have sophisticated, if they did not write, the ballads of the Hispano-Moorish frontiers, especially those which have reference to the loss of Alhamia. In any case these are founded upon Moorish legends. Certain metrical pedants, like the Marquis de Santillana, toyed with Arabic verse-forms as Swinburne did with the French rondeau or Dobson with the ballade, or as the dry-as-dusts of our universities with Greek hexameters, neglecting for the alien and recondite the infinite possibilities of their mother-tongue. These preciosities, to which many men of letters in all ages have been addicted, had no more effect upon the main stream of Castilian literature than such attempts ever have upon the literary output of a country. Some of the popular *coplas*, or couplets, however, seem to be direct translations from the Arabic, which is not surprising when we remember the considerable number of half-breeds to be found in the Peninsula until the middle of the seventeenth century. There can be no doubt, too, that Arabic was the spoken language of thousands of Christians in Southern Spain. But that it had a determined opponent in the native Spanish is becoming more and more clear—an opponent which it found as merciless as the Moor found the Spaniard.[1]

Perhaps the best measure of the decline of Arabic as a spoken language in Spain is the fact that the authors of many romances declare them to be mere translations from the Arabic—usually the writings of Moorish magicians or astrologers. These pretensions are easily refuted by means of internal evidence. But regarding the question broadly and sanely, Spanish literature could no more remain unaffected by Arab influence than could Spanish music, architecture, or handicrafts. All such influences, however, were undoubtedly late, and, as regards the romances, were much more 'spiritual' than 'material.' Christian Spain had held off the Saracen for eight hundred years, and when at last she consented to drink out of the Saracen cup she filled it with her own wine. But the strange liquor which had brimmed it before left behind it the mysterious odours and scents of the Orient, faint, yet unmistakable.

The Type of Spanish Romance

The type of Spanish romance at its best is that in which the spirit of wonder is mingled with the spirit of chivalry. Old Spain, with her glorious ideas of honour,

[1] See Dozy, *History of the Moors in Spain*, Eng. trans., and *Recherches sur l'Histoire politique et littéraire de l'Espagne* (1881); F. J. Simonet, Introduction to his *Glosario de Voces iberias y latinas usadas entre los Muzárabes* (1888); Renan, *Averroës et Averroïsme* (1866). Gayangos' *Mohammedan Dynasties in Spain* (London, 1843) is somewhat obsolete, as is Condé's *Dominación de los Arabes*.

her finely wrought sense of chivalry, and her birthright of imagination, provided almost a natural crucible for the admixture of the elements of romance. Every circumstance of climate and environment assisted and fostered the illusions with which Spanish story teemed, and above all there was a more practical interest in the life chivalric in Spain than, perhaps, in any other country in Europe. The Spaniard carried the insignia of chivalry more properly than Frenchman or Englishman. It was his natural apparel, and he brought to its wearing a dignity, a gravity, and a consciousness of fitness unsurpassed. If he degenerated into a Quixote it was because of the whole-hearted seriousness with which he had embraced the knightly life. He was certainly the first to laugh when he found that his manners, like his mail, had become obsolete. But even the sound of that laughter is knightly, and the book which aroused it has surely won at least as many hearts for romanticism as ever it disillusioned.

The history of Spanish conquest is a chronicle of champions, of warriors almost superhuman in ambition and endurance, mighty carvers of kingdoms, great remodellers of the world's chart, who, backed by a handful of lances, and whether in Valencia, Mexico, Italy, or Araucan, surpassed the fabulous deeds of Amadis or Palmerin. In a later day the iron land of Castile was to send forth iron men who were to carry her banners across an immensity of ocean to the uttermost parts of the earth. What inspired them to live and die in harness surrounded by dangers more formidable than the enchantments of malevolent sorcerers or than ever confronted knights-errant in the quest of mysterious castles? What heartened them in an

The Type of Spanish Romance

existence of continuous strife, privation, and menace? Can we doubt that the hero-tales of their native land magically moved and inspired them—that when going into battle the exploits of the heroes of romance rang in their ears like a fanfare from the trumpets of heralds at a tournament?

> And as we gat us to the fight
> Our armour and our hearts seemed light
> Thinking on battle's cheer,
> Of fierce Orlando's high prowess,
> Of Felixmarte's knightliness
> And the death of Olivier.[1]

---

[1] "The Raid," an old Spanish poem.

CHAPTER II : THE "CANTARES DE GESTA" AND THE "POEMA DEL CID"

When meat and drink is great plentye
Then lords and ladyes still will be,
    And sit and solace lythe.
Then it is time for mee to speake
Of kern knights and kempes great,
    Such carping for to kythe.

" Guy and Colbrand," a romance

THE French origin of the *cantares de gesta* has already been alluded to. Their very name, indeed, bespeaks a Gallic source. But in justice to the national genius of Spain we trust that it has been made abundantly clear that the *cantares* speedily cast off the northern mode and robed themselves in Castilian garb. Some lands possess an individuality so powerful, a capacity for absorption and transmutation so exceptional, that all things, both physical and spiritual, which invade their borders become transfigured and speedily metamorphosed to suit their new environment. Of this magic of transformation Spain, with Egypt and America, seems to hold the especial secret. But transfigure the *chansons* of France as she might, the mould whence they came is apparent to those who are cognisant of their type and machinery. Nor could the character of their composers and professors be substantially altered, so that we must not be surprised to find in Spain the *trouvères* and *jongleurs* of France as *trovadores* and *juglares*. The *trovador* was the poet, the author, the *juglar* merely the singer or declaimer, although no very hard-and-fast line was drawn betwixt them. Some *juglares* of more than ordinary distinction were also the authors of the *cantares* they sang, while an unsuccessful

The Singers of Old Spain

trovador might be forced to chant the verses of others. Instrumentalists or accompanists were known as *juglares de péñola* in contradistinction to the reciters or singers, *juglares de boca*.

The Singers of Old Spain

With the *juglar*, indeed, was left the final form of the *cantar*, for he would shape and shear it, add to or suppress, as his instinct told him the taste of his audience demanded.   Not infrequently he would try to pour the wine of a *cantar* into the bottle of a popular air, and if it overflowed and was spilt, so much the worse for the *cantar*.   Frequently he was accompanied not only by an instrumentalist, but by a *remendador*, or mimic, who illustrated his tale in dumb show.   These sons of the gay science were notoriously careless of their means of livelihood, and lived a hand-to-mouth existence.   A crust of bread and a cup of wine sufficed them when silver was scarce.   Unsullied by the lust of hire, they journeyed from hall to hall, from castle to castle, unmindful of all but their mission—to soothe the asperities of a barbarous age.

> Our long-dead brothers of the roundelay,
> Whose meed was wine, who held that praise was pay,
> Hearten ye by their lives, ye singers of to-day!

But this simple state did not last.   As the taste for the *cantares* grew, the *trovadores* and their satellites, after the manner of mankind, became clamorous for the desirable things of life, making the age-long plea of the artist that the outward insignia of beauty are his very birthright, and forgetting how fatal it is to

> Stain with wealth and power
> The poet's free and heavenly mind.

These "spirits from beyond the moon" did not, alas!
"refuse the boon." Kings, infantes, and peers indulged
the *trovador* out of full purses, flattered him by imitating
his art and his life, and even enrolled themselves in his
brotherhood. Few men of genius are so constituted as
to be able to control altogether a natural hauteur and
superiority. In these early days poetical arrogance
seems to have been as unchecked as military boastful-
ness, and the *trovadores*, pampered and fêted by prince
and noble, at length grew insufferable in their insolence
and rapacity. The land swarmed with singers, real and
pretended, the manner of whose lives became a scandal,
even in a day when scandal was cheap. The public
grew weary of the repetition of the *cantares* and the
harping on a single string. It became fashionable to
read romances instead of listening to them, and eventually we see the *juglares* footing it on the highways
of Spain, and declaiming at street-corners in a state of
mendicancy more pitiable by far than their old indigent
yet dignified conditions.

Few of the ancient *cantares* of Spain have survived,
in contradistinction to the hundred or more *chansons*
that France can show. But what remains of them
suffices to distinguish their type with sufficient clearness.
As has been indicated, we owe our knowledge of more
than one of them to the circumstance that they became
embedded in the ancient chronicles of Spain. An
excellent illustration of this process of literary em-
balming is provided by the manner in which the *cantar* of
Bernaldo de Carpio has become encrusted in the rather
dreary mass of the *General Chronicle of Spain* which
was compiled by King Alfonso the Wise (*c.* 1260),
in which it will be found in the seventh and twelfth

The Story of Bernaldo de Carpio

chapters of the third part. The poet-king states that he has founded his history of Bernaldo upon "old lays," and in the spirit as well as the form of his account of the legendary champion we can trace the influence of the *cantar*.

The Story of Bernaldo de Carpio

Young Bernaldo de Carpio, when he arrived at manhood, was, like many another hero of romance, unaware that he was of illustrious parentage, for his mother was a sister of Don Alfonso of Castile, and had wed in secret the brave and noble Count de Sandias de Saldaña. King Alfonso, bitterly offended that his sister should mate with one who was her inferior in rank, cast the Count into prison, where he caused him to be deprived of sight, and immured the princess in a cloister. Their son Bernaldo, however, he reared with care. While still a youth, Bernaldo rendered his uncle important services, but when he learned that his father languished in prison a great melancholy settled upon him, and he cared no more for the things that had once delighted him. Instead of mingling in the tourney or the dance, he put on deep mourning, and at last presented himself before King Alfonso and beseeched him to set his father at liberty.

Now Alfonso was greatly troubled when he knew that Bernaldo was aware of his lineage and of his father's imprisonment, but his hatred for the man who had won his sister was greater than his love for his nephew. At first he made no reply, but sat plucking at his beard, so taken aback was he. But kings are not often at a loss, and Alfonso, thinking to brush the matter aside by brusque words, frowned, and said sternly: "Bernaldo, as you love me, speak no more of this matter. I swear to you that never in all the days of my life shall your father leave his prison."

"Sire," replied Bernaldo, "you are my king and may do whatsoever you shall hold for good, but I pray God that He will change your heart in this matter."

King Alfonso had no son of his own, and in an ill moment proposed that Charlemagne, the mighty Emperor of the Franks, should be regarded as his successor. But his nobles remonstrated against his choice, and refused to receive a Frank as heir to the throne of Christian Spain. Charlemagne, learning of Alfonso's proposal, prepared to invade Spain on the pretext of expelling the Moors, but Alfonso, repenting of his intention to leave the crown to a foreigner, rallied his forces around him and allied himself with the Saracens. A battle, fierce and sustained, took place in the Pass of Roncesvalles, in which the Franks were signally defeated, chiefly by the address of Bernaldo, who slew the famous champion Roland with his own hand.

These and the other services of Bernaldo King Alfonso endeavoured to reward. But neither gift nor guerdon would young Bernaldo receive at his hands, save only the freedom of his father. Again and again did the King promise to fulfil his request, but as often found an excuse for breaking his word, until at last Bernaldo, in bitter disappointment, renounced his allegiance and declared war against his treacherous uncle. The King, in dread of his nephew's popularity and warlike ability, at last had recourse to a stratagem of the most dastardly kind. He assured Bernaldo of his father's release if he would agree to the surrender of the great

The Story of Bernaldo de Carpio

castle of Carpio. The young champion immediately gave up its keys in person, and eagerly requested that his father might at once be restored to him. The treacherous Alfonso in answer pointed to a group of horsemen who approached at a gallop.

"Yonder, Bernaldo, is thy father," he said mockingly. "Go and embrace him."

"Bernaldo," says the chronicle, "went toward him and kissed his hand. But when he found it cold and saw that all his colour was black, he knew that he was dead; and with the grief he had from it he began to cry aloud and to make great moan, saying: 'Alas! Count Sandias, in an evil hour was I born, for never was man so lost as I am now for you; for since you are dead and my castle is gone, I know no counsel by which I may do aught.'" Some say in their *cantares de gesta* that the King then said: "Bernaldo, now is not the time for much talking, and therefore I bid you go straightway forth from my land."

Broken-hearted and utterly crushed by this final blow to his hopes, Bernaldo turned his horse's head and rode slowly away. And from that day his banner was not seen in Christian Spain, nor the echoes of his horn heard among her hills. Hopeless and desperate, he took service with the Moors. But his name lives in the romances and ballads of his native country as that of a great champion foully wronged by the treachery of an unjust and revengeful King.

Although the *cantares* of Fernán González and the Children of Lara also lie embedded in the chronicles, I have preferred to deal with them in the chapter on the ballads, the form in which they are undoubtedly best known.

The " *Poema del Cid* "

But by far the most complete and characteristic of the *cantares de gesta* is the celebrated *Poema del Cid*, the title which has become attached to it in default of all knowledge of its original designation. That it is a *cantar* must be plain to all who possess even a slight familiarity with the *chansons de gestes* of France. Like many of the *chansons* heroes, the Cid experiences royal ingratitude, and is later taken back into favour. The stock phrases of the *chansons*, too, are constantly to be met with in the poem, and the atmosphere of boastful herohood arising from its pages strengthens the resemblance. There is also pretty clear proof that the author of the *Poema* had read or heard the *Chanson de Roland*. This is not to say that he practised the vile art of adaptation or the viler art of paraphrase, or in any way filched from the mighty epic of Roncesvalles. But superficial borrowings of incident appear, which are, however, amply redeemed by originality of treatment and inspiration. The thought and expression are profoundly national ; nor does the language exhibit French influence, save, as has been said, in the matter of well-worn expressions, the *clichés* of medieval epic.

Its Only Manuscript

But one manuscript of the *Poema del Cid* is known, the handiwork of a certain Per or Pedro the Abbot. About the third quarter of the eighteenth century, Sanchez, the royal librarian, was led to suspect through certain bibliographical references that such a manuscript might exist in the neighbourhood of Bivar, the birthplace of the hero of the poem, and he succeeded in unearthing it in that village. The date at the end is given as

Authorship of the " Poema del Cid "

Mille CCXLV, and authorities are not agreed as to its significance, some holding that a vacant space showing an erasure after the second C is intentional, and that it should read 1245 (1207 new style). Others believe that 1307 is the true date of the MS. However that may be, the poem itself is referred to a period not earlier than the middle of the twelfth nor later than the middle of the thirteenth century.

As we possess it, the manuscript is in a rather mutilated and damaged condition. The commencement and title are lost, a page in the middle is missing, and the end has been sadly patched by an unskilful hand. Sanchez states, in his *Poesías Castellanas anteriores al Siglo XV* (1779–90) that he had seen a copy made in 1596 which showed that the MS. had the same deficiencies then as now.

Its Authorship Unknown

The personality of the author of the *Poema del Cid* will probably for ever remain unknown. He may have been a churchman, as Ormsby suggests, but I am inclined to the opinion that he was a professional *trovador*. The *trouvères*, rather than ecclesiastics, were responsible for such works in France, and why not the *trovadores* in Spain?[1] That the writer lived near the time of the

---

[1] Ormsby (*The Poem of the Cid*), who wrote in 1879, seems to have had the most elementary notions of what a *cantar* was, and states that the *Poema* "was nearly contemporary with the first *chansons de gestes.*" But he is probably at least a century out in his reckoning, as the first *chansons* date from about the middle of the eleventh century. Of *trovador* and *juglar* he had evidently never heard. Yet he is anything but superficial, and on the whole his book is the best we have in English on the *Poema*. It is unlucky, too, as Saintsbury remarks, that neither Ticknor nor Southey, who wrote so widely on ancient Spanish

events he celebrated is plain, probably about half a century after the Cid sheathed his famous sword Colada for the last time. On the ground of various local allusions in the poem he has been claimed as a native of the Valle de Arbujuelo and as a monk of the monastery of Cardeña, near Burgos. But these surmises have nothing but textual references to recommend them, and are only a little more probable than that which would make him an Asturian because he does not employ the diphthong *ue*. We have good grounds, however, for the assumption that he was at least a Castilian, and these are to be found in his fierce political animus against the kingdom of Leon and all that pertained to it. That Pedro the Abbot was merely a copyist is clear from his mishandling of the manuscript; for though we have to thank him for the preservation of the *Poema*, our gratitude is dashed with irritation at the manner in which he has passed it on to us, for his copy is replete with vain repetitions, he frequently runs two lines into one, and occasionally even transfers the matter of one line to another in his haste to be free of his task.

Other Cantares of the Cid

That other *cantares* relating to the Cid existed is positively known through the researches of Señor Don Ramón Menéndez Pidal, who has demonstrated that one of them was used in the most ancient version of the

literature, were acquainted with the *chansons de gestes*. Still more luckless is it that so much in the way of Spanish translation was left to Longfellow, who shockingly mangled and Bowdlerized many fine ballads. Probably no poet was so well qualified as he to divest a ballad of all pith and virility in the course of translation. Bad as are his Spanish renderings, however, they are adequate when compared with his exploits in the field of Italian translation.

Metre of the " Poema del Cid "

Crónica General, of which three recensions evidently existed at different periods, and it is now clear that the passage in question does not come from the *Poema* as we have it, as was formerly believed.[1] The passages on the Cid in the second version of the *Crónica* are also derived from still another *cantar* on the popular hero, known as the *Crónica Rimada*,[2] or *Cantar de Rodrigo*, evidently the work of a *juglar* of Palencia, and which seems to be a *mélange* of several lost *cantares* relating to the Cid, as well as to other Spanish traditions. This version, however, is much later than the *Poema*, and is chiefly interesting as enshrining many traditions relative to the Cid as well as to the ancient folk-tales of Spain.

Metre of the "Poema del Cid"

It would certainly seem as if, like all *cantares*, the poem had been especially written for public recitation. The expression " *O señores*," encountered in places, may be taken as the equivalent of the English " Listen, lordings," of such frequent occurrence in our own lays and romances, which was intended to appeal to the attention or spur the flagging interest of a medieval audience. The metre in which the poem is written is almost as unequal as its poetic quality. The prevailing line is the Alexandrine or fourteen-syllabled verse, but some lines run far over this average, while others are truncated in barbarous fashion, probably through the inattention or haste of the copyist.[3] It seems to me

---

[1] See his *Poema del Cid* (1898).

[2] See Manuel Rivadeneyra, *Biblioteca de Autores españoles*, vol. xvi (1846–80).

[3] A good deal of controversy has arisen concerning the metre of the *Poema*. Professor Cornu of Prague (see M. Gaston Paris, in *Romania*, xxii, pp. 153, 531) has stated that the basis of it is the ballad octo-

that the *Poema*, although of the highest merit in many
of its finest passages, has received the most extravagant
eulogy, and I suspect that many of the English critics
who descant so glibly upon its excellences have never
perused it in its entirety. Considerable tracts of it are
of the most pedestrian description, and in places it
descends to a doggerel which recalls the metrical
barbarities of the pantomime. But when the war-trump
gives him the key it arouses the singer as it arouses
Scott—the parallel is an apt and almost exact one—
and it is a mighty orchestra indeed which breaks upon
our ears. The lines surge and swell in true Homeric
tempest-sound, and as we listen to the crash of Castilian
spears upon the Moorish ranks we are reminded of those
sounding lines in Swinburne's *Erechtheus* beginning :

> With a trampling of drenched, red hoofs and an earthquake of men
> that meet,
> Strong war sets hand to the scythe, and the furrows take fire from
> his feet.

But the music of the singer of the *Poema* does not
depend upon reverberative effect alone. His is the
true music of battle, burning the blood with keenest fire,
and he has no need to rely solely upon the gallop of his

---

syllable, full or catalectic, arranged as hemistichs of a longer line, but
this theory presupposes that the copyists of the original MS. must have
mistaken such a simple measure, which is scarcely credible. Professor
Saintsbury (*Flourishing of Romance*, p. 403) gives it as his opinion that
"nobody has been able to get further in a generalization of the metre
than that the normal form is an eight and six (better a seven and seven)
'fourteener,' trochaically cadenced, but admitting contraction and extension with a liberality elsewhere unparalleled." No absolute system of
assonance or rhyme appears, and we are almost forced to the conclusion
that the absence of this is in a measure due to the kind offices of
Abbot Pedro.

metrical war-horse to excite our admiration, as does the English poet.

The Poem Opens

The opening of the *Poema del Cid*, as we possess it, is indeed sufficiently striking and dramatic to console us for the loss of the original commencement. The great commander, banished (*c.* 1088) by royal order from the house of his father through the treachery of the Leonese party at the Court of King Alfonso, rides away disconsolately from the broken gates of his castle. A fairly accurate translation of this fine passage might read as follows :

> He turns to see the ruined hold, the tears fall thick and fast,
> The empty chests, the broken gates, all open to the blast.
> Sans raiment are the wardrobes, reft of mantle and of vair,
> The empty hollow of the hall of tapestry is bare.
> No feather in the falconry, no hawk to come to hand,
> A noble beggar must the Cid renounce his fathers' land.
> He sighed, but as a warrior sighs. "Now I shall not repine.
> All praise to Thee, our Father, for Thy grace to me and mine.
> The slanderous tongue, the lying tale, have wrought my wreck to-day,
> But Thou in Thy good time, O Lord, the debt wilt sure repay."
> As they rode out of Bivar flew a raven to the right,
> By Burgos as they bridled the bird was still in sight.
> The Cid he shrugged his shoulders as the omen he espied ;
> "Greetings, Cousin Alvar Fañez, we are exiles now," he cried.
> The sixty lances of the Cid rode clattering through the town ;
> From casement and from turret-top the burgher-folk looked down.
> Sore were their hearts and salt their eyen as Roderick rode by ;
> "There goes a worthy vassal who has known bad mastery."
> And many a roof that night had sheltered Roderick and his band
> But for the dread in Burgos of Alfonso's heavy hand.
> The missive broad with kingly seals had run throughout the town :
> "Who aids the Cid in banishment, his house shall be cast down."
> So as the train rode through the streets each eye was turned aside,
> All silent was the town-house where the Cid was wont to bide ;

Both lock and bar were on the gates, he might not enter there.
Then from a casement spoke a maid who had the house in care :
" My lord Don Roderick, who took the sword in happy hour,
The King hath sent a letter broad to ban from hall and bower
Both thee and all thy company, 'tis doom to shelter one ;
Never again who aids thee shall his eyes look on the sun.
Now go, and Goddës help with thee, thy pity we implore ;
In all broad Spain thou canst not lack, O Cid Campéador."

Finding no place to lay their heads within the town, the Cid with his men rode disconsolately to the plain of Glera, to the east of Burgos, where he pitched his tents on the banks of the river Arlanzon. To him came Martin Antolinez, one of his former vassals, who brought food and wine for all his train and strove to comfort him. Not a *maravedi* had the Cid, and how to furnish his men with arms and food he knew not. But he and Antolinez took counsel together, and hit upon a plan by which they hoped to procure the necessary sinews of war. Taking two large chests, they covered them with red leather and studded them with gilt nails, so that they made a brave outward show. Then they filled the chests with sand from the river-banks and locked them securely.

Money-lending in the Eleventh Century

" Martin Antolinez," said the Cid, " thou art a true man and a good vassal. Go thou to the Jews Raquel and Vidas, and tell them I have much treasure which I desire to leave with them since it is too weighty to carry along with me. Pledge thou these chests with them for what may seem reasonable. I call God and all His saints to witness that I do this thing because I am driven to extremity and for the sake of those who depend upon me."
Antolinez, rather fearful of his mission, sought out the Jews Raquel and Vidas where they counted out their

wealth and their profits. He told them that the Cid had levied much tribute which he found it impossible to carry with him, and that he would pledge this with them if they would lend him a reasonable sum upon it. But he stipulated that they must solemnly bind themselves not to open the chests for a year to come. The Jews took counsel together, and consented to hide the chests and not to look upon their contents for a year at least.

"But tell us," they said, "what sum will content the Cid, and what interest will he give us for the year?"

"Needy men gather to my lord the Cid from all sides," replied Antolinez. "He will require at least six hundred marks."

"We will willingly give that sum," said Raquel and Vidas, "for the treasure of such a great lord as the Cid must indeed be immense."

"Hasten then," said Antolinez, "for night approaches, and my lord the Cid is under decree of banishment to quit Castile at once."

"Nay," said the Jews, after the manner of their kind. "Business is not done thus, but by first taking and then giving." They then requested to be taken to where the Cid lay, and having greeted him, paid over the sum agreed upon. They were surprised and delighted at the weight of the chests, and departed well satisfied, giving Antolinez a present or commission of thirty golden marks for the share he had taken in the business.

Donna Ximena

When they had gone the Cid struck his camp and galloped through the night to the monastery of San Pedro de Cardeña, where his lady, Donna Ximena, and his two young daughters lay. He found them deeply engaged in prayer for his welfare, and they received him with heartfelt expressions of joy. Taking the Abbot aside, the Cid explained to him that he was about to fare forth on adventure in the country of the Moors, and tendered him such a sum as would provide for the maintenance of Donna Ximena and her daughters until his return, as well as a goodly bounty for the convent's sake.

By this time tidings of the Cid's banishment had gone through the land broadcast, and so great was the fame of his prowess that cavaliers from near and far flocked to his banner. When he put foot in stirrup at the bridge of Arlanza a hundred and fifty gentlemen had assembled to follow his fortunes. The parting with his wife and daughters presents a poignant picture of leave-taking :

> Sharp as the pain when finger-nails are wrenched from off the hand,
> So felt the Cid this agony, but turned him to his band,
> And vaulted in the saddle, and forth led his menie,
> But ever and anon he turned his streaming eyes to see
> Dear faces he might see no more, till blunt Minaya, irked
> To see the yearning and regret that on his heartstrings worked,
> Cried out, "O born in happy hour,[1] let not thy soul be sad :
> The heart of knight on venture bound should never but be glad.
> The heavy sorrow of to-day will prove to-morrow's joy.
> What grief can bide the trumpets' sound, what woe the battle's ploy?"

Giving rein to their steeds, they galloped forth of the bounds of Christian Spain and, crossing the river Duero on rafts, stood upon Moorish soil. Far to the west they could see the slender minarets of the Saracen city of Ahilon glittering in the high sun of noon, emblematic

---

[1] By this phrase the Cid seems to have been widely known ; in fact it appears to have served him as a sort of cognomen or nickname.

The Taking of Alcocer

of the rich treasure they had come to win in the land of the paynim. At Higeruela still more good lances rallied to the Cid's banners, border men to whom the foray was a holiday and the breaking of spears the sweetest music. As he slept that night the Cid dreamed that the Archangel Gabriel appeared to him and said: "Mount, O Cid Campeador, mount and ride. Thy cause is just. Whilst thou livest thou shalt prosper!" With three hundred lances behind him, the Cid rode into the land of the Moors. He lay in ambush while Alvar Fañez and other knights made a foray toward Alcalá. In their absence the Cid observed that the men of Castijon, a Moorish town hard by, came out of the place to work in the fields, leaving the gates open. He and his men made a dash at the gates, slew the handful of heathens who guarded them, and took the town without striking a score of blows. The men were well content at the treasure of gold and silver they found in the quaint Moorish houses. But they were merciful to the inhabitants, of whom they made servitors rather than slaves.

The Taking of Alcocer

After they had rested at Castijon, the Cid and his array rode down the valley of the Henares, passing by way of Alhamia to Bubierca and Ateca, and as he was in unknown country, and environed round by hosts of enemies, he took up a position upon a " round hill " near the strong Saracen city of Alcocer, to which he set siege. But the place was well guarded, and he saw that if he were to penetrate its defences it must be by stratagem and not by fighting alone. So one morning, after he had beleaguered Alcocer for full fifteen weeks, he withdrew his men as if retreating in disgust, leaving but one pavilion behind him. When the Moors beheld his withdrawal they exulted, and in their eagerness to see what spoil the solitary tent might contain they rushed out of the town, leaving the gates open and unguarded. Now when the Cid saw that there was a wide space between the Moors and the gates of Alcocer, he ordered his men to turn and fall upon the excited rabble of Saracens. Small need had he to ask them to smite the paynim. Dashing among the dense crowd with levelled lances, the cavaliers of Castile did fearful execution. The wretched Moors, taken completely by surprise, fled wildly in all directions, and soon the plain was littered with white-robed corpses. Meanwhile the Cid himself, with a few trusted followers, galloped to the gates and secured them, so that with much triumph the Spaniards entered Alcocer. As before, the Campeador was merciful to such of the Moors as made full surrender, saying: "We cannot sell them, and we shall gain nothing by cutting off their heads. Let us make them rather serve us."

The Saracens of the neighbouring towns of Ateca and Zerrel were aghast at the manner in which Alcocer had been taken, and sent word to the Moorish King of Valencia how one called Roderigo Diaz of Bivar, a Castilian outlaw, had come into their land to spoil it, and had already taken the strong city of Alcocer. When King Tamin of Valencia heard these tidings he was greatly wroth, and sent an army of three thousand well-appointed men against the Campeador. In his anger he charged his captains that they should take this Spanish renegade alive, and bring him where justice might be done upon him.

THE CID IN BATTLE

ELISENA AND PERION BEHOLD ONE ANOTHER

The Combat with the Moorish King

The Cid knew nothing of the coming of this host, and one morning his sentinels, pacing the walls of Alcocer, were surprised to see the surrounding country alive with Moorish scouts, flitting from point to point upon their active jennets, and shaking their scimetars in menace. His own outposts soon brought in word that he was surrounded, and his knights and men-at-arms clamoured to be led forth to do battle with the infidels. But the Cid was old in Moorish warfare, and denied them for the moment. For days the enemy paraded around the walls of Alcocer. But the Cid, with three hundred men, knew well the folly of attacking three thousand, and bided his time.

The Combat with the Moorish King

At last the Moors succeeded in cutting off the water-supply of Alcocer. Provisions, too, were running low, and the Cid saw clearly that such a desperate situation demanded a desperate remedy. Alvar Fañez, ever panting for the fight like a war-horse that hears the trumpet, urged an immediate sally in force, and the Cid, knowing the high spirit of his men, consented. First he sent all the Moors out of the city and looked to its defences. Then, leaving but two men to guard the gate, he marshalled his array and issued forth from Alcocer with dressed ranks and in strict order of battle. And here prose must once more give place to verse.[1]

[1] The passage in the *Poema del Cid* which tells of the combat that followed has perhaps a better right than any other in the epic to the title 'Homeric.' The translation which I furnish of it may not be so exact as those of Frere or Ormsby. But although I am only too conscious of its many shortcomings, I cannot bring myself to make use of the pedestrian preciseness of the one or the praiseworthy version of the other of my predecessors, both of which, in my view, fail to

Huzza! huzza! the Moorman mounts and waves his crescent blade
Hark to the thunder of the drums, the trump's fanfaronade!
Around two glittering gonfanons the paynim take their stand,
Beneath each waving banner's folds is massed a swarthy band.
The turbaned sons of Termagaunt sweep onward like the sea;
So trust they to engulf and drown the Christian chivalry.
"Now gentles, keep ye fast your seats," cries the Campeador,
"And hold your ranks, for such a charge saw never knight
    before."
But the fierce heart of Bermuez that echoed to the drum,
Cried, "Santiago, shall I stay the while these heathen come?
With this bold banner shall I pierce yon pride of paynimrie.
So follow, follow, cavaliers, for Spain and Christendie!"
"Nay, comrade, stay!" implored the Cid, but Pero shook his head.
His hand was loose upon the rein. "It may not be," he said;
Then in his destrier's flank he drove the bright speed-making
    spur:
Like a spray-scattering ship he clove the sands of Alcocer.
Lost in a sea of Saracens, whose turbans surge as foam,
He stands unshaken as a cliff when on its bosom come
Madness of ocean and the wrath of seas that overwhelm.
So rain the hounds of Máhomet fierce blows on shield and helm.
"A rescue, rescue," cries the Cid, "and strike for Holy Rood!
Up, gentlemen of Old Castile, and charge the heathen brood!"
As forth the hound when from the leash the hunter's hand is
    ta'en,
As the unhooded falcon bounds, her jesses cast amain,
But fiercer far than falcon or the hound's unleashèd zeal
Comes crashing down upon the foe the fury of Castile.
Now rally, rally, to the flash of Roderigo's blade,
The champion of Bivar is here who never was gainsaid.

---

render the magnificent spirit and chivalric dash of the original. All that
I can claim for my own translation is that it does not fail so utterly
as either in this regard. I have in places attempted the restoration
of lines which seemed to me omitted or coalesced with others, and
I must admit that this rendering of a great passage is more consciously
artificial than the others—a fault which I am unable to rectify. But
allowances must be made for the rendition of such a passage, and the
whole must be accepted by the reader *faute de mieux*.

The Combat with the Moorish King

Three hundred levelled lances strike as one upon the foe.
Down, down in death upon the sand three hundred heathen go.
The lances rise, the lances fall, how fast the deadly play!
Ah, God! the sundered shields that lie in dreadful disarray.
The snow-white bannerets are dyed with blood of Moorish slain,
And chargers rush all masterless across the littered plain.
As lightning circles Roderick's sword above the huddled foe,
With Alvar Fañez, Gustioz, and half a hundred moe
He reaps right bloodily.   But stay, the Saracens have slain
Bold Alvar Fañez' destrier; to aid him comes amain
The Cid Campeador, for sore the brave Minaya's need.
His way is barred, his stride is marred by a tall emir's steed.
His falchion swoops, his falchion stoops, down sinks the turbaned
    lord.
"Mount in his place, Minaya, mount! I need thy trenchant
    sword.
The phalanx of the foe is firm, unbroken still they stand."
The stout Minaya leaps in selle, and falchion in hand
Strews death to left and right, his trust to rout the Moor right
    soon.
But see, the Cid hath fiercely rid with blood-embroidered shoon
Upon the Moorish capitan, he cleaves his shining shield:
The haughty Moslem turns to fly—that blow hath won the field.
Bold Martin Antolinez aims a stroke at Galve's head;
The jewelled casque it cracks in twain, the infidel hath fled
Rather than bide its fellow; he and Fariz make retreat:
They caracoled to victory, they gallop from defeat.
Ne'er was a field so worthy sung since first men sang of war.
Its laurels unto thee belong, O Cid Campeador!

Fierce and sanguinary was the pursuit. The Moorish
rout was complete, and the little Castilian band had lost
but fifteen men. Five hundred Arab horses, heavily
caparisoned, each with a splendid sword at the saddle-
bow, fell into the hands of the Cid, who kept a fifth
share for himself, as was the way with the commanders
of such free companies as he led. But greatly desiring
to make his peace with King Alfonso of Castile, he

sent the trusty Alvar Fañez to Court with thirty steeds saddled and bridled in the Moorish fashion.

But the Moors, even with the dust of defeat in their mouths, were not minded to leave the Cid the freedom of their borders, and seeing that he would not be able to hold Alcocer for long against their numbers, he bargained with the Saracens of the neighbouring cities for the ransom of Alcocer. This they gladly agreed to for three thousand marks of gold and silver, so, quitting the place, the Campeador pushed southward, and took up a position on a hill above the district of Mont'real. He laid all the Moorish towns in the neighbourhood under tribute, remaining in his new encampment full fifteen weeks.

Meanwhile Alvar Fañez had journeyed to the Court and had presented the King with the thirty good steeds taken in battle. "It is yet too soon to take the Cid back into favour," said Alfonso, "but since these horses come from the infidel, I scruple not to receive them. I pardon thee, Alvar Fañez, and withdraw my banishment from thee. But as to the Cid, I say no more than that any good lance who cares to join him may do so without hindrance from me."

The War with Raymond Berenger

Now the Count of Barcelona, Raymond Berenger, a haughty and arrogant lord, conceived the presence of the Cid in a territory so near his own dominions to be an insult to himself, and in a high passion he mustered all his forces, Moorish as well as Christian, so that he might drive the Cid from the lands he held in tribute. The Campeador, hearing of the advance of this host, sent a courteous message to Count Raymond, assuring

The War with Raymond Berenger

him of pacific intentions toward himself. But the Count felt that his personal dignity had been offended, and refused to receive the messenger.

When the Cid beheld the army of Raymond marching against his position on the heights of Mont'real, he knew that his overtures for peace had been in vain, and, dressing his ranks for the fierce combat that he knew must follow, took up a position upon the plain suitable for cavalry. The lightly armed Moorish horsemen of Berenger's host rushed precipitately to the attack, but were easily routed by the Castilian cavaliers. The Count's Frankish men-at-arms, a band of skilful and warlike mercenaries, then thundered down-hill upon the lances of the Cid. The shock was terrific, but brief was the combat, for the knights of Castile, hardened by constant warfare, speedily overthrew the Frankish horsemen. The Cid himself attacked Count Berenger, took him prisoner, and forced him to deliver up his famous sword Colada, which figures so prominently in the mighty deeds which follow. A falchion which tradition states is none other than this celebrated blade, the Spanish Excalibur, is still shown at the Armeria at Madrid, and all pious lovers of chivalry will gladly believe that it is the sword taken by the Campeador from the haughty Berenger, even though the profane point out that its hilt is obviously of the fifteenth century !

Greatly content were they of the Cid's company with the victory no less than with the spoil, and a feast worthy of princes was prepared to celebrate the occasion.

In courtesy the Cid invited the defeated Count Raymond to feast with him, but he refused the invitation with hauteur, saying that his capture by outlaws had taken away his appetite. Nettled at this display of rudeness, the Cid told him that he would not see his realms again until he broke bread and drank wine with him. Three whole days did the Count refuse to touch all provender, and on the third day the Cid promised him immediate freedom if he would break his fast. This was too much for the haughty Berenger, whose hunger now out-matched his scruples. "Powers above!" exclaims the poet, "with what gust did he eat! His hands plied so quickly that my Cid[1] might not see their play." The Cid then gave him his liberty, and they parted on good terms.

> "Ride on, ride on, my noble Count, a free Frank as thou art ;
> For all the spoil thou leavest me I thank thee from my heart.
> And if to turn the chance of fate against me thou shalt come,
> Right gladly shall I listen for the echoes of thy drum."
> "Nay, Roderick, I leave in peace and peace I shall maintain ;
> From me thou sure hast spoil enow to count a twelvemonth's
>   gain."
> He drove the spur, but backward glanced, he feared for treachery ;
> So black a thought the Cid had harboured not for Christendie.
> No, not for all the wealthy world, who kept his soul in light.
> Whose heart as his so free from guile, the very perfect knight ?

The Cid Makes War Seaward

Turning from Huesca and Montalvan, the Cid began to make war toward the salt sea. His eastward march struck terror to the hearts of the Moors of Valencia. They took counsel together, and resolved to send such a host against him as they thought he might not with-stand. But he routed them with such a slaughter that they dared face him no more. Three years did the Cid

---

[1] Throughout the *Poema* and elsewhere the Cid is constantly alluded to as "Mio Cid" ("My lord"). I deal with the etymology of the name farther on, but hold to the form 'the Cid' as being most familiar to English readers.

war in that country, and his many conquests there were long to tell. He and his men sat themselves down in the land as kings, reaped its corn, and ate its bread. And a great famine came upon the Moors, so that thousands perished.

Now the Cid sent messengers to Castile and Aragon, who made it known that all Christians who came to dwell beneath his rule should fare well. Hearing this, thousands flocked to his banner, and so greatly was he reinforced that in time he was able to march against Valencia itself, the capital of the Moors of that country. With all his host he sat down before that city and beleaguered it. Nine months he environed it, and in the tenth month the men of Valencia opened the gates and surrendered the place. Great was the booty of gold and silver and precious stuffs, so that there fell to his share alone treasure to the amount of thirty thousand marks, and he grew in greatness so that not only his own followers but the Moors of Eastern Spain began to look upon him almost as their rightful lord.

Beholding his puissance, the Moorish King of Seville grew greatly afraid, and resolved to bring the whole power of his kingdom against him. Collecting an army of thirty thousand men, he marched against Valencia. But the Cid encountered him on the banks of the Huerta, and defeated him so completely that never again was he able to do him scathe.

The heart of the Cid now began to grow hopeful that his King would receive him into friendship and confidence once more. And he swore a great oath that for love of Alfonso he would never let his beard be shorn. "So," he said, "will my beard be famous among both Moors and Christians." Once more he sent Alvar

Fañez to Court with the gift of a hundred splendidly appointed horses of the purest Arab blood, praying that he might be permitted to bring his wife, Donna Ximena, and their daughters, to the possessions which he had carved out for himself by his good sword.

Meanwhile there had come to Valencia from the East a holy man, one Bishop Don Jerome, who had heard afar of the prowess of the Cid and longed to cross swords with the infidel. The Cid was well pleased with him, and founded a bishopric of Valencia for the doughty Christian, whose one thought was but to spread the worship of God and slay Saracens.

When Alvar Fañez reached the Court, he sought audience of King Alfonso, who was heartened to hear of the deeds of the Campeador, how he had routed the Moors in five pitched battles, made their lands subject to the crown of Castile, and erected a bishopric in the heart of paynimrie, so that he readily granted permission that Donna Ximena and the ladies Elvira and Sol should go to Valencia. Hearing this, Count Garcia Ordoñez, of the Leonese party, who had secured the Cid's banishment and who cordially hated him, was greatly vexed. But the two Infantes or Princes of Carrión, in Leon, seeing how the Cid grew in power and importance, resolved to ask his daughters in marriage from the King, but meanwhile kept their counsel.

The time had long passed when the Cid should have discharged his debt to the Jews Raquel and Vidas, and hearing that Alvar Fañez was at Court they came to him and begged that it might be paid. Fañez assured them that all should be done as the Cid had promised, and that only stress of constant warfare had kept his master from fulfilling his obligation to them. They were perfectly satisfied with this assurance, and so greatly had they trusted the Cid that they had never opened the chests to examine the nature of the security he had given them.

The Cid Welcomes his Family

Alvar Fañez now made ready to set out for Valencia with Donna Ximena and the Cid's daughters, whom he safely conveyed to their new home. When he heard that they were near at hand, the Cid, who had only a few days before won his famous steed Babieca in a skirmish with the Moors, leapt upon the charger's back, and rode off at a gallop to meet them and welcome them to their new possessions. Greeting them with much affection, he led them to the castle, from the towers of which he showed them the lands he had won for them. And they gave thanks to God for a gift so fair.

Now there was great stirring among the Moors of Africa when they heard of the deeds of the Cid, and they held it for dishonour that he should have redeemed so great a part of Spain from their brothers of the Peninsula. Their king, Yussef, levied a mighty army of fifty thousand men, and, crossing the seas to Spain, marched upon Valencia, hoping to regain it for the Crescent. When the Cid heard this, he exclaimed : " I thank God and the blessed Mother that I have my wife and daughters here. Now shall they see how we do battle with the Moors and win our bread in the land of the stranger ! " The host of Yussef soon came in sight, and environed Valencia so closely that none might enter or leave it, and when the ladies beheld the great army which surrounded the city they were much afraid. But the Cid bade them be of good cheer. "Hearten ye," he said, "for, see, marvellous great wealth comes to us. Here comes a dowry against the marriage of your daughters!"[1]

The Battle with King Bucar

Springing upon Babieca, the Cid led his lances against the Moors of Africa. Then began a contest great and grim. The Spanish spears were red that day, and the Cid plied his good blade Colada so terribly that the Saracens fell before his strokes like corn before the sickle. He aimed a great blow at King Yussef's helm, but the Moorish chieftain, avoiding it, gave his horse the rein and galloped off the field, his dusky host following him in headlong rout. Countless was the spoil in gold, silver, richly caparisoned horses, shields, swords, and body-armour. Too wearied with ceaseless slaughter to give chase, the Cid rode back to where his wife and daughters had sat watching the progress of the battle, his dripping sword in his hand. "Homage to you, ladies," he cried. "Thus are Moors vanquished on the field of battle." But ever mindful of his King and liege-lord, he at once dispatched Alvar Fañez and Pero Bermuez to Court, with the tent of King Yussef and two hundred horses with their caparisons. Greatly pleased was Alfonso. "I receive the gift of the Cid willingly," he said, "and may the day of our reconciliation soon arrive." The Infantes of Carrión, seeing that the reputation of the Cid increased daily, were now fully resolved to ask the daughters of the Campeador in marriage from the

[1] This passage is reminiscent of the saying of the famous Border outlaw Jock Eliot, when he and his men came upon a large haystack of which they resolved to make fodder for their horses. "Eh, man," exclaimed the humorous raider, "if ye had legs, wouldna' ye run!"

The Cid's Daughters Wed

King. Alfonso agreed to enter into negotiations with the Cid, not only for the hands of his daughters, but with the idea of effecting a reconciliation with him, for he was well aware of all the service which the Campeador had done him. So he sent for Alvar Fañez and Pero Bermuez and acquainted them with the offer of the Infantes of Carrión, requesting them to convey it to the Cid without loss of time and assuring him of his esteem.

The envoys hastened to Valencia and told the Cid how the King had sent him a gracious message, asking for the hands of his daughters for the Infantes of Carrión. The Cid was right joyful on hearing this. "What the King desires is my pleasure," he said, "though the Infantes of Carrión are haughty, and bad vassals to the Throne. But be it as God and the King wills."

Then the Campeador made great preparations and set out for the Court, and when the King knew he was approaching he went out to meet him. And the Cid went on his knees before the King and took the grass of the field in his teeth to humble himself before his lord. But Don Alfonso was troubled at the sight, and, raising him, assured him of his grace and affection, at which the Cid was greatly moved and wept joyfully. Then the King feasted the Cid bravely, and when the banquet was at an end asked for the hands of his daughters for the Infantes of Carrión. The Cid made reply that he and his daughters were in the King's hands and that Alfonso himself might give the damsels in marriage.

The Cid's Daughters Wed

After some days spent in feasting and rejoicing, the Campeador returned to Valencia with the two Infantes

75

of Carrión. He told his wife and daughters that the marriage was of the King's making and not of his, as he was not without misgivings as to the result of the alliance. Nevertheless he made great preparations, as befitted the importance of such a ceremony with two of the greatest lords in Spain, and Donna Elvira and Donna Sol were espoused to the Infantes of Carrión in the church of Santa Maria by the good warrior-bishop Jerome. The wedding celebrations lasted fifteen days, and the Cid had no reason to be dissatisfied with his sons-in-law, who bore themselves as gallantly in the lists as in the dance.

The Adventure of the Lion

The Infantes of Carrión and their wives had remained in Valencia for about two years when a mishap befell. One day, during the time of the afternoon siesta, a lion, kept for baiting in the ring, broke loose from its cage and made its way into the palace. The Campeador reclined upon a couch asleep, but his dauntless followers gathered round him to protect him, all except the Infantes of Carrión, one of whom crept beneath the couch on which the Cid slept, while the other made such speed to quit the palace that he fell across the beam of a wine-press and rent his robes. The clamour awoke the Cid, who rose, and, going to where the lion crouched, firmly placed his hand on the brute's bristling mane and led him back to his cage. Nor did the lion resist, evidently knowing his master.

The Infantes of Carrión, when they knew all danger was past, came out of hiding, looking so pale and terrified that the hardy soldiers of the Cid could not restrain their laughter. At this the haughty northern grandees felt deep insult and resentment and an unmanly feeling of revenge awoke in their hearts.

Within a few days of this incident news reached Valencia that Abu Bekr, the commander of the armies of the King of Morocco, was marching upon the city. The Cid and his captains rejoiced at the news, but not so the Infantes of Carrión, who took counsel together as to how they might avoid the fighting and return to their own territories.

Here a break occurs in the narrative, and from a later passage it is clear that the missing lines relate to a test of the courage of at least one of the Infantes, who, stung by an imputation of cowardice, armed himself and set out to fight a Moor, who, however, put him to flight. But Pero Bermuez, to save the Cid's feelings, slew the Saracen and made it appear that the Infante had done so.

A 'Secret Service' Story of " The Cid "

A most romantic tale hangs upon the first line of the next passage :

" May the time come when I deserve as much of both of you."

The line is supposed to be the last in the speech of Pero Bermuez to the Infante Don Ferrando, who had probably expressed gratitude to him. The first English author to attempt a translation of the *Poema del Cid* was John Hookham Frere, the translator of the plays of Aristophanes, who was for some years British Minister at Madrid. He made a conjectural reading of the above line, which he communicated to the Marquis de la Romana. Some years later, in 1808, when the Marquis was commanding a body of troops in the French service in Denmark, Frere was able to accredit a confidential messenger to him, assuring the

Spanish commander of the genuineness of the message he carried by mention of the amended line, the correction in which was known only to the Marquis and himself. The circumstance led to one of the most important movements in the war against Napoleon.

The Fighting Bishop

The Infantes of Carrión, who did not relish the idea of a protracted struggle with the Moors, resolved to betake themselves to the security of their own estates at the first opportunity. But, as if to shame them, the warlike Bishop Jerome appeared before the Cid armed *cap-à-pie* and entreated his permission to take part in the fighting. The Cid smilingly gave his assent, and no sooner had he done so than the doughty churchman mounted a great war-horse and, issuing out of the gates, galloped headlong against the Saracens. At the first onset he slew two of them outright, but had the misfortune to break his lance. Nothing daunted, however, this ardent disciple of the Church militant drew his sword and, brandishing it about his head like a trained knight-at-arms, flung himself once more upon the Moorish ranks with all the weight of his charger. Laying about him left and right, he killed or wounded a heathen with every blow. But the enemy closed round him, and it would have gone hard indeed with the fighting bishop had not the Cid, who had witnessed his gallantry with all a warrior's admiration for the deeds of another brave man, laid his lance in rest and, setting spurs to Babieca, plunged into the thickest of the fray. Beneath his terrific onset the lightly armed Moors gave way in terror. Wheeling, he came at them again, crashing through their ranks

The Fighting Bishop

like a tempest, and dealing death and destruction wherever he went. The Moors wavered, broke, and fled amain. The whole army of the Cid now bore down upon them, horse and man, bursting into their camp, breaking the tent-ropes, and dashing aside the gaudy Eastern pavilions where they had lodged.

Upon the terror-stricken ranks the horsemen of Castile
Came thundering down ; King Bucar's men the iron tempest feel.
And down to dust the severed arm, the severed steel-capped head
Fall lifeless, and the charger's hoofs trample the gory dead.
"Ha ! stay, King Bucar !" cries the Cid. "Now tarry, Moorish
    lord ;
You came to seek me o'er the sea, mine is the peaceful word."
"If peace is in thy naked sword and in thy charging steed,
Then I would flee it," cried the King, and spurred his horse to speed.
With hasty stride the King doth ride straight for the open sea ;
Spain's champion is at his side, never again will he
Know the delights of Algiers' halls ; Colada shines on high :
Now whether by the sword or sea, King Bucar, wilt thou die ?
The good blade shears the Moor in twain, down to the saddle-
    bow ;
So perished the Algerian lord—may every Moor die so !
And thus upon this day of fame the Cid his guerdon won,
Worth many a purse of minted marks, the noble blade Tizon !

Riding back from the fray, the Cid espied the Infantes of Carrión and welcomed them. "Now that they are brave will they be welcomed by the brave," he said, rather wistfully, to Alvar Fañez. The proud and shallow princes were wrathful when they overheard this, and the shadow of vengeance once more arose within their haughty hearts. "Let us take our leave of the Cid and return to Carrión," they said. "We have been flouted and insulted here by these banditti and their leader. On the way home we shall know how to avenge ourselves upon his daughters."

With this cowardly purpose they smilingly requested the Campeador to permit them to depart. Sorrowfully he granted it, and loading them with presents and bestowing upon them the famous swords Colada and Tizon, which he had himself taken in battle from the Moors, he requested Feliz Muñoz, his nephew, to accompany the Infantes and his daughters to Carrión.

The Infantes' Revenge

Great was the grief of the Cid and Donna Ximena at parting with the ladies Elvira and Sol, and they were not without some misgivings. But they charged Feliz Muñoz to keep good watch over their daughters, and this he promised to do. After journeying for some days the party had to traverse the great forest of Corpes, where in a glade they pitched pavilions and spent the night. In the morning the Infantes sent their suite on ahead, and, taking the saddle-girths from the horses, beat the unfortunate daughters of the Cid most cruelly. The wretched ladies begged for death rather than suffer such disgrace, but the cowardly Infantes, laughing scornfully, mocked them, cast them off, and so dealt with them that they left them for dead. "Thus," they said, "the dishonour of the affair of the lion is avenged," and mounting their horses they rode off.

As the deserted and dishonoured wives of the cowardly pair lay bleeding on the grass, Feliz Muñoz, their cousin, who had lodged during the night in another part of the forest, rode up, and seeing their piteous condition hastened to their relief. Having dressed their hurts to the best of his ability, he rode quickly to the nearest town and purchased clothing and horses for them as befitted their station. When these tidings reached the Cid in Valencia great anger rose in his heart. He did not give it vent, however, but sat moodily pondering upon the dishonour done to his daughters. At last, after many hours, he spoke. "By my beard!" he cried, "the Infantes of Carrión shall not profit by this." Soon the ladies Sol and Elvira arrived at Valencia, and he received them lovingly, but not compassionately. "Welcome, my daughters," said he. "God keep ye from evil! I accepted this marriage, for I dared not gainsay it. God grant that I see you better married hereafter, and that I have my revenge upon my sons-in-law of Carrión."

The Court at Toledo

Then the Cid dispatched messengers to King Alfonso, acquainting him of the great wrong done to his daughters by the Infantes, and pleading for justice. The King was greatly wroth at the news, and ordered the Court to sit at Toledo and the Infantes to be summoned before him to answer for their crime. They begged to be excused attendance, but the King peremptorily refused to accept any apology or subterfuge, and demanded their instant compliance with his summons. With great misgivings they journeyed to Toledo, taking with them the Count Don Garcia, Asur González, Gonzalo Asurez, and a great band of dependents, thinking thereby to overawe the Cid. The Campeador himself soon arrived at Court, with many a trusted veteran, all armed to the teeth. He wore a rich robe of red fur broidered with gold, and his beard was bound with a cord to preserve it. When he entered the Court with his men all rose to greet him save the

81

Infantes of Carrión and their party, for he seemed a great baron and the Infantes might not look at him for shame.

"Princes, barons, and hidalgos," said King Alfonso, "I have summoned ye here that justice may be done the Cid Campeador. As ye all know, foul wrong has been done his daughters, and I have set judges apart to moderate in this business and to search out the right, for wrong I will not have in Christian Spain. I swear by the bones of San Isidro that he who disturbs my Court shall quit my kingdom and forfeit my love, and he who shall prove his right, on his side am I. Now let the Cid make his demand and we shall hear the answer of the Infantes of Carrión."

Then rose the Cid, and in the Court among all these great barons and lords there was no nobler figure. "My lord the King," he said, "it is not I alone whom the Infantes of Carrión have wronged, but yourself also, who gave them my daughters in marriage. Let them first restore my swords Colada and Tizon, since they are no longer my sons-in-law."

The Infantes, hearing the Cid speak thus, thought that he would urge no more against them if they restored the swords, and so they formally handed them over to the King. But it was the Campeador's intention to punish them by every means in his power, so when he received the wondrous falchions from the hands of Alfonso he at once presented them to Feliz Muñoz and Martin Antolinez, thus showing that it was not for himself that he desired them. Having done this, he turned once again to the King.

"My liege," he said, "when the Infantes left Valencia I bestowed upon them three thousand marks in gold and silver. Let them now restore this, since they are no longer my sons-in-law."

"Nay, if we do this," cried the Infantes, "we must even pay it out of our lands in Carrión." But the judges demanded that the sum be paid in Court without delay. The treacherous princelings could not raise such a treasure in money, so the Court decided that it must be paid in kind. Then the Infantes saw that there was no help but to acquiesce, and brought many a steed and trained palfrey with their furniture to repay the Cid, borrowing from the members of their suite and entering into such obligations as would burden them for many a day.

Redress by Combat

When this matter had at last been settled, the Cid then advanced his principal grievance against the Infantes, and asked for redress by combat in the lists for the great wrong they had done his daughters. At this Count Garcia, their spokesman, rose to defend the Infantes. He pleaded that they were of princely degree, and for that reason alone were justified in casting off the daughters of the Cid. Then Fernán González, the elder of the Infantes, himself rose to approve the speech of his vassal, and cast fresh scorn upon the alliance he had made, justifying his cowardly action by his princely rank as a thing quite natural and fitting. At this Pero Bermuez opened the vials of his wrath upon the Infantes, taunting them with cowardice in the affair of the lion and casting defiance of battle in their teeth.

Enter Asur González

The argument waxed high, when at that moment Asur González, a haughty vassal of the Infantes, entered the hall.

With early viands and with wine flushed were his face and brow,
Disordered were his garments and his mantle hung full low.
He scanned the Court with bearing rude, right clownish was his
    vaunt:
"How now, my lords? What have we here? Thinkst Carrión to
    daunt?
What bruit is this about the Cid, the lordling of Bivar?
At drawing tithes from dusty millers better is he far
Than ruffling at a Cortés; he to match with Carrión!"
Then up leapt Muño Gustioz: "Ha' done, thou knave, ha' done!
Drunkard, who lookest on the wine before ye tell a bead,
Who never yet did keep thy troth, evil in word and deed,
The only boon I crave is but to have thee where my sword
May cut the false tongue from thy throat and cease thy lying word."
"Enough, enough," Alfonso cried, "I give thee my consent
To meet each other in the lists; so ends this Parliament."

The tumult which the King had endeavoured to abate
had hardly died away when two cavaliers entered the
Court. The new-comers were ambassadors from the
Infantes of Navarre and Aragon, who had come to
request the King to bestow the hands of the Cid's
daughters upon their masters. Alfonso turned to the
Cid and requested his permission to ratify the marriage
at once, and when the Campeador had humbly given
his consent he answered to the assembled nobles that
the espousals would duly take place, adding that the
combat between the disputants would be fought out on
the morrow.

This was right woeful news to the Infantes of Carrión,
who, in great fear, requested him to permit them some
delay to procure fitting horses and arms, so that at last
the King scornfully fixed the day of combat at three
weeks from that date, and the place where it was to be
fought out as Carrión itself, so that the Infantes should
have no grounds of excuse for absence or be able to

The Trial by Combat

plead that the champions of the Cid had been granted any undue advantage.

The Cid then took his leave of the King, and on parting pressed him to accept his courser Babieca. But Alfonso refused the proffered gift, saying courteously that if he accepted it Babieca would not have so good a lord. Turning to those who were to uphold his cause in the lists, the Campeador bade them an affectionate farewell, and so he departed for Valencia, and the King for Carrión to see justice done.

The Trial by Combat

When the time of truce was over the contending parties sought the lists. The Cid's men did not waste much time in arming themselves, but the treacherous Infantes of Carrión had brought with them a number of their vassals in the hope that they might be able to slay the Cid's champions by night, when they were off their guard. But Antolinez and his comrades kept good watch and frustrated their design. When they saw that there was no help for it but to meet their challengers *à outrance*, they prayed the King that the Cid's men might not be permitted to use the famous swords Colada and Tizon, for they superstitiously dreaded the trenchancy of these marvellous weapons, and bitterly repented that they had restored them. Alfonso, however, refused to listen to this appeal.

"Ye have swords of your own," he said brusquely. "Let them suffice you, and see that you wield them like men, for, believe me, there will be no shortcoming on the side of the Campeador."

The trumpets sounded and the Cid's three champions leapt upon their impatient destriers, first having made the sign of the Cross upon their saddles. The Infantes of Carrión also mounted, but none so blithely. The marshals or heralds who were to decide the rules of the combat, and give judgment in case of dispute, took their places. Then said King Alfonso : "Hear what I say, Infantes of Carrión. This combat ye should have fought at Toledo, but ye would not, so I have brought these three cavaliers in safety to the land of Carrión. Take your right ; seek no wrong : who attempts it, ill betide him."

The description of the scene that follows has more than once been compared with Chaucer's description of the combat between Palamon and Arcite in *The Knight's Tale*, and, as will be seen, a resemblance certainly exists.[1]

> And now the marshals quit the lists and leave them face to face ;
> Their shields are dressed before their breasts, their lances are in place.
> Each charger's flank now feels the spur, each helm is bending low,
> The earth doth shake as horse and man hurl them upon the foe.

---

[1] The commencement of the passage in question is as follows (lines 1741–50) :

> The heraldz laften here prikyng up and doun ;
> Now ryngede the tromp and clarioun :
> Ther is no more to say, but est and west
> In goth the speres ful sadly in arest ;
> Ther seen men who can juste, and who can ryde ;
> In goth the scharpe spore into the side,
> Ther schyveren schaftes upon schuldres thykke ;
> He feeleth through the herte-spon the prikke.
> Up sprengen speres on twenty foot on hight ;
> Out goon the swerdes as the silver bright.

The balance is, however, greatly in favour of Chaucer, whose lines, *if properly accented*, beat the original Spanish on its own ground, and this notwithstanding the absurd remark of Swinburne that "Chaucer and Spenser scarcely made a good poet between them."

The Trial by Combat

The echo of their meeting is a sound of meikle dread,
And all who hear the deadly shock count them as good as sped.
The false Ferrando and Bermuez strike lance on either's shield,
The Infant's spear goes through the boss, but the stout shaft doth
    yield
And splinters ere the point can pass thorough the other's mail.
But Pero's shaft struck home, nor did the seasoned timber fail ;
It pierced Ferrando's corselet and sank into his breast,
And to the trampled ground there drooped the Infant's haughty
    crest.
Bermuez then drew Tizon's bright blade ; ere ever he could smite
The Infant yielded him and cried, "Thou hast the victor's right."

While this combat was proceeding Antolinez and the
other Infante came together. Each of their lances smote
the other's shield and splintered. Then, drawing their
swords, they rode fiercely against one another. Antolinez, flourishing Colada, struck so mightily at Diego
that the good blade shore its way clean through the
steel plates of his casque, and even cut half the hair from
Diego's head. The terrified princeling wheeled his
courser and fled, but Antolinez pursued him with mock
fury and struck him across the shoulders with the flat
of his sword. So had the hound the chastisement of
cowards. As he felt the blade across his withers Diego
shrieked aloud and spurred past the boundaries of the
lists, thus, according to the rules of the combat, admitting
himself vanquished.

When the trumpets of the pursuivants sounded,
Muño Gustioz and Asur González ran swiftly and
fiercely together. The point of Asur's spear glanced
off Muño's armour, but that of the Cid's champion
pierced the shield of his opponent and drove right
through his breast, so that it stuck out a full fathom
between the shoulder-blades. The haughty Asur fell

heavily to the ground, but had enough of life left in him to beg for mercy.

King Alfonso then duly credited the Cid's champions with the victory, and without loss of time they returned to Valencia to acquaint their master with the grateful news that his honour had been avenged.

Shortly afterward the espousals of the Cid's daughters to the noble Infantes of Navarre and Aragon were celebrated with much pomp. The *Poema del Cid*, however, concludes as abruptly as it begins :

> So in Navarre and Aragon his daughters both did reign,
> And princes of his blood to-day sit on the thrones of Spain.
> Greater and greater grew his name in honour and in worth ;
> At last upon a Pentecost he passed away from earth.
> Upon him be the grace of Christ, Whom all of us adore.
> Such is the story, gentles, of the Cid Campeador.

The Real Cid

Cervantes' summing-up upon the *Poema del Cid* is perhaps the sanest on record. The Cid certainly existed in the flesh ; what matter, then, whether his achievements occurred or not ? For the Cid of romance is a very different person from the Cid of history, who was certainly a born leader of men, but crafty, unscrupulous, and cruel. The *Poema* is thus romance of no uncertain type, and as this book deals with romance and not with history, there is small need in this place to provide the reader with a chronicle of the rather mercenary story of Roderigo of Bivar the real.

"Mio Cid," the title under which he is most frequently mentioned, is a half Arabic, half Spanish rendering of the Arabic *Sid-y*, "My lord," by which he was probably known to his Moorish subjects in Valencia, and it is

The Real Cid

unlikely that he was given this appellation in Spain during his lifetime. But even to this day it is a name to conjure with in the Peninsula. So long as the heart of the Briton beats faster at the name of Arthur and the Frenchman is thrilled by the name of Roland the Spaniard will not cease to reverence that of the great romantic shadow which looms above the early history of his land like a very god of war—the Cid Campeador.

CHAPTER III: "AMADIS DE GAUL"

There stands a castle on a magic height
Whose spell-besetten pathways ye may climb
If that ye love fair chivalry sublime.
Come, its enchanted turrets yield the sight,
As long ago to demoiselle and knight,
Of many a satrapy of ancient rhyme,
And in its carven corridors shall Time
Display us trophies of a dead delight :

The damascene of armour in the dusk,
Shadows of banners torn from infidels,
The fragments of an unremembered glory,
Fragrant with faint, imperishable musk
Of Moorish fantasy.   Dissolve, ye spells !
Open, ye portals of Castilian story !

L. S.

MANY a casement in the grey castle of Spanish Romance opens upon vistas of fantastic loveliness or gloomy grandeur, but none commands a prospect so brilliant, so infinitely varied, or so rich in the colours of fantasy as that aery embrasure overlooking the region of marvel and high chivalry where is enacted the gallant and glorious history of Amadis de Gaul.   The window of which I speak is perched high in a turret of the venerable fortalice, and displays such a landscape as was dear to the weavers of ancient tapestries or the legend-loving painters of old Florence.   Beneath is spread a princely domain of noble meadow-land, crossed and interlaced by the serpent-silver of narrow rivers and rising northward to dim, castellated hills. Far beyond these, remote and seeming more of sky than of earth, soar the blue and jagged peaks of dragon-haunted mountains.   This scene of almost supernatural beauty presents, at the first glance, an unbroken richness of colour and radiance.   The meadow-land is populous

Amadis de Gaul

with pavilions and the air is painted with pennons and gilded with the blazonry of banners. The glitter of armour thrills the blood like the challenge of martial music. Strange palaces of marble, white as sculptured ice, rise at the verges of magic forests, or glitter on the edges of the promontories, their gardens and terraces sloping to silent and forlorn beaches. The scene is indeed " Beautiful as a wreck of Paradise."

Such seems the book of *Amadis* when first we glance through its rainbow-coloured pages. But when we gain a nearer view by the aid of the romancer's magical glass we find that the radiant scene is deeply shadowed in places. Ravines profound as night lie near the castled hills, in which all manner of noxious things swarm and multiply. The princely fortresses, the gay palaces, are often the haunts of desperate outlaws or malignant sorcerers. Hideous giants dwell in the mountains, or in the shadowy islands which rise from the pale sea, and dragons have their lairs in fell and forest. But whether it breed light or gloom, the atmosphere of *Amadis* is suffused with such a glamour that we come to love the darker places ; we feel that the horror they hold is but the stronger wine of romance, a vintage which intoxicates.

And if we remain at our point of vantage until nightfall and watch the illumination of this wondrous region by the necromancy of moonshine we shall be granted an even more inspiring draught from the strange chalice of romance. In the mystery of moonlight armour is silvered to an unearthly whiteness, blood-red lights gleam from the turrets of the magicians, and the sylph-like shapes of sorceresses flit from sea to forest like living moonbeams. From the deserts between the hills and the distant mountains come the cries of ravening monsters, and all the fantastic world of Faëry is vivid with life.

What marvel then that when this surpassing picture was unveiled to the eyes of a nation of knights it aroused such a fervour of applause and appreciation as has been granted to few works in the history of literary effort? The author of *Amadis* displayed to the chivalry of Spain such a world as it had dreamed of. Every knight felt himself a possible Amadis and every damsel deemed herself an Oriana. The philosophy and atmosphere of the book took complete possession of the soul of Spain, banishing grosser ideals and introducing a new code of manners and sentiment. The main plot and the manifold incidents which arise from it were coherently and skilfully arranged, and were not made up of isolated and disconnected accounts of combats, or tedious descriptions of apparel, appointments, or architecture, interspersed with the boastful bellowings of rude paladins or vociferous kings, as the 'plots' of the *cantares de gesta* had been. Moreover, the whole was powerfully infused with the love-philosophy of chivalry, in which woman, instead of being the chattel and plaything of man, found herself exalted to heights of worship, and even of omnipotence, undreamed of by the ruder singers of the *cantares*.

Origin of the "Amadis" Romances

The first Peninsular version of *Amadis* appeared in a Portuguese dress, and was the work of a Lusitanian knight, Joham de Lobeira (1261–1325), who was born at Porto, fought at Aljubarrota, where he was knighted upon the field by King Joham of happy memory, and died at Elvas. But Southey's protestations notwithstanding, everything points to France as being the

Origin of the " Amadis " Romances

original home of the romance, and there is even a reference in Portuguese literature to the circumstance that a certain *Pedro* de Lobeira translated *Amadis* from the French by order of the Infante Dom Pedro, son of Joham I.   The original French tale has vanished without leaving a trace that it ever existed, save in the Peninsular versions to which it gave birth, and we are no more fortunate as regards the Portuguese rendering. A manuscript copy of Lobeira's romance was known to exist at the close of the sixteenth century in the archives of the Dukes of Arveiro at Lisbon, and appears to have been extant as late as 1750.   After that period, however, it disappears from the sight of the bibliophile, and all the evidence points to its having been destroyed at the earthquake at Lisbon in 1755, along with the ducal palace in which it was housed.

Its fame, as well as its matter, was, however, kept alive by the Spanish version, and if we must regard Portugal as the original home of *Amadis* in the Peninsula, it is to the genius of Castile that we owe not only its preservation, but its possible improvement.   At some time between 1492 and 1508 Garcia Ordoñez de Montalvo, governor of the city of Medina del Campo, addressed himself to the task of its translation and adaptation. At what precise date it was first printed is obscure. Early copies are lacking, but we learn that the Spanish conquerors of Mexico remarked upon the resemblance of that city to the places of enchantment spoken of in *Amadis*.   This occurred in 1519, not 1549, as stated by Southey.   They may, perhaps, have referred to the Portuguese version, but in any case an edition of *Amadis* is known to have been published in that year, and another at Seville in 1547.   Reference has already been made to the numerous translations of the romance in all languages, and to the equally manifold continuations of it by several hands, but it is necessary to remark that only the first four books of *Amadis*—that is, those which constitute the *Amadis* proper—were written by Montalvo, the remainder being the independent and original work of imitators.[1]

Elisena and Perion

The action of the romance begins at an obscure and indefinite period, described as following almost immediately upon the death of our Redeemer, at which time, we are told, there flourished in Brittany a Christian king named Garinter, who was blessed with two lovely daughters. The elder, known as 'the Lady of the Garland,' because of her fondness for wearing a coronel of flowers, had some years before the period of the story's commencement been wed to King Languines (Angus) of Scotland, and had two beautiful children, Agrayes and Mabilia. Elisena, the younger daughter, was famed for her beauty throughout the lands of Christendom, but though many powerful monarchs and princes had asked her hand in marriage, she would wed with none, but gave herself up to a life of holiness and good works. In the opinion of all the knights and ladies of her father's realm, one so fair grievously transgressed the laws of love by remaining

[1] See the work of Rivadeneyra, *Biblioteca de Autores españoles*, vol. xl (1846–48), where the romance is prefaced in a brilliant and scholarly manner by Gayangos. Its origins are ably discussed by Eugène Baret, *Études sur la Redaction Espagnole de l'Amadis de Gaule* (1853); T. Braga, *Historia das Novellas Portuguezas de Cavalleria* (1873); and L. Braunfels, *Kritischer Versuch über den Roman Amadis von Gallien* (1876).

Elisena and Perion

single, and it came to pass that the beautiful and saintly Elisena earned from the more worldly of her gay critics the name of 'the Lost Devotee.'

If Elisena was devoted to a life of austerity her royal father was equally partial to the pleasures of the chase, and spent much of his time in the green forest-land which occupied the greater part of Lesser Britain in those remote days. On one of those occasions, as he rode unattended in the greenwood, as was his wont, he chanced to hear the clash of arms, and, riding to a clearing whence came the sounds of combat, he saw two knights of Brittany attacking an armed stranger, whom he guessed by his armour and bearing to be a person of rank and distinction, and who bore himself with such courage and address that he succeeded in slaying both his opponents.

As the stranger was in the act of sheathing his weapon he observed Garinter, and rode forward to meet him, saluting him with a courteous mien. He complained that in a Christian country an errant knight did not expect such treatment from its inhabitants as had been meted out to him, to which the King sagely replied that in all countries evilly disposed people were to be found as well as good folk, and that the slain knights had been traitors to their liege lord and well deserved their fate.

The stranger then proffered the information that he sought the King of Brittany with tidings of a friend, and on learning this Garinter revealed his identity. The knight then informed him that he was King Perion of Gaul, who had long desired his friendship. Garinter insisted that his brother monarch should accompany him to his palace, and Perion consenting, they turned their horses' heads toward the city.

Arrived at the palace, they sat down to a rich banquet,

which was graced by the Queen and the Princess Elisena. No sooner did Elisena and Perion behold one another than they knew that a great and deathless love had sprung up between them. When the Queen and Princess had risen from the banquet Elisena divulged her love for Perion to her damsel and confidante, Darioleta, and asked her to discover whether the King of Gaul had pledged his troth to any other lady. Darioleta, who was not easily abashed, went straight to Perion, who avowed his love for Elisena in passionate terms and promised to take her to wife. He begged the damsel to bring him to where Elisena was, that he might have the happiness of expressing his love in person, and she returned to the Princess with his message. So impatient was Elisena to hear from Perion's own lips that he loved her, that, recking not of time or tide, she sought the apartment in which he was lodged, where she remained until dawn, detained by his protestations of affection and her own devotion to the noble and knightly monarch who had so suddenly made her regard her former mode of life as savourless and melancholy.

Ten days did Perion sojourn at the Court of Garinter. At the end of that time it became necessary that he should depart, but before he took his leave he plighted his troth to Elisena, and left her one of two duplicate rings he wore, as a pledge of his faith. Search as he might, however, he failed to find his good sword, a tried and trusty weapon, and at last was forced to abandon the search for it.

The Birth and Casting Away of Amadis

When her lover had gone Elisena was plunged in the deepest grief, and all the comfort which Darioleta could

The Birth and Casting Away of Amadis

bestow upon her failed to rouse her from the lethargy of sorrow into which she had fallen. In her father's kingdom, as in modern Scotland, an old law existed which provided that if two persons solemnly took each other in marriage by oath no further ceremony was necessary to render the union legal, although it was usual to have it ratified later by both Church and law. Perion and Elisena had taken these vows upon themselves, but the Princess dreaded the wrath of her father, whom the lovers had not consulted, and when a little son was born to her she was in great fear of the consequences, for she knew her father to be both proud and hasty and prone to act before he learned the truth of a matter. The worldly and quick-witted Darioleta had, however, no scruples regarding the manner in which she resolved to save her mistress and herself from the King's wrath, and despite the protestations of Elisena, who in her weakness was unable to restrain her, she built a little ark of wood, made it water-tight with pitch, and, regardless of the tears and lamentations of her mistress, placed the new-born baby boy therein with Perion's sword, which she had abstracted from his sleeping-chamber. Then she wrote upon a piece of parchment, "This is Amadis, son of a king," covered the writing with wax so that it might be preserved from obliteration, and, securing it to the betrothal ring which Perion had given to Elisena, fastened it by a silken cord round the infant's neck. Then with the utmost caution, lest any one should observe her action, she carried the tiny vessel to the river which ran at the foot of the palace garden and launched it upon the swift, deep waters.

The little ark was rapidly carried out to sea, which was not more than half a league distant, and it had scarcely emerged upon the tossing billows when it was sighted by the mariners of a Scottish vessel which bore a Caledonian knight, Gandales, back from Gaul to his home in the North. At his orders the sailors launched a boat, and having secured the tiny vessel, brought it to the ship, when the wife of Gandales, delighted with the beauty of the infant it held, decided to adopt him as her own. In a few days the vessel put into the Scottish port of Antalia,[1] and Gandales carried the little Amadis to his castle, where he brought him up with his own son, Gandalin.

Some years afterward, when Amadis was about five years old, Languines, the King of Scotland, and his Queen, 'the Lady of the Garland,' and sister to Elisena, paid a visit to the castle of Gandales, and were so greatly attracted by the child's grace and beauty that they expressed a desire to adopt him as their own. Gandales acquainted them with what he knew of Amadis's history, and the royal pair promised to regard him as their own son. Amadis, because of the circumstances of his strange discovery, was known to every one as 'the Child of the Sea,' and indeed this mysterious and poetic name cleaved to him until his identity had been proven beyond cavil. He showed no reluctance to accompany his new guardians, although he was grieved at having to part with his first foster-parents, but the little Gandalin would in no wise be separated from him, and begged so hard to be permitted to share his fortunes that at last King Languines took both the boys under his protection.

[1] Anstruther, in Fife? The Spaniards would know the place through their intercourse with the Flemings, who traded considerably with it. A Spanish vessel put into Anstruther during the flight of the Armada round the coasts of Scotland.

Perion's Dream

Perion's Dream

Let us return to King Perion. Occupied once more with the affairs of his kingdom, he still knew great heaviness of spirit because of a dream that he had had while at the Court of Garinter. It seemed to him in his dream that some one entered his sleeping-apartment, thrust a hand through his side, and, taking out his heart, cast it into the river that flowed through King Garinter's garden. Crying out in his anguish, he was answered by a voice that another heart was still left to him. Troubled by memory of the dream, which he could not unriddle, he called together all the wise men of his realm and requested them to attempt its solution. Only one of them could unravel the mystery, and the sage who did so assured him that the heart which had been abstracted represented a son which a noble lady had borne him, while the remaining heart symbolized another son who would in some manner be taken away against the will of her who had cast away the first.

As the King left the wise man's presence he encountered a mysterious damsel, who saluted him and said : " Know, King Perion, that when thou recoverest thy loss the kingdom of Ireland shall lose its flower " ; and ere the King could detain or question her she had gone.

In course of time King Garinter died, and Perion and Elisena were formally wedded. But when Perion asked his wife if she had borne him a son, so bitterly ashamed was she of the part she had been forced to play in the matter of the child's disappearance that she denied everything. Later, two beautiful children were born to them, a son and a daughter, called Galaor and Melicia.

When Galaor was but two and a half years old, the
King and Queen, at that time sojourning at a town
called Banzil, near the sea, were walking in the gardens
of the palace there, when suddenly a monstrous giant
rose out of the waves and, catching up the little Galaor,
made off with him before anyone could prevent him.

The monster, dashing into the water, clambered on
board a ship and put out to sea, crying out joyfully, as
he did so: "The damsel told me true!" The parents
were deeply afflicted at the loss of their son, and in her
grief Elisena admitted the casting away of Amadis.
Then Perion knew that what the wise man had told
him regarding the loss of the two hearts was the truth
indeed.

Now the giant who had stolen the little Galaor was not
of the race of evil monsters, but was generous in disposition and gentle in demeanour. Indeed, he took as
much care of the child as if he had been one of his own
gigantic brood. He was a native of Lyonesse, was
known as Gandalue, and was the master of two castles
in an island of the sea. He had peopled this island
with Christian folk, and gave the little Galaor into the
keeping of a holy hermit, with strict orders to educate
him as a brave and loyal knight. He told the hermit
that a damsel—the same who had addressed King
Perion so strangely, and who was a powerful sorceress—
had assured him that only a son of Perion could conquer
his lifelong and ruthless enemy, the giant Albadan,[1]

[1] I think I can see in this giant Albadan the giant Albiona, one of the
two monsters, sons of Neptune, who, according to Pomponius Mela,
attacked Hercules in Liguria. The name Albion was once given to
the whole of Britain, and later, as Alba and Albany, to Scotland, whose
people were known as Albannach. This is said to mean 'the White,' in

who had slain his father, and had taken from him the rock Galtares. And so Galaor was left in the care of the hermit.

Oriana

About this time King Lisuarte of Britain chanced to put into a port of Scotland, where he was honourably received by King Languines. With Lisuarte was his wife Brisena, and his beautiful little daughter Oriana, the fairest creature in the world. And because she suffered so much at sea, her parents decided to leave her for a space at the Court of Scotland. Amadis was now twelve years old, but seemed fifteen, so tall and hardy was he, and the Queen bestowed him upon Oriana for her service. Oriana said that 'it pleased her,' and Amadis cherished those words in his heart, so that they never faded from his memory. But he knew not that Oriana loved him, and was greatly in awe of the lovely and serious little maiden of ten, for whom he conceived a high and noble affection. Very beautiful was the silent love of these children for one another. But silent it remained, for Amadis was fearful of presumption and Oriana the most modest of little damsels.

High thoughts of chivalry now began to stir in the heart of Amadis, so that at last he requested King Languines to grant him the boon of knighthood. Languines was greatly surprised that a mere boy should crave such a heavy burden of honour, but approved his desire, and gave orders that arms should be made for

allusion to the cliffs of Dover! It is much more probable that it signified 'the place or region of the god Alba,' 'the country of the white god.' All the Scottish gods were giants, like the Fomorians of Ireland.

him. He sent to Gandales, the knight who had found Amadis in the sea, acquainting him with the lad's purpose, and Gandales dispatched a messenger to Court with the sword, ring, and parchment which he had found in the ark along with the sea-borne baby.[1]

These things were delivered to Amadis as belonging to him, and when he showed them to Oriana she begged for the wax that contained the parchment, not knowing it held anything of moment, and accordingly he gave it to her. Shortly after this King Perion arrived on a visit to Languines, to ask his help against King Abies of Ireland, who had invaded Gaul with all the force of his kingdom. Amadis, knowing Perion's great reputation as a warrior, much desired to be knighted by his hand, and asked the Queen to crave the boon on his behalf. But she seemed sad and distraught, and heeded him not. He inquired of Oriana the cause of the Queen's sadness, and she replied: "Child of the Sea, this is the first thing ye ever asked of me."

"Ah, lady," replied Amadis, "I am not worthy to ask anything from such as you."

"What?" she exclaimed. "Is then your heart so feeble?"

"Aye, lady," he replied, "in all things toward you, save that it would serve you like one who is not his own, but yours."

"Mine!" said Oriana, mystified; "since when?"

"Since 'it pleased you,'" replied Amadis, with a smile. "Do you not remember your words when the Queen offered me for your service?"

---

[1] Strange that a sword and a ring should so often be the test of identity in such tales! So it was, as regards the first of these tokens at least, with Theseus, Arthur, and many another hero. On this head see Hartland, *The Legend of Perseus* (1894–96).

Amadis Goes on Adventure

"I am well pleased that it should be so," said Oriana shyly, and beholding Amadis much overcome at her gracious answer, she slipped away to ask the Queen the cause of her sorrow.

The Queen told her that she was deeply distressed because of her sister Elisena, whose kingdom had been invaded, and, returning to Amadis, Oriana explained to him why his royal mistress had left his appeals unanswered. Amadis at once expressed a desire to proceed to Gaul to fight against the Irish invaders, and Oriana applauded his intention. "You shall go to the wars as my knight," she said, simply but graciously. Amadis kissed her hand, and requested her to ask the Princess Mabilia, Perion's daughter (and Amadis's sister) to bring it about that her father should confer the honour of knighthood upon him. The little damsel readily consented to do so, and King Perion joyfully acquiesced in the young man's eager desire to embrace the profession of arms. So, asking him to kneel, he bestowed upon him the accolade, fastened the knightly spurs upon his heels, and girded the sword to his side.

Amadis Goes on Adventure

Now Amadis resolved to set out for Gaul at once, so, taking a tender leave of Oriana and accompanied by Gandalin, his foster-brother, he rode off from the palace at nightfall. They had not gone far when they encountered the mysterious sorceress who, as we have seen, took such an interest in the fate of our hero, and whose name was Urganda.[1]

[1] Urganda, as Southey remarks, is a true fairy, resembling Morgan le Fay in her attributes, but, as Scott says, she has no connexion with the more classic *nymphidæ*. But is not this *dea phantastica* identical with Morgan, and her name merely a Hispanic rendering of the Celtic fairy's?

The fay greeted Amadis in a most gracious manner, and presented him with a lance, which she told him would, within three days, "preserve the house from which he was descended from death." With her was another damsel, and when Urganda had departed her companion remained and announced to Amadis that she would journey with him for three days, and that she was not a familiar of the sorceress, but had encountered her by chance. They had not ridden far when they came to a castle, where they heard a squire lamenting loudly that his master was beset therein by its inmates. Amadis spurred his horse into the courtyard, and beheld King Perion fiercely attacked by two knights and a number of men-at-arms. With a cry of defiance he fell upon the attackers, striking left and right and dealing such terrific blows that the caitiff knights who had assailed the King were slain and their retainers put to flight.

Perion at once recognized Amadis as the youth he had knighted not long since. Leaving the castle, they came to a fork in the road, where they parted, with mutual promises to meet in Gaul. The damsel who had so far accompanied him now told Amadis that she was in reality a messenger from Oriana, whereat Amadis trembled so with joy at hearing his lady's name that had not Gandalin supported him he had fallen from the saddle. The damsel then took her leave, saying that she would acquaint her mistress of his welfare.

After several other adventures which it would be tedious to recount, Amadis arrived with Gandalin at the Court of King Perion, in Gaul. They had scarcely rested themselves when they heard the clarions of King Abies of Ireland sound for an attack upon the city, and, mounting

Amadis Goes on Adventure

their destriers, sallied forth, with Agrayes and other knights, to give the men of Ireland battle. A stubborn contest ensued, in which Amadis performed prodigies of valour. Perion came up with his men, but they found themselves greatly outnumbered by the host of King Abies, and were forced to give ground. However, the day was retrieved by Amadis, who charged with such fury that neither horse nor man might withstand him, and in the press he slew, among others, Daugavel, a favourite of Abies. Hearing this, Abies grieved full sorely, and, encountering Amadis, challenged him to a mortal combat on the following day. They met, and after a fierce duel, which lasted several hours, Abies was slain, and the war was thus ended at a blow.

Now Melicia, Perion's daughter, lost a ring which had been given her by her father, the same indeed as that which the King had worn when first he met Elisena, and the exact counterpart of the ring he had bestowed upon her, and which she had tied to the neck of Amadis when he was cast adrift. Rather than that her father should know of this loss, Amadis gave Melicia his own ring. But the King himself recovered the lost jewel, and made inquiries regarding the resemblance between the rings, asking his daughter where she had procured its counterpart. Through her explanation, and his recognition of the sword which Amadis wore, Perion felt certain that Amadis could be no other than his long-lost son, and when the young knight recounted the circumstances of his history, how that he had been found in the sea, the last doubts of his parents regarding his identity were quite dissipated, and they were overjoyed at recovering him, publicly acknowledging him as prince of the realm.

We must now follow the fortunes of Galaor, brother of Amadis, who had been so suddenly snatched away in his infancy by the giant. In due time he grew to be a youth of courage and address, and as he had heard that at no Court did chivalry flourish so gallantly as at that of King Lisuarte of Britain, he resolved to journey thither in the hope of receiving the honour of knighthood. His giant foster-father accompanied him, and they had travelled but two days when they came to the castle of a felon knight, whom, with his retainers, they saw attacking a single champion. Galaor spurred to the rescue, and by his aid the caitiff crew were slain or routed. Galaor conceived such an affection for the stranger that he requested knighthood at his hands. This was cheerfully granted, and after Amadis—for the stranger knight was none other—had taken his departure, Galaor, beholding a damsel close at hand, asked her if she was aware of the name of the knight he had assisted. The damsel, who was the sorceress Urganda, replied that his name was Amadis, and that he was own brother to Galaor. On hearing this Galaor was overjoyed, but his satisfaction was mingled with a deep regret that he had not discovered their relationship ere they had taken leave of one another.

Not content with having enlightened Galaor, Urganda hastened after Amadis, who was on his way to the Court of King Lisuarte at Windsor. She told him that his rescuer was his brother Galaor, who had been stolen in youth, whereat he was both overjoyed and sorrowful.

Greatly heartened by the strange encounter, Galaor still pressed on to the goal of his adventure, the rock Galtares, which he hoped to free for ever from the tyrannous rule of the monster who usurped it. A few days' journey brought him to the fortalice, and at his defiance the giant issued from his castle, armed at all points, mounted upon a gigantic charger, and mouthing the most terrible threats imaginable. He rode fiercely at the young knight, hoping to end the combat at a blow. But, striking out wildly with his club, he smote down his own horse, came thundering to the ground, and Galaor spurred his courser over his prostrate body. In doing so, however, he fell from his charger, and received a terrible buffet from the giant. Recovering himself, he drew his sword and severed the monster's arm at the shoulder. This blow practically ended the combat, for Galaor with another sweep of his good blade beheaded his gigantic adversary.

Amadis, arriving at the Court of King Lisuarte, mingled with its chivalry, and partook of its adventures with such zest that he came to be known as one of the most illustrious knights in Christendom. His adventures at the Court of Lisuarte would fill a goodly volume, and included a war of extermination against the giants, the defeat of the usurper Barsinan and the enchanter Archelaus, as well as a score of other exploits, even a meagre account of which would overflow the pages set apart for the description of this romance. His adventures are intertwined with those of his brother Galaor, whom he even once meets in fierce combat, neither recognizing the other because of his armour.

Lisuarte's Vow

Now, while Lisuarte held court in London an aged knight entered and displayed such a marvellously wrought crown and mantle that the King eagerly offered him any price he might ask for them. The knight declared that he would return on a certain day and claim his reward, and the King agreed to keep the crown and mantle with all care, upon pain of losing that which he loved best. The knight was an emissary of the false enchanter Archelaus, and the gauds he had shown Lisuarte were made by magic art, so that when the King desired to wear them and unlocked the coffer in which they were kept he found they had vanished. The aged knight returned, and demanded his recompense. Lisuarte was forced to admit the loss of the crown and mantle, and the creature of the cunning magician demanded the Princess Oriana in pledge of the King's vow. In true romantic compliance with his promise, Lisuarte weakly acquiesced, and the knight rode off with Oriana, whom he at once placed in the power of Archelaus, and Lisuarte himself fell into a trap set by the artful enchanter.

Learning of this treason while at some distance from the Court, Amadis and Galaor hurried to Windsor, resolved to frustrate the necromancer's wicked intention, which was to wed Oriana to the pretender to the British throne, the false Barsinan, whom Amadis had already worsted. Galaor speedily delivered Lisuarte from his enemies, and Amadis, searching high and low for his lady, at last encountered her in a forest, through which she was being carried by Archelaus. On beholding the doughty champion, whose reputation was only too well known to him, the enchanter hastily made off, leaving Oriana with her lover, who conducted her back to Court.

The Firm Island

With the commencement of the Second Book we enter a strange and mystic atmosphere. Indeed the book

The Firm Island

may be called the *cor cordium* of romance, its mirror, its quintessence. It introduces us to Apolidon, son of a King of Greece, who is described as a valiant knight and powerful necromancer. Abandoning his inheritance to a younger brother, he sailed from Greece into the Great Sea, where he discovered an island inhabited by peasants only, and ruled by a frightful giant, which was known as the Firm Island, fated to be celebrated in the pages of romance along with many another insular paradise.

Slaying the monstrous tyrant, Apolidon dwelt in the isle until, on the death of his brother, he returned to sit upon the Grecian throne. But ere he left the place he laid a potent enchantment upon it to the purpose that no knight or lady might dwell there save such as were equal in valour to himself or in beauty to his lady Grymenysa.

The wonders of this magical island well merit description, and as much of the action of our romance centres there let us embark upon the fairy galley which lies ever ready in the harbours of legend, sail thither, and set foot upon its enchanted beaches. Perhaps it is only through the rainbow lenses of poesy that we can view this wondrous region aright, so I have essayed a description of the isle in verse.

THE FIRM ISLAND

Prince Apolidon the Mage
Raised a mystic hermitage
On an island in a shipless sea
By necromantic potency,
Carving the granite gateways of its cliffs
With interdicting seals and hieroglyphs,
That his unequals might not habit there,
Nor drink that island's consecrated air.

Legends & Romances of Spain

White terraces o'erhung the black abyss,
Fair as the gardens Queen Semiramis
Piled above Babylon: the glittering height
Seemed as the day empillared on the night.
And from the ocean-green of myrtle's shadow
Rose a pavilion, which from afar
Seemed to the eyes of shipmen as a star
Shattered on a distant meadow.
Betwixt this palace and the shipless sea
The wizard set an arch of glamourie,
Byzantine, builded as from golden air.
Its fretted alcove held an image rare,
In whose uplifted hand there burned and shone
The brazen brightness of a clarion.
And should a lady or a knight,
Lesser in beauty or in might
Than wise Apolidon the wight
Or Grymenysa fair
Seek to traverse the magic vault,
Or make the palace by assault,
The brazen trump would blare,
And vomit such a horrid blast
That, fainting from the garden cast,
The wretch would perish there.
But, should a knight of equal fame
Or lady of unblemished name
Seek entrance by the port,
The trumpet, with a high fanfare
Of praise, would waken all the air
Of that celestial court.
Two crystal pillars marked the magic line;
A tablature of jasper, serpentine,
Surround by arabesques like carven flame,
On which would flash the lineage and name
Of that illustrious paladin or dame,
Gleamed in the Grecian pavement; who did pass
Those pillars frozen in Phœnician glass
Would see, 'mid splendour like reflecting ice,
The lord and lady of that paradise
Moulded in immortality of brass.

The Firm Island

Still deeper in those labyrinths of pleasure
A siege right perilous the Mage did make
For Grymenysa's fair, mysterious sake,
For glory of a love withouten measure,
Setting nine seals of Babylonian doom
Upon the entrance to her ivory room,
That but the highest hearts the world had seen
Might know the rapture of its air serene.
And that no sordidness might pass therein
He sentinelled the door with savage jinn,
Invisible and with the flaming powers
Of Sheol in their guarding scimetars.
And all the webs of his weird soul were woven,
In mazy mystery of charm and spell,
Around the shadows of that citadel,
Where oft his wizard prowess had been proven.
So did he leave the place of his delight
To sinful spirits in a magic night,
Calling on Siduri and Sabitu,
And Baphomet, in syllables of might.
And when the moon was in her thinnest phase
He left that island in the shipless sea,
No man knew how, nor evermore did he
Return unto its labyrinthine ways.
Still in the dawn's white fire the shepherd sees
Shapes whiter than the dawn, and whisperings
Sigh through the shadows of the myrtle-trees,
Like to the mutterings of invisible kings
Who speak of blessed, heart-remembered things.

Before he had quitted this marvellous island Prince
Apolidon had placed a governor over it, and had commanded that any who failed to pass the Arch of Honour
and still survived the dread blast of the trumpet should
without ceremony be cast out of the island, but that such
as sustained the ordeal were to be entertained and served
with all honour. And he willed that when the island
should have another lord the enchantment should cease.

Now the spell had been laid upon the island for about a hundred years when Amadis, who had taken a fond farewell of Oriana, and was on adventure bound, encountered a damsel who told him of the wonders of the Firm Island, which, she said, was scarcely two days' sail from where he then sojourned. Amadis replied that he could desire nothing better than to essay such an adventure, and the damsel's father, a knight of large estate, agreed to guide him there so that he might essay the perilous adventure. When at last they came to the Firm Island they beheld the pavilion, the walls of which were hung with the shields of those who had tried the adventure but failed, for though several had passed the arch none had penetrated to the pavilion. And when Amadis saw that so many good knights had been undone his heart misgave him.

Amadis Passes the Archway

Amadis was accompanied by Agrayes, son of King Languines of Scotland, who decided to attempt the passage of the arch at once. As he passed through it the trumpet held by the image emitted sweet music, and he entered the pavilion. Then Amadis approached the archway, and the trumpet blew louder and more melodiously than it had ever done before. Both knights approached the forbidden chamber. They saw the jasper slab, on which they read: "This is Amadis of Gaul, the true lover, son of King Perion." As they looked upon it Amadis's dwarf, Ardian, ran to his master and told him that Galaor and Florestan, his brothers, who had also accompanied him on the adventure, had attempted the passage of the arch, but had been attacked on all sides by unseen hands, and

THE FIRM ISLAND

THE PROUD CIRCUMSTANCE OF CHIVALRY

were left for dead. Amadis and Agrayes at once retraced their steps, and found the young knights lying as in a deep swoon. While Amadis was giving his brothers such assistance as he could, Agrayes tried to enter the forbidden chamber, but he too was struck senseless.

When Galaor and Florestan had somewhat recovered from the effects of the blows they had received from invisible assailants, Amadis felt that for the honour of his lady, Oriana, he must attempt the great adventure of entering the forbidden chamber, into which no knight had yet penetrated. Summoning all his courage to his aid, he crossed the line of the spell between the pillars, and immediately felt himself assaulted by the unseen warriors who had defeated his comrades. A terrific uproar of voices arose, as if all the knights in the world were assailing him, and the blows were doubled in force and violence. But, nothing daunted, and strong in memory of his lady, he fought on. Sometimes he was beaten to his knees, and once his sword fell from his hand, yet he struggled on until he reached the door of the chamber, which opened as if to admit him. A hand came forth and, seizing his, drew him in, and a voice exclaimed: "Welcome is the knight who shall be lord here, because he surpasses in prowess him who made the enchantment and who had no peer in his time." The hand that led him was large and hard, like that of an old man, and the arm was sleeved with green satin. As soon as he was in the chamber it vanished, and Amadis felt his strength return to him.

When Florestan and Galaor and the people of the island heard that the adventure had at last been achieved, they crowded into the now disenchanted palace and gazed upon its wonders. It was full of the most marvellous treasures and works of art, but nothing more excellent was there than the statues of Apolidon and Grymenysa.

Oriana's Cruelty

At the time Amadis had left Britain and had said farewell to Oriana he dispatched his dwarf, Ardian, back to the palace for the pieces of a sword which a lady had given him in all good faith, asking him to avenge her father's death on a cowardly murderer. Amadis, like a good knight, had promised to keep the broken blade until he had avenged the dead man. Oriana, seeing the dwarf return, asked him the reason, and Ardian told her that Amadis had promised a lady ever to keep a certain sword, for which he had been sent back. Then he fetched the blade and galloped off. Oriana, putting a wrong construction upon the dwarf's words, and suspecting Amadis of unfaithfulness to her, wrote him a cruel letter, which she entrusted to a page with instructions to find him at all costs. After much journeying he traced Amadis to the Firm Island, and delivered the letter into his hands.

When Amadis had perused the cold and bitter words of his lady he seemed to the messenger as a man distraught. The page told him that he was forbidden to carry any reply to Oriana. Amadis in terrible grief called for Ysanjo, the governor of the island, and requested him as a loyal knight to keep secret all that he might see till after his brothers had heard Mass on the morrow. Then he commanded Ysanjo to open the gate of the palace privily so that he might withdraw his horse and arms therefrom without being observed by anyone. Accompanied by the honest Ysanjo, for whom he had formed a high esteem, he betook himself to a chapel of the Virgin hard by. He prayed fervently that she would intercede with her Divine Son to have mercy upon him, as he felt that his days would be few. Then he rose and, taking an affectionate leave of the Governor, mounted his horse and, without shield, spear, or helmet, rode off.

Now Gandalin, squire to Amadis, and son of the Scottish knight Gandales, who throughout all these adventures had never left his master, took counsel with Durin, the messenger who had brought Oriana's cruel letter to the Firm Island, and resolved to follow the distraught knight, lest he should come to harm. They soon found him sleeping beside a fountain, worn out with the violence of his sorrow, and mercifully allowed him to slumber on. But when night had fallen Amadis awoke and, remembering his wretchedness, broke into pitiful lamentations for his evil fate. The youths concealed themselves, for they did not wish him to know of their presence. But Amadis, catching sight of Gandalin, was angry with him for having followed him. To arouse him from his lethargy Gandalin told him that a knight, like himself abandoned by his lady, was in the neighbourhood, threatening vengeance upon any whom he might encounter. Amadis, minded to throw away his life, leapt on his horse at hearing this, and accompanied Gandalin in search of the crazy challenger. They soon came up with the unknown, and Amadis hurled a fierce defiance at him. A stubborn combat ensued, and Amadis, by a desperate blow, struck his opponent senseless. Leaving the wounded knight with Durin, Amadis rode on, still followed by the faithful Gandalin.

Galaor, Florestan, and Agrayes, hearing of Amadis's plight and his hurried departure, resolved to follow him.

Meanwhile the object of their search rode onward, allowing his horse to choose its own path, and given over to weeping and lamentation. While the anxious Gandalin slept, the crazed lover eluded him, and traversed the wildest parts of the savage country which they had penetrated. Ere long he came to a plain at the foot of a mountain, where he encountered a hermit, and begged the holy man for leave to remain with him. The hermit greeted him kindly, and Amadis confided his history to the good old man, who told him that he dwelt on a high rock full seven leagues out at sea. And the hermit gave him the name Beltenebros, or 'the Fair Forlorn,' as he was at once so comely and so sore distracted.

The Poor Rock

In due time they reached the sea-shore, and, giving his horse to the mariners, Amadis accompanied the hermit on board a vessel and sailed to the Poor Rock, as the holy man had named his place of hermitage. And here Amadis partook of the austerities of the hermit, "not for devotion but for despair, forgetting his great renown in arms and hoping and expecting death—all for the anger of a woman!"

Durin, Oriana's messenger, journeyed back to the British Court and told his mistress how Amadis had received her letter, and of the manner in which her knight had achieved the adventure of the Firm Island. Then Oriana knew that Amadis must have remained true to her. When she learned that he had gone into the desert to die, her shame and anguish knew no bounds, and she wrote a letter of deep contrition to her lover, and dispatched it to him by one of her

The Poor Rock

women called 'the Damsel of Denmark,' a sister of Durin.

After they had set out, the knight whom Amadis had vanquished on the evening of the day on which he learned of Oriana's cruelty arrived at the British Court, bringing with him the armour of Amadis, which he had found, some time after his encounter with him, at the edge of a deep fountain. And when she heard his story Oriana believed her lover to be dead, and in great grief shut herself in her apartments, refusing all comfort.

Meanwhile, calling to mind the great misery he had endured, Amadis made this song in his passion :

> Farewell to victory,
> To warlike glory and to knightly play.
> Ah, wherefore should I live to weep and sigh ?
> Far greater honour would it be to die !
>
> With kindly death my wretchedness shall cease,
> And from my torments shall I find release.
> Love will be unremembered in the shade,
> The deep unkindness of a cruel maid,
> Who in her pride hath slain not me alone,
> But all the deeds for glory I have done ![1]

At this time the lady Corisanda, who loved Florestan, chanced to visit the Poor Rock, and her damsels heard the story of Amadis, who told them that his name was Beltenebros, but that the song had been made by one Amadis, whom he had known. On her return to the

---

[1] Scott girds fiercely against Southey's interpolation of Anthony Munday's translation of these verses in his *Amadis*, and with justice. The above translation is only slightly more tolerable, but it is at least sense. Poor Tony was bitten by the absurdities of euphuism, and his lines are mere nonsense. But there is even less excuse for a modern translation to backslide into the style of the eighteenth century.

British Court, Corisanda's maidens sang the song to
Oriana as the composition of Amadis. And she
knew that Amadis and Beltenebros were one and the
same.

Now the Damsel of Denmark, who had been sent to
search for Amadis, was driven by tempest to the foot of
the Poor Rock.[1]   Landing with Durin and an attendant,
Enil, she found Amadis praying in the chapel, and when
he beheld the Damsel's face he fainted away.

This extreme sensitiveness to love is characteristic of
the late Middle Ages, however absurd and overdrawn
it may appear to us.   That Amadis fainted at the mere
sight of one who had served his lady seems to us
ridiculous, and that he should imprison himself upon a
barren rock for the remainder of his life because she
had been unkind to him is to the modern reader more
than a little grotesque.

> Shall I, wasting in despair,
> Die because a woman's fair?

But we must deal gently with the ideas of the past,
as with one of those faded samplers of our great-
grandmothers, which, if we handle it carelessly, is apt to
fall to pieces.   When we think of the manner in which
Dante and Petrarch had established the worship of
woman, and how the Courts of Love had completed the
work they had begun, can we wonder that men bred
in this creed, and regarding the worship of womankind
as second to that of God alone, were apt to become

---

[1] She had previously visited Scotland and embarked there "for Great
Britain," and while on this voyage was driven on the Poor Rock,
which would seem to have been 'somewhere' in the Mediterranean!
Strange that geography should have been so shaky at such a period
and among a people who had done so much for discovery and navigation.

The Poor Rock

disconsolate and despairing if the object of their devotion condemned or deserted them? Again, exalted and sensitive minds in all ages have been peculiarly amenable to feminine criticism, as we can see in perusing the biographies of such men as Goethe. Genius, too, which itself nearly always abundantly partakes of the nature of the feminine, is prone to adopt this ultra-reverent attitude, as the sonnets of Shakespeare and the poems of Lovelace and many another singer show. The rough, manly common sense of the average male is too often denied it, and, man and woman in itself, it must suffer the emotions of both sexes.

But, if maintained within rational bounds, this reverence for women in general and for the best type of woman in particular must be regarded as one of the great binding forces of humanity, a thing which has accomplished perhaps more than aught else for the world's refinement and advance. And here, even in a work of romance, which perhaps, after all, is the fitting place for such an exhortation, I would appeal to the younger generation of to-day to look backward with eyes of kindness upon the tender beauty and infinite charm of a creed which, if it is not entirely dead, is in a manner moribund. I do not ask our youths and maidens to imitate its fantastic features or its extravagances. But I do entreat them to regard its fine spirit, its considerate chivalry, and, above all, the modest reserve and lofty intention which were its chief characteristics. It is a good sign of the times that the sexes are growing to know each other better. But we must be wary of the familiarity that breeds contempt. Let us retain a little more of the serious beauty of the old intercourse between man and woman, and learn to beware of a flippancy of attitude and laxity of demeanour which in later years we shall certainly look back upon with a good deal of vexation and self-reproach.

When he had regained consciousness, the Damsel of Denmark gave Amadis Oriana's letter, beseeching him to return to her and receive her atonement for the wrong she had done him. He took leave of the good hermit, and, embarking upon the ship in which the Damsel had arrived, set sail for the Firm Island, where he rested, as he was yet too weak to make the long journey to England. But at the end of ten days he took Enil for his squire and, accompanied by Durin and the Damsel, set out for the English Court.

Oriana Repentant

Meanwhile Galaor, Florestan, and Agrayes, having searched in vain for Amadis, arrived at London in a most disconsolate frame of mind. Oriana, hearing of their want of success, betook her to the castle of Miraflores, some leagues from the city. In its ancient garden she came to feel that Amadis was still alive, and, full of remorse for the manner in which she had dealt with him, she resolved that no further shadow should fall upon their love. The description of Miraflores in the romance is very beautiful, and the impression we receive of Oriana walking in its quiet and umbrageous alleys may perhaps best be rendered in verse.

> Miraflores, fountain-girded,
> Where the trees are many-birded,
> And the orchard and the garden
> Of the forest seem a part ;
> In the stillness of thy meadows,
> In the solace of thy shadows,
> I await the blessed pardon
> That will ease a breaking heart.

Oriana Repentant

Miraflores, name of beauty!
May I learn a lover's duty,
In the evening and the morning,
In this fair and fragrant place;
May I know the bliss of pardon
In thy battlemented garden;
Come to hate the hate of scorning,
And to love the love of grace!

Now a herald came to King Lisuarte at Windsor giving him defiance in the name of Famongomadan, the giant, Cartadaque, his nephew, giant of the Defended Mountain, and Madanfaboul, giant of the Vermilion Tower; from Quadragante, brother of King Abies of Ireland, and Archelaus the Enchanter, all of whom were to join against Britain on behalf of King Cildadan[1] of Ireland, who had quarrelled with Lisuarte. The knight, however, made one condition which he said would ensure peace, and that degrading enough. For he announced that, should Lisuarte give his daughter Oriana as damsel and servant to Madasima, the daughter of Famongomadan, or in marriage to Basagante, his son, the allied giants and kings would not advance against him, but would remain in their own lands. Lisuarte rejected the proffered terms with quiet dignity.

Now Amadis had slain King Abies long before, and it was revenge against him the ill-assorted allies desired, and Florestan, who was present, hearing this, challenged the ambassador to battle. This the knight, whose name was Landin, promised him on the completion of the war, and they exchanged gages of battle.

When the knight had departed, Lisuarte called for his little daughter Leonora to come with her damsels and

---

[1] 'Cildadan' I take to be Cuchullin (*pron.* Coohoolin, or Coolin), the hero of the well-known Irish epic.

dance before him, a thing he had not done since the news that Amadis was lost. And he asked her to sing a song which Amadis, in sport, had made for her. So the child and her companions made music and chanted this little lay:

> White rosebud, Leonore,
> Unblemished flower,
> Pure as a morning in the fields of May,
> Thy perfume haunts my heart,
> Why dost thou bloom apart,
> Hid in the shadows of thy modesty?
>
> Or, if thou mayst not be,
> Blossom of purity,
> Mine own to wear and cherish, as the leaves
> Embrace thee and enfold,
> Be not so white, so cold:
> Bloom also for the lonely heart that grieves![1]

Gandalin journeyed to Miraflores to acquaint Oriana with the news that Corisanda had arrived at Court and had been reunited to Florestan. Delighted as she was at this intelligence, she could not help comparing the happy condition of the lovers with her own, and burst into tears. But even as she wept the Damsel of Denmark was announced. Oriana listened to her tidings with a beating heart, and when the Damsel gave her a letter from Amadis, in which she found his ring enclosed, she all but swooned with excess of joy.

Amadis lay in a distant nunnery, recovering from the wasting sorrow from which he had suffered so long.

[1] It was Munday's translation of these verses from the French which chiefly aroused the scorn of Scott, and it is in dread of the memory of that scorn that I offer these lines, which partake much more of the nature of an adaptation than a translation, the original Spanish being much too stiff and artificial for rendition in English.

Amadis Slays Famongomadan

When he felt stronger, he donned green armour, so that he might not be known, and travelled toward London. On the eighth day of his journey he encountered the giant knight Quadragante, he who among others had defied King Lisuarte. Amadis unhorsed the gigantic warrior, who yielded himself vanquished and promised to deliver himself up to Lisuarte.

Amadis Slays Famongomadan

Proceeding on his way, Amadis passed some tents pitched in a meadow which were occupied by a party of knights and damsels in the service of the Princess Leonora. The knights insisted upon his breaking a lance with them. He unhorsed them all and rode on. While he was in the act of drinking from a well not many miles farther on, he espied a wagon full of captive knights and damsels in chains. Before it, on a huge black horse, rode a giant so immense that he was terrible to behold, and Amadis knew him for Famongomadan, who had sent his challenge to Lisuarte. Amadis, who was much wearied by his recent encounter with the knights, did not then desire to meet him, but when he saw that Leonora was in the wagon along with the other damsels he leapt on his destrier and, looking toward Miraflores, where Oriana was, awaited the giant's onset.

Seeing him, Famongomadan thundered down upon him like a human avalanche. His great boar-spear transfixed Amadis's horse, but the lance of the paladin ran its way clean through the monster's carcass and broke off short in his body. At this his son Basagante ran to the rescue, but Amadis, disengaging himself from his fallen steed, drew his sword and severed one of Basagante's legs from the trunk. But his falchion snapped in twain with the violence of the blow, and a fierce struggle for Basagante's axe ended in Amadis wrenching it from his opponent's grasp and smiting off his head. Then he slew Famongomadan with his own spear, and, releasing the knights in the wagon, requested them to carry the bodies of the dead gaints to King Lisuarte and say that they were sent by a strange knight, Beltenebros. And mounting the great black horse of Famongomadan, he galloped off.

At long last Amadis came to Miraflores and met with Oriana, and great was the love between them. Eight days he sojourned in the castle with his lady; then he rode away to assist Lisuarte in his war against Cildadan of Ireland, who, as we have seen, had challenged the King's supremacy in Britain. Cildadan and his giant allies were vanquished and the Irish king sorely wounded by Amadis.

Now Briolania, the lady from whom Amadis had received the broken sword, visited Oriana, and told her in confidence that she was enamoured of Amadis, who on his part had told her that he loved her not, whereat Oriana was both relieved and not a little amused. And now the whole Court knew that Beltenebros and Amadis were one and the same, and great was the wonder at the puissance of his single arm.

But Amadis, who knew that adventure was the duty and lot of a knight, desired once more to go in quest of it, and with him went ten knights, his friends and kinsmen, greatly to the discontent of Lisuarte, whom mischief-makers tried to incense against Amadis, for removing the best and bravest of his Court.

Meanwhile Briolania had betaken herself to the Firm

The Firm Island

Island, where she was much disturbed by signs and portents of a very terrible nature. She passed between the Arch of True Lovers. But when she attempted to penetrate to the Forbidden Chamber she was violently cast out. So, sad at heart, she returned to her own country. Shortly after this Amadis arrived at the island, greatly to the joy of all therein.

Here we learn something further regarding the topography and natural history of the Firm Island, which was nine leagues long and seven wide, full of villages and rich dwelling-houses. Apolidon had built himself four wonderful palaces in the isle. One was that of the Serpent and the Lions, another that of the Hart and the Dogs. The third was called the Whirling Palace, for three times a day, and as often in the night, it whirled round, so that they who were in it thought it would be dashed to pieces. The fourth was that of the Bull, because every day a wild bull issued out of an old covered way and ran among the people as though he would destroy them. Then he entered a tower, from which he emerged ridden by an aged ape, which flogged him back to the place whence he had come.[1]

News reached the island that Gromadaza of the Boiling Lake, the wife of Famongomadan, had sent her defiance to Lisuarte, who in consequence had resolved to behead her daughter Madasima and other damsels of the race of giants unless she gave up her castles and yielded her kingdom to him. Amadis and his knights thought it

[1] I take this incident to be a reminiscence of the Minotaur story. Indeed the Firm Island appears to me, both from its geographical proximities and its whole phenomena, as a borrowing of Cretan or Minoan story. The "old covered way" from which the bull emerges is surely the Labyrinth. Is the wise old ape Dædalus?

ill in Lisuarte to take such measures against women, and dispatched twelve of their number to act as champions to the distressed giantesses. This action naturally gave colour to the stories of the mischief-makers at Lisuarte's Court, who desired to put Amadis to shame. But Lisuarte was of too noble a mind to listen to them, and on the arrival of the knights he set the damsels free.

Amadis Quarrels with Lisuarte

But Fate and the counsels of wicked men are often stronger than the nobility of kings. His advisers urged Lisuarte to attempt the siege of the Island of Mongaza, the last stronghold of the giants, and held only by their womenkind. Amadis and his company conceived this proposal as unchivalrous, and when Lisuarte heard of their opinion he grew wroth and sent his defiance to Amadis in the Firm Island. Amadis replied that Madasima, the daughter of Famongomadan, having wed with Galvanes, a friend of both Lisuarte and himself, the island could not be held as sheltering the enemies of Lisuarte any longer, and that he would defend it with his whole force. And he set sail for the island with a large and well-equipped army. There they found a garrison which had taken possession in the name of Lisuarte, and which they dispossessed.

Leaving a suitable force in the island, Amadis, who was becoming anxious regarding Oriana, set sail for his own land of Gaul, and, putting in at an island for supplies, chanced then to rescue his brother Galaor and King Cildadan from the clutches of a tyrannous giant, who had entrapped them. Arrived in Gaul, Amadis greeted his parents, whom he had not seen for some years. In the meantime Lisuarte had himself landed in the Isle of Mongaza, and had defeated the troops of Galvanes, its rightful lord, but he dealt reasonably and kindly with his vanquished foes and contented himself with making Galvanes, and Madasima, his wife, do homage to him.

For some time Amadis led a life of ease, hunting and feasting, and contenting himself with such news of his lady as he could obtain. We are told that by these means his great renown became obscured, although the unbiased reader might think that he had already achieved sufficient fame to last a lifetime. "Damsels who went to him to seek revenge for their wrongs cursed him for forsaking arms in the best of his life."

But Amadis had strong reasons for acting as he did, for a letter from Oriana had informed him that she had borne him a little son, and she beseeched him not to leave Gaul until such time as he heard further from her. She did not acquaint him with the circumstance that the infant had been lost, but of this we shall hear more anon. Later Oriana wrote desiring Amadis not to take arms against her father, and not to quit Gaul, unless it were to take his part. So Amadis resolved to assist Lisuarte against the Kings of the Isles, with whom he was about to do battle, and who had invaded his kingdom.

Now the Damsel of Denmark had taken the little son of Amadis and Oriana and had carried him by night through a gloomy forest, in order that her mistress might not be disgraced. Left alone for a moment, the child had been carried off by a lioness, from which it had been rescued by a hermit, Nasciano, who had called him Esplandian, and educated him along with his own nephew. The good man brought the lads up as hunters, and not the least strange thing about this remarkable child was the circumstance that a lioness had affectionately attached herself to him, refusing to leave him, either when at home or in the chase.

Meanwhile Amadis, calling himself 'Knight of the Green Sword,' had resolved to do away with the ill reports of his unchivalrous sloth. Taking only Ardian the dwarf with him, he entered Germany, where he passed four years in adventure without word or message from Oriana. Passing into Bohemia, he remained at its Court for a space.

One day Lisuarte, going to the chase with the Queen and his daughters, came to the mountain where the hermit Nasciano dwelt, and encountering Esplandian, resolved to adopt him, and the hermit showed him a letter, written by Urganda, which had been tied to Esplandian's neck when Nasciano found him. The letter was addressed to King Lisuarte himself, and advised him to cherish the boy, who one day would deliver him from the greatest danger. So Lisuarte resolved to attach Esplandian, and Sargil, his foster-brother, to his service. And when the hermit told how he had rescued Esplandian from the lioness Oriana knew him to be none other than her own son, for she had heard that the infant left on the threshold of the nunnery had been seized by a wild beast and carried off.

In the course of his adventures, which were numerous and stirring, Amadis was sorely wounded by a monster which he had slain, and was cured of his hurt by a certain lady called Grasinda, to whom he was grateful for her kindness and assistance, and he promised to do her will in any adventure she might choose for him.

'The Greek Knight'

About the same time El Patin, Emperor of Rome, resolved to ask King Lisuarte for the hand of Oriana. Hearing this, Queen Sardamira of Sardinia, who loved El Patin, came to Britain along with the ambassadors of the Roman Emperor, and, meeting Oriana, gave her some account of Amadis, telling her how on one occasion he had conquered El Patin in battle and how that emperor owed him a mortal grudge.

Galaor, who suspected the love of Amadis and Oriana, went to Lisuarte, strongly advising him not to give Oriana in marriage to the Emperor, and set out for Gaul, hoping to receive some news of Amadis. At the same time Florestan betook himself to the Firm Island, to acquaint Agrayes of the troubles besetting Oriana, and to carry him news of his lady Mabilia, who longed to see him once more.

'The Greek Knight'

But, as fortune would have it, Amadis, now calling himself 'the Greek Knight,' accompanied by the lady Grasinda, arrived in Britain. Amadis, desiring to remain *incognito*, gave explicit orders to all in his train not to divulge his name. He learned that Oriana was about to be given to the Emperor, and resolved to take his measures accordingly. Grasinda, however, mindful of his vow to her to embark in any adventure she might choose for him, sent a letter to King Lisuarte stating that she held herself fairer than any lady at his Court, and that did any knight deny this he must do battle with her champion, the Greek Knight. The Roman ambassadors requested of Lisuarte that they might be permitted to take up the challenge, and to this he acceded.

The combat duly took place between Amadis and the knights of Rome, to the entire discomfiture of the latter. But the day came on which Lisuarte had promised the Emperor to send Oriana to him, and although she swooned at the thought of being taken to Rome, her stubborn father had her carried on board ship, said farewell to her, not unkindly, and watched the Roman galley as it bore his daughter from the white shores of Britain.

Amadis, hearing of the King's intention, went on board his own ship, and lay in wait for the Roman vessel which was carrying off his adored lady. Attacking the Italian craft with impetuosity, he quickly overcame those on board, rescued Oriana, and at once set sail with her for the golden shores of the Firm Island.

After a voyage of seven days the vessel of Amadis anchored in the haven of the Firm Island. The lady Grasinda had by this time arrived there, and now came out to welcome Oriana, whom of all ladies in the world she most desired to see, because of her great renown, which was everywhere spread abroad. And when she beheld Oriana "she could not believe that such beauty was possible in any mortal creature."

Oriana and the other ladies were lodged in a tower of the palace wrought by the magic skill of Apolidon, and by her request no knight was permitted to enter this tower till some terms might be made with the King, her father. Amadis was well aware that the defiance he had thrown in the teeth of Lisuarte and the Emperor of Rome by his abduction of Oriana must lead to serious consequences, so he dispatched messengers to his many friends throughout the world asking that they would send succour to him in his necessity.

War with Lisuarte

The enmity which had arisen betwixt his two ancient enemies, Amadis and King Lisuarte, presented an opportunity to the wily enchanter Archelaus which he had no intention of letting slip. He therefore approached several other spirits of discord and proposed to them that if strife commenced between Amadis and the British King they with their forces should conceal themselves in the neighbourhood of the engagement, and when one side or the other had achieved victory, they should fall upon the remnants of both armies and overwhelm them in a common ruin. This dastardly plan commended itself to the malcontent lords and petty kings to whom the wizard proposed it, and they resolved to carry it into effect.

War with Lisuarte

Meanwhile Amadis had dispatched an embassy to the Court of Lisuarte, requesting the hand of Oriana, but the stubborn old monarch gave a stern refusal and sent him his defiance. El Patin, Emperor of Rome, had by this time arrived in Britain, and was busy concerting measures against Amadis. Soon a mighty host was gathered together, and marched to seek the army of Amadis, who, taking time by the forelock, had invaded Britain, and now advanced to meet the forces of Lisuarte and the Emperor.

The friends of Amadis had not failed him. In the first place his father, King Perion, was behind him with the whole force of Gaul. Ireland had sent a large contingent, and his old friends, the King of Bohemia and the Emperor of Constantinople, had furnished him with well-equipped legions, all of which were under the skilled leadership of King Perion. Moreover, the army was accompanied by Oriana, Grasinda, and the other dames and princesses who had come to the Firm Island, and their presence heartened the champions to deeds of high emprise. Meanwhile Archelaus the enchanter and his allies dogged the progress of Lisuarte's forces in the hope of taking them at a disadvantage.

Presently the armies came within sight of one another. Their meeting-place was a great plain, and for miles nothing was to be seen but the blaze of armour and gay surcoats, the waving of plumes and banners, and all the proud circumstance of chivalry. For two days the armies lay in sight of one another. Then they advanced to the charge with such a tumult of drums and cymbals, trumpets and clarions that it could be heard many a league away. They met with a crash like thunder, and the noise which arose from the clash of swords upon armour was like that of a thousand hammers upon as many anvils.

Amadis led the van. Challenged by Gasquilan, the haughty King of Sweden, he charged him, and dashed him from the saddle with such force that he lay as dead. But in the encounter Amadis fell from his horse. Quadragante, who was close to him, unhorsed a Roman knight, and gave his destrier to the steedless hero, who, followed by Gandalin and other paladins, attacked the flank of the Romans with great fierceness. Meanwhile Quadragante did fearful execution on their front, few of the enemy being able to withstand his giant might for long. The Roman army now showed signs of falling into confusion, but at that moment the Emperor came up with a reinforcement of five thousand men. He headed the charge in person, crying, "Rome! Rome!" and brandishing a great sword in his hand. Encountering

War with Lisuarte

Quadragante, he received such a buffet from the giant knight as made him give back and seek shelter among his own men.

Now Amadis, surrounded by his bravest paladins, performed deeds of valour which were a wonder in the eyes of both friends and enemies. The Romans began to give ground before the terrific blows he dealt on all sides, and at last broke and fled. So greatly had his forces suffered, however, that he refrained from pursuing his beaten enemies, and as yet the army of Lisuarte had taken no part in the fighting, so that he thought it better to spare his own men, who must meet Lisuarte's force anon.

On the following day King Lisuarte marshalled his army, and now King Perion came up with his forces, which had been held in reserve. The battle had not been long in progress, however, when Amadis encountered the Roman Emperor, and with such a blow as even he had seldom delivered ended his career. When the Romans and Britons saw that their leader was slain they began to give way, and Lisuarte, observing this, sought to withdraw his men in good order. Seeing that he retreated, and fearing for Lisuarte's personal safety, Amadis took advantage of the darkness which was now falling to withdraw his troops rather than pursue, so that the King was able to effect an orderly retiral.

When the holy hermit Nasciano heard of the great discord between the kings he resolved to make an endeavour to prevent further slaughter, and although he was old and infirm he succeeded in making his way to the camp of King Lisuarte. He did not arrive, however, until the two battles which have just been described had been fought. Making himself known to the King, he revealed to him that Oriana had promised marriage to Amadis and that Esplandian was their son. On hearing this the King was greatly troubled, and blamed the lovers for their secrecy, remarking, with justice, that many valuable lives would have been spared had they seen fit to trust him. He requested the hermit to approach Amadis with a view to the conclusion of peace between them, and this the good man was only too pleased to do. Accompanied by Esplandian, he betook himself to the camp of Amadis, where he was courteously received. The hermit first revealed Esplandian's identity to the boy's father, and Amadis cordially embraced his son. But he did not forget his pacific mission. Before he left Amadis he had smoothed over all the differences between him and the proud old King Lisuarte, and it was arranged that their ambassadors should meet, with the object of cementing a generous and lasting peace.

The Treachery of Archelaus

Meanwhile the vindictive enchanter Archelaus, with his malcontent associates, had been anxiously watching the trend of affairs, and when their spies informed them that hostilities were at an end between Lisuarte and Amadis they resolved to attack the old King's forces without delay. But the sight of their army on the march was witnessed by Esplandian as he was returning to Lisuarte's headquarters, and he hastily retraced his steps to the camp of Amadis to warn him that treachery was on foot. On learning his tidings Amadis and King Perion at once set out to rescue Lisuarte's exhausted forces from the danger which menaced them. But before Amadis and his knights could come up with

the army of Archelaus, Lisuarte and his remaining
squadrons had been attacked by the troops of the wizard
and his allies, who had inflicted upon them a crushing
defeat. The aged monarch was compelled to escape
as best he could from the stricken field, and, seeking
refuge in a neighbouring town, prepared for a last desperate defence against his implacable enemies. The
place was fiercely attacked by Archelaus, and as fiercely
defended by Lisuarte and such knights as remained to
him. But as the sorcerer was on the point of taking
the town by storm Amadis and his paladins appeared,
and routed him after a sanguinary struggle. Archelaus
and his associates were bound in chains, and were rather
foolishly released upon giving security for their future
good behaviour.

The meeting of Lisuarte and Amadis was cordial in the
extreme, and it was apparent that their old friendship
would speedily be renewed. Lisuarte summoned his
barons and nobles together, and when they had all
assembled publicly announced the espousal of Amadis
and Oriana.

Now the whole company, including Lisuarte, Perion,
and their queens, Florestan, Galaor, Agrayes, and many
others, journeyed to the Firm Island, where it was
unanimously considered that the nuptials of Amadis and
Oriana might most appropriately take place. On their
arrival at that enchanted spot princely preparations
were made to mark the event in a manner befitting
such an occasion, for not only were Amadis and
Oriana at last to be united, but numbers of their friends
were to take upon them the vows of marriage at the
same time. In the midst of the preparations the beneficent sorceress Urganda made her appearance, riding

upon a great dragon, and was affectionately welcomed by those over whose fortunes she had so diligently presided.

The Wedding of Amadis and Oriana

When all was ready and the day of the wedding had at last arrived, a brilliant assembly mounted their palfreys and proceeded to the church, where the hermit Nasciano [1] celebrated Mass. When the ceremony had duly been performed, Amadis asked of Lisuarte that ere the revels began Oriana might be permitted to make test of the adventure of the Arch of True Lovers, as the enchantment still held good so far as ladies were concerned. To this the King gave his consent. As Oriana approached the image raised its trumpet and blew such a strain of sweetness as had never yet been heard in the island, and from the mouth of the trumpet fell flowers and roses in such abundance that they covered the ground. Without any hesitation Oriana passed on to the adventure of the Forbidden Chamber. As she passed between the pillars she felt hands invisible violently pushing her backward, and three times did they thrust her past the pillars. But by reason of her surpassing faithfulness and beauty she won, despite opposition, to the enchanted portal, where the hand which had admitted Amadis was thrust out, and she entered the chamber, while the voices of viewless singers softly chanted the praises of her beauty and constancy. Now all the assembled company who had beheld this last marvel entered the chamber, and the marriage feast

[1] It is scarcely necessary to indicate to the reader that the name Nasciano is borrowed from that of Nasciens, the hermit king of Grail romance.

The Wedding of Amadis and Oriana

was spread therein. The long endurance of Amadis and Oriana was over, and at length united to each other and to their son Esplandian they looked forward to an existence of such happiness as is only vouchsafed to mortals in the unclouded pages of old romance.

So ends this brave old tale, in which we read of manners and modes of thought so widely removed from those of our own time as almost to appear like those of the people of another planet. The conduct of knight and damsel is, perhaps, a little strained. No matter how absurd a promise or fantastic the circumstances in which it was extracted, it is still regarded as binding, and if we admire the romantic nature of such a code we are tempted to smile at the seriousness with which bearded knights and all-powerful monarchs give way before the quibble of magicians whose lures and devices would be laughed at by a modern schoolboy. Nevertheless, in perusing the story we experience a strong conviction of its author's purity of soul and integrity of purpose.

From the reader who has followed me through the mazes of this enchanting romance I must ask pardon for having omitted in my rendering of it many passages of rare beauty and touching humanity. My business in this volume, however, is to present the thread of the story, to describe its main incidents, and, keeping as closely as possible to the adventures and doings of its principal characters, to supply an outline of the whole. I might readily have enhanced the brilliancy and readableness of my account if I had chosen to narrate isolated adventures and the incidents of more surpassing excellence with which it teems. But my purpose, as I have said, is to provide readers who have little time to peruse an original text with the story in brief. At the same time I have attempted to conserve the true spirit of the romance, and if I have failed to do so that must in some measure be attributed to the difficult task of compression with which I was confronted. In the words of one who 'set' *Amadis* to verse, I may say, with justice :

> To tell as meet the costly feast's array,
> My tedious tale would hold a summer's day.
> I let [1] to sing who mid the courtly throng
> Did most excel in dance or sprightly song,
> Who first, who last, were seated on the dais,
> Who carped of love and arms in courtliest phrase. [2]

---

[1] Forbear.
[2] William Stewart Rose, *Amadis de Gaul: A Poem in Three Books* (London, 1803).

CHAPTER IV: THE SEQUELS TO "AMADIS DE GAUL"

"Inferior as these after-books of *Amadis* certainly are, they form so singular an epoch in the history of literature that an abridgment of the whole series into our language is to be desired."—SOUTHEY

IN dealing with the literatures of the Peninsula, a task for which he was eminently well equipped, Southey followed an instinct of natural discrimination which seldom played him false. Feeble as some of the 'after-books' of *Amadis* undoubtedly are, we cannot afford to ignore them, if only because of the literary phenomena they present. In these fantastic tales the imagination which had flowered so luxuriantly in *Amadis* became overblown. They are, indeed, the petals fallen from the fading rose—so quickly did the wonderful blossom of chivalric fiction droop and wither.

The first of these sequels, called *The Fifth Book of Amadis*, is more generally known as *Esplandian*, as it chiefly refers to the adventures of that hero. Cervantes is, perhaps, rather more unkind to this romance than its peculiar merits deserve, for he makes his critical curate say of it: "Verily the father's goodness shall not excuse the want of it in the son. Here, good mistress housekeeper, open that window and throw it into the yard. Let it serve as a foundation to that pile which we are to set a-blazing presently."

The first edition of *Esplandian* was published at Seville in 1542. The greater part of it seems to have been composed by Montalvo, the original translator of *Amadis*. But whereas when he penned that work he acted the part of a translator only, in *Esplandian* he undertook the *rôle* of authorship proper, and that he failed to

discern the wide distinctions which separate these tasks is
rather painfully apparent. It seems to me, however, a
mistaken criticism which brands *Esplandian* as entirely
lacking in merit, and I suspect that more than one of
the censorious folk who have thus entreated it have not
perused it in the original, or have merely taken Cervantes'
word regarding its lack of quality. It is notorious that
many English critics seem to believe it possible to pass
a verdict upon works written in Spanish without possessing more than a nodding acquaintance with the
language, and the absurd idea obtains among many
men of letters, who ought to know better, that, given a
knowledge of Latin and French, the acquisition of the
Castilian tongue is merely a matter of a little reading.
Esplandian possesses many quaint beauties, and the
fairy 'machinery' and rather distinguished simplicity
of its atmosphere make it most pleasant and delectable
to peruse. Where, too, may we encounter a better or
more representative example of romantic extravagance
at its best?—for *Esplandian*, without exhibiting the
grosser faults of its descendants, has the rich and varied
colour of that imaginative excess which is the birthright
of all true poets, and in the discipline of which all are
not successful. I quite admit, however, that *Esplandian*
is food for the enthusiast, and I do not recommend
its perusal to unromantic souls. It is not for the bar-
bers and curates of this world, and pity 'tis that they who
cannot appreciate its spirit should attempt to influence
others to its detriment.

Esplandian spent his childhood at the Court of his grandfather, King Lisuarte, and had scarcely been knighted
when he felt the call of high adventure. His wishes
in this respect were speedily gratified, for shortly after

the gilt spurs had been placed on his heels he fell into
a deep swoon, which seemed to portend enchantment
of no common order. As he slept, the people of the
Firm Island, whence he had journeyed to have knighthood conferred upon him, beheld a vast mountain of fire
approach the shore, from which issued the sylph-like
form of the enchantress Urganda the Unknown, sailing
through the air upon the back of an enormous dragon.
Some time prior to these events Amadis, to whose
custody the malicious Archelaus had been entrusted,
had injudiciously released that firebrand of the magical
world, only to learn shortly afterward that the unscrupulous wizard had taken advantage of his new-found
liberty to work his wiles once more upon the all too
unsuspecting Lisuarte, who seemed incapable of profiting
by experience, and who now paid for his credulity by
incarceration in the deepest dungeons of the necromancer's castle. Urganda announced to the distracted
son-in-law that it would be necessary for Esplandian to
execute a mission of vengeance, and ere it was possible
to question her further she bore away the youth on the
back of the winged monster she bestrode.

The enchantress conveyed the sleeping Esplandian to
a mysterious vessel called the *Ship of the Great Serpent*,
and on waking it was with no little exaltation of spirit
that he found himself on its deck. As he was wafted
across the smooth ocean he felt a thrill of pleasure
arising from the magical ease with which the enchanted
galley skimmed the waves. In time he beheld a rocky
islet standing in the midst of a forsaken sea, and going
ashore he found it to be barren and showing no other
sign of habitation than a tall tower, which crowned its
topmost height. He climbed the eminence upon which

it stood, and discovered the ancient fortalice to be completely deserted. Exploring its recesses, he observed a stone in which a richly ornamented sword was firmly embedded, but as he attempted to grasp this the air was rent by the bellowings of a frightful dragon, which descended upon him with such velocity that ere he could prepare himself for its onset it had coiled its enormous folds round his body in an effort to break through the plates of his armour and crush him to death. Man and monster wrestled to and fro in a death-grapple, and so terrific were their exertions that the earth shook and the castle rocked beneath them as they swayed and writhed in a deadly embrace. At length Esplandian succeeded in freeing his right hand from the dragon's encircling folds, and, drawing a magic sword which Urganda had bestowed upon him, passed it through the monster's scaly hide. Mortally wounded, the dragon relaxed its grip, and its huge body became rigid in death. When he had assured himself that it was quite dead, Esplandian quitted the castle and returned to the shore, a weird light which came from the enchanted sword, which he had extracted from the boulder, guiding his footsteps through the gathering dusk.

Re-embarking on the *Ship of the Great Serpent*, he was speedily wafted to a rugged country known as the Forbidden Mountain, a stronghold on the borders of Turkey and Greece. At a distance he perceived a castle, and was making his way thither when he encountered a hermit, who warned him to avoid it, and told him that a prince of renown was imprisoned therein. At once it occurred to Esplandian that this must be none other than Lisuarte, and the castle the stronghold of the wicked Archelaus, and this surmise naturally made

Esplandian

him resolve to inquire into the character of the place.
As he neared the gate he saw that it was guarded by
a giant sentinel, who, on espying him, rushed at him
fiercely, brandishing a formidable club. Avoiding the
onset of his gigantic adversary, Esplandian slew him
with the sword of power, and was about to enter the
castle when he was suddenly confronted by Archelaus
in person. A bitterly contested struggle ensued. The
enchanter, enraged at the stripling's audacity in seeking
to probe the mysteries of his stronghold, and in the
knowledge that he came of the race of his detested
enemy Lisuarte, attacked Esplandian with great fury.
But his blind rage could not avail against the cooler
courage of his youthful antagonist, who succeeded in
dispatching him with the magic sword, thus for ever
putting an end to his necromantic enormities. A
nephew of the slain enchanter next assaulted the young
knight, but he too fell before the magic falchion of
Urganda. Next Arcobone, the mother of Archelaus,
a witch deeply versed in the mysteries of the occult arts,
sought to vanquish him by the force of her anathemas,
but the powers of counter-charm concealed in Esplandian's blade saved him from the fury of the dread sybil,
who felt herself bound to obey his behests. He commanded her to reveal the place of Lisuarte's confinement, and had the satisfaction of releasing his aged
relative.

As Esplandian and Lisuarte were about to leave the
island, the fleet of Matroed, eldest son of Arcobone,
arrived off its shores, and the young hero found himself
forced to do battle with a fresh enemy, for, relying upon
his ability to defeat such a youthful adversary with ease,
Matroed made the combat a strictly personal one, and

he and Esplandian were engaged in deadly fight until the waning of the sun. But at length the many wounds which the pagan warrior had received forced him to discontinue the struggle, and he begged Esplandian to permit him to die in peace. At this juncture a holy man arrived, and the expiring heathen requested his blessing, which was piously granted.

Assuming the name of 'the Black Knight,' from the colour of his armour, Esplandian now ruled in the Forbidden Mountain as lord of the castle he had subdued. But he was not permitted to remain in quiet for long, as the fortalice was speedily invested by Armato, the Soldan of Turkey, with a great army. Attracting numerous followers to himself, however, Esplandian defeated the paynims, and took their sovereign prisoner. Encouraged by this success, he carried the war into the heart of the Turkish dominions and captured the principal city.

Before entering upon his career of adventure Esplandian had met Leonorina, daughter of the Emperor of Constantinople, of whom he had become greatly enamoured, and during the course of his war with the Turks he had dispatched many messengers to her, assuring her of his undying affection. He now learned that she had taken umbrage at his long absence, so, when the capital of Turkey had fallen to his sword, he speedily set out for Constantinople. Arrived there, he purchased a cedar chest of exquisite workmanship, which he entrusted to certain messengers, commanding them to bear it to the lady. When she opened it in the privacy of her own apartment, to her mingled confusion and delight her long-absent lover himself emerged from its recesses. In Spanish romance it is inevitable

that the loves of the hero and heroine should remain
unknown to the lady's relatives, not only because this
was demanded by the romantic susceptibilities of the
average Spanish reader, but because Spanish opinion
would have been seriously affronted by the idea of
parental compliance in any intercourse between the
lovers prior to marriage, save of the most formal kind.
This sorry condition of affairs still obtains among the
middle and upper classes of Spain and Spanish America,
and we can scarcely suppress amusement when we hear
of ardent youths unable to converse confidentially with the
maidens to whom they are formally affianced otherwise
than by assuming some ridiculous disguise, or through
the kind offices of servants. Not infrequently young
Spanish couples whose engagement is quite *en règle*, and
to whose union not the slightest opposition is made,
arrange and carry out an elopement, purely because of
the romantic atmosphere surrounding such a proceeding.
It is circumstances such as these which enable us to
appreciate the firm hold of romance upon the Spanish
heart.

But Esplandian had but little time for dalliance, as the
Turks were once more arrayed against him in the field.
He had, however, a firm ally in Urganda, but, to counter-
balance this, the infidels were supported by the
enchantress Melia, the sister of Armato, the defeated
soldan, who had succeeded in making his escape upon
the back of a flying dragon, dispatched for that purpose
by this Turkish witch. With all speed he levied a
large army, and set siege to Constantinople. Numerous
as the sands of the sea were his allies, one of whom was
a beautiful Amazonian queen, who brought with her to
the scene of hostilities a squadron of fifty griffins, which

flew over the city much in the manner of devastating aircraft, belching fire and smoke on the heads of the unhappy folk below.

So dire was the loss of life in this combat between the forces of Christendom and paganism that at last it was agreed that the question of pre-eminence should be settled by the issue of a double combat. Amadis and Esplandian were selected on the one side, and the Amazon queen and a celebrated pagan soldan on the other. The heathens were defeated, but so enraged were they at their downfall that they rushed to the attack with every available man (and woman) in their hosts. But the Christians, mightily encouraged by the victory of their champions, repulsed them with terrific loss, and drove them from the bounds of the Grecian dominions. The Greek Emperor, probably only too happy to rid himself of the burden of such a troublous inheritance, resigned his crown to Esplandian, who espoused his Leonorina and settled down to the task of governing the Hellenic realm.

Relieved from the pressure of military duties, in which she had proved herself no inefficient ally, the sage Urganda had now leisure to pay some attention to the private affairs of her mortal charges. On consulting her magic mirror and other divinatory apparatus, she was desolated to find that Amadis, Galaor, Esplandian, and indeed all of her favourite champions, were soon to pay the debt of nature. Had her prophetic soul been enabled to envisage the immensities of fiction to which their future adventures were to give rise, she would undoubtedly have allowed nature to take its course, so we must conclude that her powers of vision were limited. Resolved to frustrate unkindly Fate, she summoned her *protégés* to the Firm Island, and advised them, if they desired to escape mortality, to obey the injunctions she would now place upon them. They anxiously assured her that these would be carried out to the letter, and with the best possible grace submitted to be cast into a magic sleep, from which, it was decreed, they were not to awaken until disenchanted by Lisuarte, son of Esplandian, who, on gaining possession of a certain magic sword, would be enabled to bring them once more to life with renewed vigour.

The Sixth Book of the *Amadis* series is concerned with the adventures of Florisando, his nephew, but as its hero is not in the line direct, and is, moreover, intolerably tiresome, we may well pass him over with a mere mention of his existence.

Lisuarte of Greece

More sprightly is Lisuarte of Greece, hero of the seventh and eighth books, which are believed to have been written by Juan Diaz, Bachelor of Canon Law, and published in 1526. Lisuarte is not, however, the sole hero of this romance, Perion, a later son of Amadis and Oriana, claiming a considerable share of the exploits which fall to be recounted in the volume. This young warrior, hearing of the prowess and address in arms of the King of Ireland, resolved to gratify a desire to be knighted by him, and for this purpose embarked for the Green Isle. While traversing St George's Channel, or its romantic equivalent, he encountered a damsel cruising in a boat managed by four apes. The animals begged Perion to accompany their mistress for the fulfilment of a great enterprise, so, quitting his own vessel, he embarked in the boat along with the apes and the lady. His attendants, chagrined by his acceptance of the adventure thus thrust upon him, turned their vessel eastward and sailed on until they eventually arrived at Constantinople, where they reported his virtual disappearance, on learning of which his kinsman Lisuarte decided to go in quest of him.

In the meantime young Perion had arrived with his strange fellow-wanderers in the kingdom of Trebizond, which, as we are all aware, is readily accessible from the Irish coast. In that city he had seen and fallen in love with the daughter of the Emperor, but did not have much leisure to pay his addresses to her, as the Lady of the Apes rather unduly hurried him in the preliminaries of the task she had set him. They had scarcely left Trebizond when Lisuarte arrived in the city, and promptly fell in love with Onoloria, the Emperor's remaining daughter. But one day, as the lovers were enjoying each other's society, an enormous giantess entered the Court and requested a boon from Lisuarte, which, in true romantic fashion, he granted without inquiring its nature. It proved to be his attendance for a year wherever the gigantic damsel chose to demand it. The giantess was, indeed, a pagan spy, and had concocted this device to withdraw Lisuarte, who was one of the great props of Christian Greece, from the support of the Hellenic throne at a difficult and dangerous time.

When Lisuarte had quitted Trebizond on the adventure in which he was an unwilling partaker, the Emperor of that country, father of his *inamorata*, was informed of the true character of the prodigious damsel who had carried him off by a letter which was closed with sixty-seven seals and which announced that Constantinople

Lisuarte of Greece

was about to be besieged by Armato, the Turkish Soldan, who had placed himself at the head of a league of sixty-seven princes for the purpose of waging war against the imperial city. Meanwhile Lisuarte was given into the care of the King of the Giants' Isle, whose daughter Gradaffile fell in love with him, procured his escape, and followed him to Constantinople, whence he at once betook himself for the purpose of combating the infidels who invested it. In this task he was assisted by Perion, who now arrived in Greece, after having accomplished the behest of the Lady of the Apes.

In course of time Lisuarte became conscious that duty now called him to effect the release of his sleeping ancestors from the spell in which they had been cast for the purpose of prolonging their existences. After many adventures, which we spare the reader, he obtained possession of the fatal sword and proceeded to the Firm Island, where he broke the enchanted sleep into which Amadis, Esplandian, and the rest had been lulled by the far-sighted Urganda. These, naturally refreshed by their long slumber, and longing for martial exercise, at once assisted him in routing the pagan forces before Constantinople, and achieving peace once more. Lisuarte, freed from his patriotic labours, now bethought himself of his lady-love, and turned his steps to the city of Trebizond. Perion had also gone thither from a similar reason, but on the request of the Duchess of Austria had accompanied that lady to her dominions, which were in the grip of a usurper. On his return from this chivalrous task he encountered his kinsman Lisuarte, and both champions were in the act of preparing their wedding festivities when Perion and the

Emperor of Trebizond were carried off by pagan treachery in the midst of a hunting expedition. Lisuarte, following on their track, was also seized by the enemy, and imprisoned along with those he had sought to succour.

Amadis of Greece

The Ninth Book carries on the adventures and exploits of the race of Amadis, who in more senses than one may be said to be immortal. It was first published in 1535 at Burgos, a place of many literary associations, and purports to have been imitated in Latin from the Greek, after the manner of the famous Troy romance *Dares and Dictys*, and at a later time translated into the Romance language by the potent and wise magician Alquife, evidently a supposititious Moor pressed into the service of the most imaginative but undisciplined writer who fabricated it. *Amadis of Greece*, indeed, approaches the sublime of imaginative excess and fictional unreason, and in its extravagant pages we are confronted with such a maze of marvel that to provide an intelligent account of it is a task of no little difficulty.

Following the wild career of the romancer with the halting step of modern incredulity, we learn that Amadis of Greece was, like his forbears, a child unwanted, the son of Lisuarte and Onoloria, Princess of Trebizond, born shortly after the period of their interrupted wedding. While the infant was being baptized at a fountain in a wild and deserted place, to which he had been conveyed for the purposes of secrecy, he was carried off by corsairs, who sold him to the Moorish King of Saba. Distinguished by the representation of a sword upon his breast, he adopted the name, when knighted by the pagan monarch, of 'The Knight of the Flaming Sword.' Soon after he had entered the ranks of chivalry he was falsely accused of cherishing a secret love for the Queen of Saba, and, dreading the wrath of his benefactor, he made his escape, and embarked upon a career of adventure—which, indeed, it would have been difficult for anyone of his lineage to have avoided.

A pagan in religion and sentiment, he came to the vicinity of the Forbidden Mountain which his grandfather had been instrumental in liberating from the clutches of the infidel, and, reversing the pious work then accomplished, he defeated and expelled those who held it for the Emperor of Greece. Aroused by the menacing turn events had taken, the great Esplandian himself, now Emperor of Constantinople, hastened to the scene of hostilities and engaged in single combat with the doughty new-comer, only, however, to suffer defeat at his hands, an event which never could have entered into the calculation of the enthusiastic author who composed the romance of that hero, who would have been horrified at the mere thought of the eclipse of his invincible 'star.' Shortly after this Amadis encountered the King of Sicily. Their acquaintance commenced with a combat, as it was indeed essential that it should, as the only fitting means of introduction between gentlemen of errant tendencies, but when they came to know and esteem each other they patched up a comradeship which was the more powerfully cemented by the passion of Amadis for the martial monarch's lovely daughter.

In the course of his voyage to Sicily, Amadis chanced to visit an island, where he found the Emperor of Trebizond, Lisuarte, Perion, and Gradaffile in a state of enchanted slumber. As we have seen, they had been spirited away by the emissaries of paganism. It chanced that at this time Amadis of Gaul, who was evidently not yet too old for adventurous pursuits, encountered the Queen of Saba, who was everywhere searching for a champion to defend her against her husband's false charges of conjugal infidelity. Amadis espoused her quarrel, and accompanied her to Saba, where he did battle with and overcame her accuser. He also succeeded in establishing her innocence, and that of his namesake, Amadis of Greece, to the satisfaction of the King her husband.

After he had freed his ancestors from their charmed sleep, Amadis of Greece betook himself to Sicily. He had not been long in the island when he heard a knight reciting amorous verses in the vicinity of the palace. At once his jealous heart leapt to the conclusion that the singer was chanting the praise of his princess. Almost crazed by his suspicions, he searched everywhere for his supposed rival, but without success, dogging his footsteps, but always failing to come up with him. During this chase he met with many adventures. But at last he seems to have convinced himself that his suspicions were groundless and that the singer he had heard had had no designs upon the heart of his *inamorata*.

Whilst these events were passing, Lisuarte, the father of our hero, had returned to Trebizond, and had formally requested the hand of Onoloria. But Zairo, Soldan of Babylon, had seen this princess in a dream, and, accompanied by his sister Abra, had arrived at Trebizond to demand her in marriage. The Emperor was quite prepared to grant his suit, but not so Lisuarte, who had prior claims to the lady, and his opposition so enraged the Soldan that he resorted to warlike measures and set

siege to "many-towered Trebizond." After the siege
had progressed for some time champions were selected
from either army to decide the pretensions of the rival
parties. But the Soldan's paladins were defeated by
Gradaffile, daughter of the King of the Giant's Isle, who
disguised herself as a knight, and whose Amazonian fury
the unfortunate Babylonians could scarcely be expected
to confront with any chance of success. The Soldan,
however, after the manner of the baffled in romance,
broke the rules of the tourney and carried off Onoloria
by a stratagem.

As his fleet sailed with all speed from Trebizond, it
encountered that of Amadis of Gaul, who was hastening
to the relief of that city, and had evidently not been
retarded in his passage of the Dardanelles by any considerations of international law. In the circumstances
it is scarcely necessary to chronicle the Soldan's overthrow, or dwell upon his untimely fate.

But the will to evil of the race of Babylon was not extin-
guished by the decease of the short-lived if romantically
named Zairo. By his death his sister Abra succeeded
to the throne of Semiramis. While sojourning at
Trebizond in the happy days before hostilities had
broken out between her brother and Lisuarte, she had
fallen under the spell of that champion's attractions, and
after the manner of Eastern womanhood as depicted by
the writers of romance, made the first advances to the
object of her affections. Let us hope that he did not
repulse her as rudely as did blunt Sir Bevis of Hamton,
when the fair Saracen Josiana sent her envoys to him to
acquaint him with her passion :

> He said, if ye ne were messengers,
> I should ye slay, ye iossengers.

I ne will rise one foot fro' grounde
For to speak with an heathen hounde.
She is a hound, also be ye:
Out of my chamber swith ye flee.

But repulse her Lisuarte did, and all the fury of a woman scorned burned in the breast of the fair Babylonian. Out of the depths of her vengeance she sent emissaries to all the kingdoms of the earth, asking that the knighthood of every realm should assist her to destroy Lisuarte. One of her damsels while on this quest met with Amadis of Greece, who, still a pagan, was easily inveigled into promising that he would never rest until he had presented the lady Abra with the head of Lisuarte. On the arrival of Amadis at Trebizond a dreadful combat between father and son ensued, which was mercifully broken off by the timely appearance of Urganda, who, following her usual custom, made parent and child known to one another.

But the young Amadis was not to be exempt from the amorous advances of pagan princesses any more than his father had been. Niquea, the daughter of an Eastern soldan, had fallen in love with him by report, and had sent him her picture by the hands of a favourite dwarf. The lady's undoubted attractions were, however, seriously counterbalanced by the circumstance that all who beheld her resplendent beauty either died on the spot or were deprived of reason. Her father, in the exercise of ordinary wisdom, shut her up in an almost inaccessible tower, to which her relatives (who, like most family friends, were rather apt to discount her charms) alone had the *entrée*.

Notwithstanding the former strong attachment of Amadis to the Princess of Sicily, he had no sooner set eyes on the portrait of Niquea than he renounced his former allegiance and devoted his affections to the Oriental beauty. In order that he might delight his eyes with the original of the portrait which had so enchanted him, he disguised himself as a female slave, and gained access to the tower in which Niquea was interned. They plighted their troth to each other, and Amadis remained in the tower in his disguise. Needless to say, Niquea's good looks wrought him no bale.

We now return to the fair but vindictive Abra, who, having marshalled an immense army, marched against Trebizond. After a furious encounter, the forces of paynimrie were duly routed. But as Onoloria had in the meantime been so obliging as to shake off the trammels of mortality, Lisuarte, at the persuasion of his platonic friend Gradaffile, agreed to cement a lasting peace by espousing the Babylonian queen, who was thus lucky in love if unlucky in war.

Niquea, tiring of her virtual imprisonment, succeeded in eloping with Amadis, and soon afterward arrived with him at Trebizond, where their nuptials were celebrated. Later she gave birth to a son named Florisel de Niquea, the subject of a future tale.

This romance, like that of *Esplandian*, ends with the enchantment of the Greek heroes and princesses in the Tower of the Universe by the spells of the wise magician Zirfea, who warned them that by this means alone could they escape mortality. But, unlike the enchantment of the Firm Island, the spell which they must needs undergo in this tower of marvels was not of a somnolent character, so that the enchanted paladins and their lady-loves were enabled to cultivate each other's society for a century or so, an advantage at which they had small occasion to grumble, when their long separation as relatives is taken into account. Even did they tire of one another's society, they were not likely to fall under the more dreadful spell of boredom, since the accommodating magician who undertook their enchantment had provided an apparatus by means of which they could behold every event which took place in the world, a vehicle of solace and amusement which Madame d'Aulnoy introduced into one of her fairy fictions.

Cervantes' barber and priest were especially caustic regarding *Amadis of Greece* and its immediate successors. " Into the yard with them all," quoth the priest, " for rather than not burn the queen Pintiquinestra and the shepherd Darinel with his eclogues and the devilish intricate discourses of its author, I would burn the father who begot me, did I meet him in the garb of a knight errant."

Florisel of Niquea

The composition which chiefly seems to have excited the wrath of Cervantes' unromantic churchman and even more unpoetic barber is the Tenth Book of *Amadis*, which is entitled as above, and is feigned to be written by no less a person than Cirfea, Queen of the Argives, who doubtless composed it in the intervals of repose stolen from the more important duties of royalty. Her Majesty does not degrade her exalted position by revealing to us the fee which she received from the Valladolid publishers who produced the work in 1532, but if one may place a value on her compositions without breaking the dread law of *lèse-majesté*, it might be suggested that a penny a line would amply remunerate the literary output of this most imaginative sovereign. In a word, Cirfea, or the scribbler who sought to shelter himself behind her royal robes, is tiresome to a degree, and her pastoral absurdities can scarcely be described otherwise than in a vein of humorous tolerance. The one thing that renders her work of any importance is that she was probably the first to import the sylvan element into romance, and is thus the creator of that long line of artificial and over-amorous shepherds and shepherdesses whose tears and sighs fall upon or are wafted over the poetic pages of the seventeenth and eighteenth centuries, and the insistence of whose plaints makes one dread to open a volume which seems in any way reminiscent of *l'esprit de bergères*.

The romance introduces us to Sylvia, the daughter of Lisuarte and Onoloria, who was, in the course of nature, removed from her parents in infancy, and was brought up to a pastoral life in the neighbourhood of Alexandria, which, if it enjoyed a reputation in her day as a sheep-rearing district, must have owed it to the well-known properties of sand as a medium for the fattening of those animals for the market. As Sylvia grew up she became conscious of her beauty, and, relying upon her good looks, and no doubt also upon her pretty name, she enslaved to her will the handsome swain Darinel, whose appellation, like that of his lady-love, is racy of the land of the Pharaohs. Sylvia conceived it as being correct in a shepherdess to be 'cruel' to her lover, who, thus setting the fashion for many a future sonneteer, complained bitterly of her indifference, and signified his intention of ending his days by exposing himself to the fury of the elements on a mountain-top—rather a prolonged operation, one would think, in a region especially

suited to pulmonary patients. Probably finding that the
climate of Egypt scarcely lent itself to the consumma-
tion of such a fate, he betook himself to the region of
Babylonia, where, in the intervals of searching for
mountains in a land where they are tantalizingly absent,
he found time to make a friendship with Florisel,
whose good nature must have been sorely tried by his
plaintive apostrophes to his mistress's eyebrow. So
glowing, indeed, were Darinel's descriptions of Sylvia's
charms that Florisel became infected with his unhappy
comrade's emotion, so that at last, unable to combat the
passion which was consuming him, he disguised himself
as a shepherd and prevailed upon the luckless Darinel
to conduct him to Sylvia's abode. But although
Florisel had paid her the great compliment of walking
all the way from Babylon for a glance from her bright
eyes, she showed herself every whit as cold to him as
she had been to Darinel.

One evening, when Florisel deigns to grant the reader
a blessed intermission from his pleadings to the fair
shepherdess, he described to her how the prince
Anastarax, brother of Niquea, had been enclosed in a fiery
palace by the enchantments of the potent magician Zirfea.
On hearing the story, the petulant Sylvia fell headlong
in love with Anastarax, and persuaded Florisel and
Darinel, who no longer hankered after Alpine rigours,
to attempt the deliverance of the fire-encircled prince.
But when they arrived in the vicinity of the tower in
which he was detained they learned that the adventure
was reserved for Alastraxare, a fair Amazon, daughter
of Amadis of Greece and the Queen of Caucasus. The
reader is now compelled to follow the fortunes of this
female Hercules, whose tongue-encircling name has

proved a stumbling-block to generations of printers. These are spread over many pages. The little party from Alexandria went in search of this heroine, and encountered many adventures, as per arrangement with the booksellers. Chief among these was the amorous dalliance with Arlanda, princess of Thrace, who had fallen in love with Florisel by report, as ladies had a disconcerting habit of doing in the days of high romance. She donned the clothes of the immaculate Sylvia, and thus beguiled him to a moonlight rendezvous, where she succeeded in gaining his favour while he was under the impression that she was the shepherdess whom he had vainly pursued so long.

In the course of their wanderings Sylvia became separated from the rest of the party during a great storm, and, retracing her steps, made her way back to the flaming prison of Anastarax. Meanwhile Florisel and Darinel arrived on the coast of Apollonia, where the former happily forgot the charms of the capricious little shepherdess, who by this time had been duly discovered as the daughter of Lisuarte, and had been united to her beloved Anastarax. But it was not because he suffered from a failing memory that Florisel became oblivious of Sylvia, but rather on account of the bright eyes of the Princess Helena of Apollonia.

The sequence of the tale is now broken up in a manner calculated to aggravate the most hardened of readers. Florisel was not left much leisure to enjoy the society of the fascinating Apollonian princess, as the deliverance of his kindred from the enchanted tower had all along been reserved for him. When at last he had satisfied the promptings of duty, he set his face once more toward Apollonia, but was not, of course, destined to arrive on the shores of that delectable kingdom without undergoing still further adventures. Landing at Colchos, he met with Alastraxare, who had found happiness with Falanges, a brilliant warrior of Florisel's train. Arriving at last in Apollonia, he found the Princess Helena on the eve of a marriage with the Prince of Gaul, a match ordained by the lady's politic father. But Florisel would have belied the adventurous blood which he drew from a long line of heroes who had never yet remained inactive in such a contingency if he had failed to defeat the tyrannical father's intentions, so, as our royal authoress remarks, he repeated the exploit of Paris in the tale of Troy by carrying off this second Helen.

Like its prototype of Homeric story, this action very naturally precipitated the kingdoms of the East and West, real and apocryphal, into a condition of chaotic warfare. Assisted by the Russians, who even at that distant epoch appear to have had a predilection for the task of social demolition, the countries of the West poured their myriads upon the plains of Constantinople, and inflicted a serious reverse upon the Hellenic arms. But the erratic Slavs, true to type, turned later upon their allies of the Occident, drove them from the shores of the Golden Horn, and finally secured Florisel in the possession of the capital of the East and the Princess Helena.

Here the august Cirfea might with all judiciousness have written "Finis" with her golden pen to this amazing history. But at this stage of events, if a phrase so familiarly colloquial may be employed regarding one so exalted, she 'gets her second wind,' probably in view of the circumstance that her bargain with the

Florisel of Niquea

booksellers of Valladolid stipulated that their patrons were to be regaled with so many thousand lines of her glowing periods, an arrangement in which she was probably loath to disappoint them, for reasons to which, as a crowned head, she should have been superior. But her domain of Argolis is proverbially a poor country, whose populace possesses a rooted and hereditary bias against taxation. Be that as it may, she was not the last Balkan sovereign to supply herself with pin-money by literary labours. Equipping herself, therefore, with a fresh ream of parchment from the Department of Archives (for Government paper has proverbially been everybody's property, even from the times of Khammurabi), she cast about for fresh situations and addressed herself to the task of 'spinning out.'

When the treacherous Russians had accounted for the armies of the West, they embarked for their own country, there to hatch fresh schemes for the further disturbance of a harassed Europe. But Amadis of Greece was in no mind that a people who owed so many debts to civilization (to say nothing of vast pecuniary obligations) should escape unpunished for their original adherence to the enemy. Pursuing them, but losing track of their vessels, he came to the inevitable desert island, where he resolved to stay and do penance for his infidelity to the Princess of Sicily. Quite naturally, that lady herself landed on its shores, and, after upbraiding her unfaithful lover, very sensibly advised him to return to his sorrowing wife Niquea, which he at last consented to do.

When, after a reasonable interval, Amadis did not return to Constantinople, the imperial city was in an uproar, and Florisel and Falanges elected to go in quest of him. They arrived in time at the island, where, under the assumed name of Moraizel, the former fell in love with and espoused its queen, Sidonia, who, however, did not scruple to show her preference for his companion. But Florisel soon tired of his island bride, who bore him a beautiful little daughter, Diana, destined to prove the heroine of the eleventh and twelfth books of this interminable history.

Agesilan of Colchos

The young Agesilan of Colchos was prosecuting his studies at Athens when he chanced to see a statue of the beauteous Diana. Irresistibly attracted by it, he resolved to search for and behold the original, so, donning the garb of a female minstrel, he fared to the Court of Queen Sidonia, the royal maiden's mother. Here he was employed as a companion to the princess. But when a succession of adventurous knights arrived in the island he could not refrain from giving them battle in the guise of an Amazon, with results invariably in his favour.

Learning from the Queen how she had been neglected by Florisel, Agesilan obligingly offered to bring her the head of the erring warrior, revealing, at the same time, his own personality. Sidonia, who bore her husband a deep grudge for his desertion of her, readily accepted his championship. So Agesilan repaired to Constantinople and defied the recreant to mortal combat. It was arranged that the encounter should take place in the dominions of Sidonia, but on the would-be combatants arriving in these regions they found them beleaguered by the ubiquitous Russians, who, not content with the freedom of their own vast steppes, seem to have hankered after a place in the sun in a more genial clime. It was scarcely fair to the ebullient Slavs to launch two such renowned paladins upon them at one and the same time, but, the brief battle over, victory seems to have made Florisel and Sidonia forget their estrangement, and all went merry as a marriage bell, Agesilan being duly affianced to Diana.

It was agreed, however, that the splendours of Constantinople would provide a more fitting background to their nuptials, and accordingly all set sail for the Golden Horn, having first been honoured by a visit from Amadis of Gaul in person, who, notwithstanding his patriarchal years, still continued to prove the delights of errantry. He was accompanied by Amadis of Greece, who, though almost as venerable as his great-grandfather, could yet break a lance with any like-minded champion.

They had not proceeded far from the shores of the island when they were beset by a furious tempest, in which Agesilan and Diana were separated from the rest of their kindred and cast upon a desert rock, where they would have perished had not an accommodating knight, mounted upon a hippogriff, who chanced to be flying overhead, picked them up and carried them to his home in the Canary Islands. But their preserver's disinterestedness vanished on beholding the beauty of Diana, so, when Agesilan was off his guard, he bore her to a distant part of the Green Island, as his demesne was called. His amorous dream was, however, destined to be rudely broken in upon, for at that moment a party of corsairs landed, and seeing in Diana a prize who would bring them a large sum in the nearest slave-market, promptly bore her off.

Agesilan, on being unable to find Diana, suspected

treachery, so mounted the hippogriff and set out in search of her. Having in vain surveyed the island from the back of the winged monster, in his despair he took to flying at large. Whether from 'engine trouble' or causes even more obscure, he was forced to alight in the country of the Garamantes, the king of which had been struck blind as a punishment for his over-weening pride. Moreover, the unfortunate monarch was doomed to have the food prepared for him devoured daily by a hideous dragon. From this monster Agesilan delivered him. The whole incident is an unblushing imitation of a passage in *Orlando Furioso* (can. xxxiii, st. 102 ff.), in which Senapus, King of Ethiopia, is visited by a like misfortune, and has his food daily destroyed by harpies until relieved by Astolpho, who descends in his dominions on a winged steed. But the author of *Agesilan* is no whit more guilty than Ariosto himself, for both incidents are derived originally from the story of Phineus and the harpies in the *Argonautica* of Apollonius Rhodius.

Agesilan, pursuing the quest of Diana, arrived at the Desolate Isle. The god Tervagant (Termagaunt, Tyr Magus = 'Tyr the Mighty') had fallen in love with the queen of this country, and on being repulsed by her let loose a band of demons upon her possessions, who ravaged them far and wide. The god's oracle had announced that he would not be appeased unless the inhabitants daily exposed a maiden on the sea-shore until such time as he found one as much to his taste as the Queen. Each day a hapless damsel was chained to a rock on the desolate shores of the island, and was promptly devoured by a monster which rose out of the sea. This naturally rendered the supply of maidens in the vicinity rather scarce, so in order to save one of the local ladies for another occasion, Diana, who had been brought to the island, was tied to the rock one morning and, like another Andromeda, of whose myth the incident is a paraphrase, was left to the mercy of the monster. Agesilan, soaring through the air on his hippogriff, witnessed her plight, descended to her aid, and, after a terrific combat, slew the monster which had been about to devour her.

Having accounted for the grisly satellite of Tervagant, he placed the almost unconscious Diana upon his aery steed, whose head he turned in the direction of Constantinople; but on the way thither this now practised airman caught sight of the ship of Amadis from which he and his mistress had been separated in the tempest. Alighting on the vessel with all the skill of a seaplane pilot on the deck of a 'mother-ship,' he greeted his astonished kindred, and the party eventually reached Constantinople, where the wedding of the principal characters was solemnized.

Silvio de la Selva

Silvio de la Selva, son of Amadis of Greece and a certain Finistea, is the hero of the twelfth and last book of the *Amadis* series. He first came into prominence by the gallant display he made against the Russians at the siege of Constantinople, and when the Tsar of that turbulent folk showed a desire to plunge Europe into the distractions of war once more he was not the last to unsheath his falchion and assure the twelve dwarfish ambassadors of the Muscovite that the confederacy of one hundred and sixty monarchs which he had brought together had a small chance of returning to their respective dominions. The resultant siege, with its sallies and combats *à outrance*, we shall forbear to describe, only remarking *en passant* that, in the mercantile phrase, its details are 'up to sample.' But if the Greek princes bethought them to escape the consequences of having incurred the enmity of the turbulent Russ merely by defeating him in the field, they were destined to receive a rude awakening, for by one fell stroke of necromantic art the entire galaxy was spirited away. Once more the inhabitants of the romantic city on the Bosphorus were plunged into the deepest consternation ; but, nothing daunted at the task which now confronted them, the knights and paladins of the family — in themselves an army of no mean dimensions—set out in search of their honoured relatives. But we are not yet liberated from the tangle of plot and counterplot excogitated by the expiring hackery of Castile, and the dying candle of the great romance of *Amadis* does not flare up and flicker out with the rescue of the heroes and heroines who have swaggered through its pages in almost immortal sequel of intrigue and battle. For, the princesses having been brought safely back to Constantinople, it was discovered that during their absence some of them had been blessed with little olive branches, many of whose adventures are related, until the bewildered reader, lost in the maze of their story, like Milton's Satan, looks round in desperation for any outlet of escape, exclaiming with the fallen great one :

"Me miserable, which way shall I fly?"

But, like the doomed archangel, he must 'dree his weird,' and wade through the adventures of Spheramond, son of Rogel of Greece, and Amadis of Astre, son of Agesilan—or, better still, he may do as we did, and, reverently closing the worm-eaten volume, restore it to the library, where its embossed back is, perhaps, rather more appreciated than its grotesque contents.

Instead of being hurled from the throne by an incensed and neglected populace, the line of Amadis continued to flourish exceedingly, and perhaps the secret of its success as a dynasty lies in the fact that it was more habitually resident in fire-ringed castles or enchanted islands than in its palace in the metropolis, which it seems to have chiefly employed as a convalescent establishment in which to recover from wounds delivered by magic swords and the poisonous bites of 'loathly' dragons, rather than as a seat of governmental activity and imperial direction.

We have seen how the great theme of *Amadis of Gaul* burst upon Spain in a blaze of glory, and how, mangled by the efforts of fluent hacks, it sank into insignificance amid the derision of the enlightened and the gibes of the vulgar. It is as if our own peerless British epos of Arthur, that thrice heroic treasury of the deeds of those who

> Jousted in Aspremont or Montalban,
> Damasco, or Morocco, or Trebizond,

had been seized upon by Grub Street and prostituted to the necessities of scribblers. We cannot give thanks enough to the god of letters that it has escaped such a doom, though this has been more by virtue of good hap than through that of any protecting influence. The sequels of *Amadis* descend by stages of lessening excellence until at length they approach the limits of drivel. But does this sorrowful circumstance in any way dim the glory of the first fine rapture? Nay, no more than darkness can cloud the memory of morning. The knightly eloquence of the original characters may degenerate in rodomontade; the lofty and delicate imagery of the primary books may merge into unspeakable vulgarities of invention; the tender beauty which enchants the first love idyll may become coarse intrigue. But no work of art is to be judged by its imitations. With the exception of the Fifth Book, the remaining *Amadis* romances are as oleographs placed beside a noble painting. Unrestrained in execution, daubed in colours of the harshest crudity, uneven in outline and distressing in *ensemble*, they are more fitted for the scullions' hall than the picture-gallery. Yet they may not be passed over in a work dealing with Spanish romance, and they point a moral which in this twentieth century it is fitting that we should digest—that if a nation acquiesce in the debasement of its literary standards and revel in the worthless and the excitement of meretricious fiction, it will cease to excel among the comity of peoples. Literature is the expression of a nation's soul. And what species of soul is that which voices itself in crudely jacketed novelettes, redolent of a psychology at once ridiculous and unhealthy? Have we no Cervantes to shatter this ignoble thing to the sound of inextinguishable laughter? Is not the sad lesson of *Amadis* one for the consideration of our own people? Spain was never so great as when its first books roused her chivalry to an ardour of knightly patriotism, and she was never so little as when the printing-presses of Burgos and Valladolid and Saragossa flooded her cities with a mercenary and undistinguished fiction, prompted by commercial greed, and joyfully received by a public avid for the drug of sensation.

168

CHAPTER V : THE PALMERIN ROMANCES

Let *Palmerin of England* be preserved as a singular relic of antiquity.
CERVANTES

IT would seem to have been a foible with the early critics of Spanish romance to seek to discover a Portuguese origin for practically all of its manifestations. They appear to have argued from the analogy of *Amadis* that all romantic effort hailed from the Lusitanian kingdom, yet they are never weary of descanting upon the Provençal and Moorish influences which moulded Spanish romance! It is precisely as if one said : "Yes, the Arthurian story displays every sign of Norman-French influence, but all the same, it was first cast into literary form in Wales. England ? Oh, England merely accepted it, that's all."

The *Palmerin* series ran almost side by side with *Amadis* in a chronological sense, and tradition ascribed its first book to an anonymous lady of Augustobriga. But there is reason to believe, from a passage in *Primaleón*, one of its sections, that it was the work of Francisco Vasquez de Ciudad Rodrigo. No early Portuguese version is known, and the Spanish edition of the first romance of the series, *Palmerin de Oliva*, printed at Seville in 1525, was certainly not the earliest impression of that work. The English translation, by Anthony Munday, was published in black letter in 1588.

Palmerin de Oliva

No sooner did *Palmerin de Oliva* appear than it scored a success only second to that of *Amadis*, its resemblance to which can scarcely be called fortuitous, and, as in the case of that romance, translations and continuations were multiplied with surprising rapidity.

The commencement of *Palmerin de Oliva* carries us once more to the enchanted shores of the Golden Horn. Reymicio, the Emperor of Constantinople, had a daughter named Griana, whom he had resolved to give in marriage to Tarisius, son of the King of Hungary, and nephew to the Empress. But Griana had given her heart to Florendos of Macedon, to whom she had a son. Dreading the wrath of her father, she permitted an attendant to carry the infant to a deserted spot, where it was found by a peasant, who took it to his cottage, and brought it up as his own son, calling the child Palmerin de Oliva, because he had been found on a hill which was covered with a luxuriant growth of palm and olive trees.

When the boy grew up he accepted his humble lot with equanimity. But on learning that he was not the son of a peasant he longed for a life of martial excitement. Adventure soon afforded him a taste of its dazzling possibilities. While traversing a gloomy forest in search of game he encountered a merchant beset by a ferocious lion. He slew the beast, and learned that the traveller was returning to his own country from Constantinople. Attaching himself to the man of commerce, Palmerin accompanied him to the city of Hermide, where his grateful companion furnished him with arms and a horse. Thus accoutred for the life chivalric, he betook himself to the Court of Macedon, where he received the honour of knighthood from Florendes, the son of the king of that country, and his own father.

A quest soon presented itself to him. Primaleón, King of Macedon, had long been a sufferer from a grievous sickness. His physicians assured him that could he

Palmerin de Oliva

obtain water from a certain fountain his malady would disappear. But the spring in question was guarded by an immense serpent of such ferocity that to approach its lair meant certain death. Knight after knight had essayed the adventure, only to be crushed in the monster's venomous folds, so that the life-giving waters the ailing King so sorely required continued to be withheld from him. This condition of affairs seemed to Palmerin to present him with an opportunity for distinguishing himself, and without realizing the strenuous nature of the task before him he leapt into the saddle and cantered off in the direction of the serpent-guarded fountain.

The Fairy Damsels

Very conscious of the honour of knighthood which but so lately had been conferred upon him, and inordinately proud of the gilded spurs which glittered on his mailed heels, Palmerin was not a little pleased that he had succeeded in attracting the attention of a bevy of young and beautiful ladies, who stood where field and forest met, watching his rather haughty progress with laughing eyes. Had he been less occupied with himself and his horse, which he forced to curvet and caracole in the most outrageous fashion, he would have seen that the damsels before whom he wished to cut such a fine figure were of a beauty far too ethereal to be human, for the ladies who watched him with such amusement were princesses of the race of Faery, and had waylaid the young knight with the intention of giving him such aid as fairies have in their power.

Palmerin greeted them with all the distinction of which he was capable.

"God save you, fair damsels," he said, bowing almost to his horse's mane. "Can you tell me if I am near the serpent-guarded fountain?"

"Fair sir," replied one of the sylphs, "you are within a league of it. But let us entreat you to turn back from such a neighbourhood as this. Many famous knights have we seen pass this way to do battle with the monster who guards its waters, but none have we seen return."

"It is not my custom to turn my back upon an enterprise," said Palmerin loftily. "Did I understand you to say the fountain lies within a league of this place?"

"Within a short league, Sir Knight," replied the fairy. Then, turning to her companions, she said: "Sisters, this would seem to be the youth we have awaited so long. He appears bold and resolute. Shall we confer upon him the gift?"

Her companions having given their assent to this proposal, the fairy then enlightened Palmerin regarding the true character of herself and her attendant maidens, and assured him that wherever he went, or whatever adventure he undertook, neither monster nor magician would have the power to cast enchantment upon him. Then, directing him more particularly to the lair of the serpent, they disappeared in the recesses of the forest.

Riding on, he speedily came within view of the fountain, but had scarcely beheld its silver waters bubbling from a green hill-side when a horrible hissing warned him of the proximity of its loathly guardian. All unafraid, however, he spurred his terrified horse forward. A blast of fire, belched from the monster's mouth, surged over him, but he bent low in the saddle and avoided it. Then, dashing at the bristling head, poised on a neck thick as a pillar, and armoured with dazzling scales, he

PAMERIN ENCOUNTERS FAIRIES AT THE EDGE OF
THE WOOD

PARTENOPEX IN MELIOR'S CHAMBER

Palmerin de Oliva

struck fiercely at it with his falchion. The serpent tried to envelop horse and man in its folds, but ere it could bring its grisly coils to bear upon them Palmerin had smitten off its head.

Returning to Macedon, the young hero was at once overwhelmed by the applications of importunate monarchs that he should assist them in one enterprise or another. All of these Palmerin achieved with such consummate address that his fame spread into all parts of Europe, and we find him as far afield as Belgium, where he delivered the Emperor of Germany from certain traitor knights who besieged him in the town of Ghent. It was during this adventure that he met and became enamoured of the Emperor's daughter, the beauteous Polinarda, who had on one occasion appeared to him in a dream. But the young paladin felt that if he were to render himself worthy of such a peerless lady he must subdue many knights in her name, and undertake adventures even more onerous than those through which he had already come scathless. Learning, therefore, of a great tournament in the land of France, he journeyed thither, and bore off the prize.

Returning to Germany, Palmerin found the Emperor engaged in a war with the King of England, at the instance of the King of Norway, who had requested his assistance against the British monarch. This partisanship did not, however, appeal to Trineus, the Emperor's son, who, enamoured of the princess Agriola, daughter of the English king, privately departed with Palmerin, his object being to aid the father of his lady-love. After undergoing many adventures, the companions succeeded in carrying off the English princess, but while voyaging homeward were attacked by a furious

173

tempest and were driven on the shores of the Morea. When the elements subsided Palmerin landed on the neighbouring island of Calpa, to engage in the sport of hawking, and during his absence the vessel in which he had left his friends was seized by Turkish pirates, who carried Agriola as a present to the Grand Turk. Trineus was even less happily situated, for being marooned upon an island, which we must surely regard as that of Circe, he was immediately transformed into a dog. To add to this indignity, his transformation did not take the shape of any of the more noble varieties of the canine race, but that of a tiny lap-dog, such as are found in ladies' boudoirs.

In the meantime Palmerin, all unconscious of the fate of his friends, was discovered in the island of Calpa by Archidiana, daughter of the Soldan of Babylon, who at once pressed him into her service, refusing to allow him to depart. Archidiana had from the first conceived a violent passion for the handsome young adventurer, whose embarrassment was heightened by the knowledge that her cousin, Ardemira, had likewise fallen in love with him. The knight, however, stoutly repelled the fair advances, and Ardemira took her repulse so much to heart that she burst a blood-vessel and expired, shortly after the party had arrived at the Babylonian Court. Hearing of her demise, Amaran, son of the King of Phrygia, to whom she had been affianced, hastened to Babylon, and precipitately accused Archidiana of her death, offering to make good his assertion by an appeal to arms. Palmerin, as in duty bound, espoused the princess's quarrel, slew Amaran in single combat, and by doing so won the good graces of the Soldan, whom he assisted in the war with Phrygia which followed.

Palmerin de Oliva

The Soldan, elated by his military successes, resolved to extend his empire, and with this object in view fitted out a great expedition against Constantinople, which Palmerin was forced to accompany. But during a tempest which the Babylonian fleet encountered he commanded the seamen of his own vessel to steer for the German coast. On reaching it he made his way to the capital, and made himself known in secret to Polinarda, with whom he spent some time.

But his heart misgave him regarding the fate of his friend Trineus, and he resolved to set out in quest of that unhappy prince. Journeying across Europe, he arrived at the city of Buda, where he learned that Florendos, Prince of Macedon, had recently slain Tarisius, who, it will be remembered, was his rival for the hand of the Princess Griana, and whom she had been forced to marry by her tyrannous father, the Emperor of Constantinople. Florendos had, however, been taken captive by the kinsmen of Tarisius, and had been sent to Constantinople, where he was condemned to be burnt at the stake, along with Griana, who was believed to be his accomplice. On hearing of the impending fate of those who, unknown to him, were his parents, Palmerin at once repaired to Constantinople, where he maintained their innocence, defeated their accusers, the nephews of Tarisius, in a combat *à outrance*, and succeeded in saving them from the terrible fate which had awaited them. While he lay in bed recovering from his wounds he was visited by the grateful Griana, who, from a mark upon his face and the account of his exposure as an infant, knew that he must be her son. On hearing her story the Emperor joyfully received Palmerin and acknowledged him as his successor.

The Quest for Trineus

But his new accession to power did not render Palmerin unmindful of his vow to search for his lost friend Trineus. Sailing over the Mediterranean in quest of him, he fell in with an overwhelming force of Turks, and was taken prisoner. Brought to the palace of the Grand Turk, he succeeded in liberating the princess Agriola from the power of that tyrant. Effecting his own escape, he came to the palace of a princess to whom Trineus in his shape of a lap-dog had been presented by those who had found him. This lady had contracted a severe inflammation in the nose (unromantic detail!), and requested Palmerin to accompany her to Mussabelin, a Persian magician, whom she believed to be able to remove the distressing complaint. But the sage informed her that only by means of the flowers of a tree which grew near the Castle of the Ten Steps could she be cured.

Now the castle of which the magician spoke was guarded by enchantment. But that dread power was harmless to Palmerin, ever since the fairy sisters had provided him with an antidote against it. Making his way to the magic castle, he secured the flowers of the healing tree, and also took captive an enchanted bird, which was destined to announce the hour of his death by an unearthly shriek. He further ended the enchantments of the castle, and when they finally dissolved, Trineus, who had accompanied him in canine shape, was restored to his original form.

The subsequent adventures of Palmerin bear such a strong likeness to those already related of him as to render their recital a work of supererogation. From the Court of one soldan he proceeds to that of another, enchantment follows enchantment, as combat treads upon the heels of combat. Finally Palmerin and Trineus return to Europe, and wed their respective ladies.

Cervantes' curate is perhaps too hard upon *Palmerin de Oliva*. "Then, opening another volume, he found it to be *Palmerin de Oliva*. 'Ha! have I found you?' cried the curate; 'here, take this *Oliva*; let it be hewn in pieces and burnt, and the ashes scattered in the air.'" This notwithstanding, there are some brilliant passages in the romance we have just outlined—grains of gold-dust in a desert of unrestrained and undisciplined narrative—such flashes of genius as we find here and there in Shelley's *Zastrozzi*, *St Irvyne*, and the other hysterical outpourings of his Oxford days.

Primaleón

There is no doubt regarding the thoroughly Spanish character and origin of *Primaleón*, son and successor to *Palmerin de Oliva*, although, owing to the prejudice of the time for mystery and Orientalism, its author, Francisco Delicado, saw fit to announce it as a transla-tion from the Greek. The first edition was printed in 1516, and several translations shortly followed, that in English, by Anthony Munday, being dedicated to Sir Francis Drake, and published in 1589. This translation, however, dealt only with that portion of the romance which related to the exploits of Polendos, but Munday completed the whole in editions published in 1595 and 1619. The adventures of Polendos constitute, however, by far the best part of the work.

Polendos was the son of the Queen of Tharsus.

Returning one day from the chase, he beheld a little old woman sitting on the steps of the palace, from which he removed her by a most ungallant but forceful kick. "It was not in this manner that your father Palmerin succoured the unfortunate," cried the crone, on picking herself up. Polendos thus learned the secret of his birth, for he was indeed the son of Palmerin and the Queen of Tharsus, and, exalted by the intelligence, he burned to distinguish himself by feats of arms worthy of his sire. Departing for Constantinople to make himself known to his father, he encountered many adventures on the way. Arrived at the imperial city, he did not long remain there, but set out to rescue the Princess Francelina from the power of a giant and a dwarf, who held her in bondage in an enchanted castle. Returning to Constantinople, he greatly distinguished himself at a tournament held on the occasion of the marriage of one of the Emperor's daughters, and Primaleón, the real hero of the story, son of Palmerin and Polinarda, desirous of emulating the exploits of his half-brother, was duly knighted, and took part in the *mêlée*. The rest of the romance is occupied with the adventures of this young hero and those of Duardos (Edward) of England. In the course of his adventures Palmerin had slain the son of the Duchess of Armedos, who vowed that she would only give her daughter in marriage to the man who could bring her the head of Primaleón. One by one Primaleón slew the lovers of Gridoina, the Duchess's daughter, so that in time she came to detest the mere mention of his name. But one evening Primaleón arrived at her castle, and, not knowing who he was, she fell deeply in love with him. The child of their affections was Platir, whose exploits were recounted by the same author, and published at Valladolid in 1533. We may well pass over this very indifferent romance, and bestow our attention and interest upon its more entertaining successor.

Palmerin of England

This is perhaps the best of the series. The first Spanish edition was believed to be lost; but a French translation from it was published at Lyons in 1553, and an Italian one at Venice in 1555. Southey maintained that there never was a Spanish original of this story, and that it was first written in Portuguese. But this hypothesis was upset by Salva's discovery of a copy of the lost Spanish original, written by Luis Kuxtado [1] and published at Toledo in two parts, in 1547 and 1548. Southey attempted to show in his English translation of *Palmerin of England* that a consideration of its *mise en scène* would afford irrefragable proof of its Lusitanian origin—surely a good illustration of the dangers and fallacies connected with this species of reasoning. An argument of equal cogency could be advanced for its original English authorship, as most of its action takes place within the borders of the 'perilous isle' of Britain, in which respect it follows *Amadis*, its model.

In *Palmerin of England* we are provided with a biographical sketch of the hero's parents. Don Duardos, or Edward, son of the King of England, was wedded to Flerida, daughter of Palmerin de Oliva. While engaged in the chase, he lost his way in the depths of an English forest, and sought shelter in a mysterious

---

[1] For a brief account of this Toledan poet, who translated Ovid's *Metamorphoses*, see Antonio, *Bib. Nov.*, t. ii, p. 44.

castle, where he was detained by a giantess, Eutropa, whose brother he had slain. But Dramuziando, her nephew, son of the giant whom Duardos had sent to his death, was of milder mood than his terrible aunt, and conceived a strange friendship for the captive Duardos.

In the meantime Flerida, alarmed at Duardos' absence, set out to search for him, accompanied by a train of attendants, and while traversing the forest in the hope of tracing him gave birth to twin sons, who were baptized in the greenwood by her chaplain. The ceremony had scarcely come to an end when a wild man, an inhabitant of the forest recesses, burst from the undergrowth, and, seizing upon the infant princes, carried them off. None might stay him, for he was accompanied by two lions of such size and ferocity that their appearance struck terror into the hearts of the stoutest of Flerida's retainers.

The savage conveyed the infants, who had been named Palmerin and Florian, to his den, where he resolved to give them to the lions. Flerida returned disconsolately to the palace, and dispatched a messenger to Constantinople with news of her losses. On receiving this intelligence, Primaleón and a number of the Grecian knights took ship for England, and, learning of the imprisonment of Duardos in the castle of the giantess, they essayed his deliverance. But they made the mistake, common to errantry, of attempting to do so singly and not in a body, and so, one by one, fell a rather easy prey to the giant Dramuziando, who forced them to combat each new enemy who approached.

The sylvan savage who had destined the royal twins as food for his lions had reckoned without his wife,

Palmerin of England

whose motherly instincts prompted her to save the children from a fate so dire. Having prevailed upon her uncouth mate to spare them, she brought them up along with her own son Selvian. In course of time they became expert in the chase and woodcraft, and on one of his excursions in the forest while following the slot of a red deer Florian encountered Sir Pridos, son of the Duke of Wales, who took him to the English Court, where he was brought before his mother, Flerida. Attracted to the savage youth, she adopted him, and trained him in the usages of civilization, calling him 'the Child of the Desert.'

Florian had not long been lost to the sylvan family when Palmerin and Selvian, wandering one day by the sea-coast, observed a galley cast upon the shore by the violence of a tempest. From this vessel Polendos (whose prior adventures were recited in the romance of *Primaleón*) disembarked, having come to England with other Greek knights in search of Duardos. Palmerin and Selvian requested him to take them on board his vessel, which put to sea once more, and shortly afterward arrived at Constantinople, where they were brought before the Emperor, who, of course, was in ignorance of the extraction of Palmerin, but knew of his high rank from letters he had received from a certain Lady of the Bath, who seems to have acted as the hero's good genius. The Emperor, impressed by such an introduction, knighted Palmerin, whose sword was girded to his side by Polinarda, the daughter of Primaleón. During Palmerin's residence at Constantinople a tournament was held, in which he and a stranger knight, who bore for his device a savage leading two lions, greatly distinguished themselves. The stranger departed still *incognito*, but was afterward discovered to be Florian, who was thenceforth known as 'the Knight of the Savage.'

Palmerin fell an easy victim to the charms of the princess Polinarda, but the precipitate nature of his wooing, prompted, probably, by his sylvan upbringing, offended the courtly damsel, and she forbade him her presence. In despair at her coldness, he quitted the Grecian capital, and journeyed toward England, under the name of 'the Knight of Fortune,' taking Selvian as his squire. On the way he encountered a wealth of adventure, in which he was uniformly successful, and at last arrived in the dominions of his grandfather. But while passing through the forest inhabited by his savage foster-father he came face to face with him, and recounted his adventures. Pressing on, he came to a castle in the neighbourhood of London, the castellan of which begged of him to do battle with the Knight of the Savage, who had slain his son. Arriving in London, he defied Florian, but the Princess Flerida intervened and forbade the combat, which was not resumed, for Palmerin having at last overcome Dramuziando and set Duardos at liberty, the birth of the twin brothers was revealed by Doliarte, a magician, and confirmed by their savage foster-father.

The Castle of Almaurol

Spurred on by the love of adventure, Florian and Palmerin disdained to lead a life of ease at Court, and set out on their travels. We cannot follow them here through the maze of exploit into which they are plunged, but many of their trials, especially those undergone by Palmerin in the Perilous Isle, are among the most interesting and attractive in the series which bears his name. In several of the passages the amiable giant Dramuziando figures to advantage, but his aunt, the vindictive Eutropa, still retains her ill-will to the family of the Palmerins, and is constant in the exercise of her machinations against them. These are, however, challenged and countered by the skill of the magician Doliarte. The chief scene of adventure is the castle of Almaurol, where, under the care of a giant, dwelt the beautiful but haughty Miraguarda, whose lineaments were pictured on a shield which was suspended over the gate of the castle. It was guarded by a body of knights, who had become enamoured of the original, and when other paladins arrived vaunting the charms of their ladies these gave them battle. Among these victims of the fair Miraguarda was the giant Dramuziando, but during his custody of the picture it was purloined by Alhayzar, the Soldan of Babylon, whose lady, Targiana, daughter of the Grand Turk, had commanded him to bring it to her as a trophy of his prowess.

The writer of the romance appeared to think it necessary at this point to recall his heroes to Constantinople in order to espouse them to their respective ladies. Palmerin was united to Polinarda, and his brother Florian to Leonarda, Queen of Thrace, so that the lovers were made happy. These espousals, however, by no means bring the romance to a conclusion, for we learn that matters had become complicated by the passion of the daughter of the Grand Turk for the newly wedded Florian. That gay young prince, while residing at the Court of the lady's father, had taken the liberty of eloping with her, and although she was now safely married to Alhayzar, Soldan of Babylon and picture-thief, she still retained a strong affection for her former lover, which was mingled with resentment that he should have deserted her charms for those of the Queen of Thrace. To ease the clamours of her jealous heart, she employed a magician to work woe upon the Thracian queen, who, while she took the air in the gardens of her palace, was pounced upon by two enormous griffins, and conveyed to a magic castle, where she was transformed into a huge serpent. Her disconsolate husband found in her deliverance an adventure quite to his taste, and, having consulted the wise Doliarte, succeeded in discovering the place where his wife was imprisoned and in freeing her from the enchantment which had been laid upon her.

In accomplishing this, however, he seriously offended the proud Alhayzar, who determined to avenge the affront placed upon his queen, and demanded the person of Florian from the Emperor of Constantinople. On receiving the imperial refusal which naturally followed his request, he invaded the Greek territories, with an army of two hundred thousand men, recruited from all the kingdoms and satrapies of the Orient, real and imaginary. Three sanguinary battles occurred, in one of which Alhayzar was slain and the pagan army totally annihilated.

Cervantes' Eulogy

Cervantes launches into an extravagant eulogy of this romance. "This *Palmerin of England*," he says, "let it be kept and preserved as a thing unique, and let another casket be made for it such as Alexander found among the spoils of Darius. . . . This book, Sir Comrade, is of authority, for two reasons: the one because it is a

right good one in itself, and the other because the report
is that a wise king of Portugal composed it. All the
adventures at the Castle of Miraguarda are excellent,
and managed with great skill ; the discourses are courtly
and clear, observing with much propriety and judgment
the decorum of the speaker. I say then, saving your
good pleasure, Master Nicholas, this and *Amadis de
Gaul* should be saved from the fire, and all the rest be,
without further search, destroyed."

Saving *your* good pleasure, Master Cervantes, I would
come to an issue with you regarding this. For though
Palmerin of England is the best romance of those which
recount the adventures of that line, still it does not bear
away the bell quite so easily as you say. Indeed, its
merits are not transcendently above those of its kind,
and its faults are of the same character. Again, true
Spaniard as you are, do you not praise it so greatly
because you believe it to be the work of a king? And
do you not demean yourself to the level of a newspaper
critic when you doom to extinction those romances
which you have not read? Further, as a Castilian
gentleman, do you agree with the author's most
despiteful entreatment of that sweet sex for whose sake
all romances were written? No good knight, no good
man, could have penned so many stupidities concerning
their envy, their fickleness, their lack of reason, as he
has done ; and still worse, he has made them mere
puppets, moving as the strings are pulled. For one
thing I thank him, however—his character of the
magician Doliarte, a wise sage dwelling in the Valley
of Perdition, lost in contemplation of mysterious things.
Nay, for a greater thing I have to thank him also, the
colours of the marvellous, the intoxicating magic with

which he has suffused his story; and if the rush of it, the spell of it, transported you to the forests of Faery and blinded you to the book's demerits, you are perhaps to be excused if your enchanted eyes refused to behold them and saw only the outward glamours of that rainbow world.

CHAPTER VI: CATALONIAN ROMANCES

Romances from a coast of love and wine,
Echoing the music of adventurous swords,
Murmur of necromancy's dark ingyne,
And speech that holds the ghosts of curious words.

THE literary genius of Catalonia was unquestionably a lyrical one, as befitted a province so happily endowed by nature, clothed with the purple mantle of vineyards, and laved by the calm beauty of a dreamy ocean. Epic has her home in rugged and wind-swept lands, where the elemental trumpets of the air arouse the soul of man to fiercer song and fill the memory with the clash of war. But on sheltered strands, mellow with sun and painted in the ripe colours of plenty, a softer and more dreamy music mimics the æolian sound of the zephyrs which steal like melodious spirits through orchard and vineyard. Yet this province of the Trovadores was not without its legends of chivalric enterprise, and indeed produced two romances of such intrinsic merit that they may be regarded as occupying an unassailable position in the literature of the Peninsula.

Partenopex de Blois

The beautiful and highly finished romance of *Partenopex de Blois* was written in the Catalonian dialect in the thirteenth century, and printed at Tarragona in 1488. That the tale was originally French is highly probable, but it is no mere translation, and the treatment it has received in the course of adaptation has undoubtedly made it a thing as wholly Catalonian as *The Cid* is Castilian. Here is the story of the knight Partenopex.

On the death of the Emperor Julian of Greece the rule of his kingdom devolved upon his daughter Melior, a maiden of extraordinary talents, who was, moreover, possessed of a deep knowledge regarding the hidden sciences. Notwithstanding her ability, however, her advisers did not think it fitting that she should rule alone, and insisted that she should address herself to the task of selecting a husband. They granted her a space of two years in which to make choice of a suitable consort, and in order that she might be able to select a *parti* of a rank sufficiently illustrious to match with her own, she dispatched embassies to all the principal courts of Europe, bidding their members to inquire diligently into the credentials of all eligible princes.

At this time there lived in France a youth of much beauty and promise in arms called Partenopex de Blois, nephew to the King of Paris. While following the train of his royal uncle in the chase one day, in the green shades of the Forest of Ardennes, he became separated from the rest of the party and lost his way. Forced to spend the night in the forest, he awoke with the dawn, and, in trying to find his bearings, came to the seashore. To his surprise, he beheld a splendid vessel moored near to the land. In the hope that its crew would be able to direct him as to the path he should take to reach home, he went on board the ship, but found her deserted. He was about to quit the vessel when she began to move, and, gaining speed, cleaved the water with such velocity that to attempt to leave her was impossible. After a voyage as short as it was swift, Partenopex found himself moored in a bay in a country of the most enchanting description.

Disembarking, the youth walked inland, and soon came to the walls of a stately castle. He entered, and, to his surprise, found it as deserted as the vessel which had brought him thither. The principal chamber was illuminated by the sparkle of countless diamonds, and the young knight, who was by this time famished with hunger, was pleased to see an exquisite repast spread on the table before him. He was soon to learn the magical nature of all things in that enchanted castle, for the dainties with which the table groaned found their own way to his lips, and when he had refreshed himself sufficiently a lighted torch appeared as if suspended in the air, and preceded him to a bed-chamber, where he was undressed by invisible hands.

As he lay in bed thinking upon the extraordinary nature of the adventure which had befallen him a lady entered the apartment, and introduced herself as Melior, the Empress of Greece. She told the young knight that she had fallen in love with him from the account of her ambassadors, and had contrived to bring him to her castle by dint of the powers of magic she possessed. She commanded him to remain at the castle, but warned him that if he attempted to see her again before two years had elapsed the result would be the loss of her affection. She then quitted the apartment, which was entered in the morning by her sister Uracla, who brought him the most splendid apparel.

The Mysterious Castle

In the mysterious castle of Melior Partenopex found no lack of entertainment, for the extensive grounds by which it was surrounded afforded him the pleasures of the chase, and in the evenings he was amused by the sweet strains of invisible musicians. Everything possible and impossible was done to render his stay pleasant and memorable. But in the midst of the delights with which he was surrounded he learned that his country had been attacked by a host of enemies. He communicated to his invisible mistress his desire that he should be permitted to fight for the land of his birth, and when she had received his assurance that he would return she placed at his service the magic vessel in which he had come to her coasts, and by its aid he shortly regained the shores of France.

Partenopex was making his way as quickly as possible to Paris to place his sword at the service of his king, when he encountered a knight whose conduct toward him brought matters to the arbitrament of a combat. When they had fought for a space Partenopex discovered that his opponent was none other than Gaudin, the lover of Uracla, the sister of Melior, and from being at daggers drawn the two young knights became the closest companions, and rode on together to where the Court sat at Paris.

Shortly after his return to the capital Partenopex was presented to the Lady Angelica, niece of the Pope, who promptly fell in love with him. Animated by the mistaken belief that 'All's fair in love,' she intercepted his letters from Melior, and thus learned of his passion for the wonder-working Empress of Constantinople. Enlisting on her side a hermit of great sanctity, she bade him repair to Partenopex and denounce his lady-love as a demon of darkness, who was so lost to all good that she even partook of the outward semblance of a fiend in possessing a serpent's tail, black skin, white eyes, and red teeth. This story Partenopex stoutly refused to credit, but when hostilities had come to an end and he had returned to the enchanted castle the hermit's tale still agitated his mind, and he resolved to put it to the test, for Melior had visited him in the dark and he knew not how she appeared.

So one fateful night, when all the castle was plunged in slumber, the young knight equipped himself with a lamp and made his way to the chamber where he knew Melior slept. Entering softly, he held the lamp above the form of his sleeping mistress, and when he beheld her warm human beauty he knew that false slander had been spoken of her. But, alas! as he gazed at her recumbent loveliness a drop of oil from the lamp he held fell upon her bosom and she awoke. Furious that her commands had been broken, she would have slain her unhappy lover on the spot, but at the intercession of Uracla, who had entered the chamber on hearing her sister's exclamations of anger, the incensed Empress at last permitted him to depart without scathe.

The unfortunate Partenopex quitted the castle in all haste, and in time came once more to the green shadows of Ardennes, where he resolved to perish in strife with the savage beasts which haunted its dark recesses. But although they devoured his steed they seemed unwilling to encounter the knight himself. The neighings of his charger brought Uracla, who had been searching for him, to the spot, and she succeeded in inducing him to accompany her to her castle in Tenedos, there to await a more complacent attitude on the part of her sister. Returning to the wrathful Empress, she at last persuaded her to send forth a decree that she would bestow her hand upon the victor in a tournament she was about to proclaim.

Preparations for the tournament proceeded apace, and Partenopex awaited the day in Uracla's castle in Tenedos. But he was not permitted to remain in peace, for Parseis, one of Uracla's maidens, conceived a passionate attachment to him, which she avowed to him while they were taking a short trip in a boat. Partenopex, taken aback, was about to protest, when the frail vessel was caught up by a terrific tempest, and the pair were driven upon the coast of Syria. On landing they were seized by the people of that country, who bore the knight to their king, Hermon, and he was cast into prison.

A sad plight was that of Partenopex, for he heard that Hermon and other knights had departed to the tournament of Melior at Constantinople, while he had perforce to remain in durance vile and renounce all hope of regaining his place in the affections of his lady by force of arms.

But Partenopex succeeded in interesting the Queen in his affairs, and she assisted in his escape from his Syrian prison. He arrived at Constantinople just in time to participate in the tournament. Many and powerful were his opponents, the most formidable being the Soldan of Persia, but at length he overcame them all, and when he asked to be permitted to claim his reward he was received by Melior with every mark of forgiveness and rejoicing.

The Type of 'Partenopex'

The romance of Partenopex is undoubtedly of the same class as those of Cupid and Psyche and Melusine, in which one spouse must not behold another on pain of loss. The loss invariably occurs, but poetical justice usually demands that recovery should take place after many trials. Frequently the husband or wife takes beast or reptile shape, as in the grand old romance of *Melusine*, to which *Partenopex* bears a strong resemblance, and by which I think it has certainly been sophisticated. But in the story with which we have been dealing the reputed semi-reptilian form which the heroine is said to possess is proved to be the figment of the brain of a jealous rival, and in this we have a valuable variant of the main form of the legend, illustrating the rise within it of more modern ideas and the skilful utilization of an antique form to the uses of the writer of fiction. The tale of *Partenopex de Blois* certainly deserves fuller study at the hands of folk-lorists than it has yet received, and I hope they will peruse its Catalonian as well as its French form, thus rendering their purview of the tale more embracive.

Tirante the White

The grand old tale of *Tirante the White* was the work of two Catalonian authors, Juan Martorell and Juan de Gilha, the latter completing the work of the former. Martorell states that he translated the romance from the English, and it certainly seems as if portions of the work had been sophisticated or influenced by the old English romance of *Sir Guy of Warwick*. I cannot, however, discern any signs of direct translation, and think it very probable that the author's statement in this regard is one of those polite fictions employed by the romance-writers of Old Spain to render their efforts more mysterious or to guard themselves against the merciless critics with whom the Peninsula seems to have swarmed in a period when well-nigh everybody was bitten with the craze for *belles-lettres*. The romance was first printed at Valencia in 1490. It contains reference to the Canary Islands, which were first discovered in 1326, and were not well known even in Spain until the beginning of the fifteenth century, so that we may perhaps be justified in fixing the date of its composition about that period, especially as it alludes to a work on chivalry entitled *L'Arbre des Batailles*, which was not published until 1390. The book was translated into Castilian and produced at Valladolid in 1511, and was followed by Italian and French translations by Manfredi and the Comte de Caylus respectively, but the latter has dreadfully mutilated the original, and has even altered its main plot as well as many of its lesser incidents, and has imported into it an unhealthy atmosphere which we do not find in the work as given us by Martorell.

On the occasion of the marriage of a certain King of England with a beautiful and accomplished princess of France the most extraordinary efforts were made to signalize the *entente* thus ratified by a tournament of the most splendid description. Learning of these martial preparations, Tirante, a young knight of Brittany, resolved to participate in them, and with a number of youthful companions who had a like object in view he took ship for England, where in due time he landed, and proceeded to Windsor. But the fatigues of the voyage overtook him and he fell asleep, lulled into slumber by the jog-trot of his weary charger.

It is not to be wondered at that in this manner he became separated from his brisker companions, and that on awaking he found himself alone on the broad highway. Setting spurs to his destrier, he pushed on for a few miles, but feeling the necessity for rest and refreshment he cast about for a halting-place, and was cheered by the sight of a humble lodging, which he believed to be a hermitage, nestling among the trees at some distance from the roadside and almost concealed in the leafy shadows. Dismounting, he entered the place, and was confronted by a person whose hermit's garb ill suited him, and whose disguise was soon penetrated by the practised eye of knighthood, so that Tirante was scarcely surprised to observe that the recluse was engaged in reading the book known as *L'Arbre des Batailles*, a work which descants with learning and insight upon the precepts and practice of chivalry.

The Hermit Earl

The hermit was, indeed, none other than William, Earl of Warwick, a renowned champion, who, tired of the frivolities of the Court, had gone on a pilgrimage to Jerusalem. Arrived at the Holy Sepulchre, he had spread a report of his death, had returned to England in the disguise of a pilgrim or palmer, and had taken up his abode in the hermitage where Tirante discovered him, and which was not far from the castle where his countess resided. But his retirement was not destined to last long, for when the great King of the Canary Islands landed in England with a formidable army, the Earl, beholding the widespread consternation occasioned by his invasion, took up arms once more. The advance of the raiders was, however, so swift that the King of England was speedily driven from Canterbury and London, and was compelled to seek refuge in the town of Warwick, where he was hotly besieged by the

Canarese forces. At this crisis the Earl came to his assistance, slew the King of the Canaries in single combat, and dispersed his army in a pitched battle. This accomplished, he revealed himself to his countess, and once more retired to his hermitage. All of these details agree in a measure with those of the old English romance of *Sir Guy of Warwick*.

Tirante made himself known to the hermit Earl, told him that he was so called because his father was lord of the marches of Tirraine, situated in that part of France which was opposite the coast of England, and that his mother was daughter to the Duke of Brittany. He further told his host that he was resolved to take part in the great tournament held to celebrate the royal wedding, whereupon the Earl read him a chapter from the book he had been perusing regarding the whole duty of a knight. This he followed by a lecture upon the use of arms and the exploits of ancient paladins. When he had finished he observed that the hour was late and that as Tirante was ignorant of the roads he had better hasten upon his way, and, pressing the youthful champion to accept the book from which he had been reading, he bade him farewell.

A twelvemonth passed. Tirante, having shown his superiority at the tournament, was returning with some forty of his companions from the Court, when they once more passed the Earl's retreat, and halted to pay their duty to him. Interested to learn of the warlike pageant, he inquired who had most distinguished himself, and was told that Tirante had borne off the prize. A French lord called Villermes, having objected to his wearing a favour given him by the fair Agnes, daughter of the Duke of Berri, had defied him to mortal combat, and

Tirante the White

had required that they should fight armed with bucklers of paper and helmets of flowers. Villermes was slain in the encounter, but Tirante, having recovered from eleven wounds, shortly afterward slew four knights, brothers-in-arms, who proved to be the Kings of Poland and Friesland and the Dukes of Burgundy and Bavaria. A certain subject of the King of Friesland, rejoicing in the name of Kyrie Eleison, or 'Lord have mercy upon us,' and descended from the ancient giants, now arrived in England to avenge his master's death. On beholding his sovereign's tomb, however, he expired from grief on seeing the arms of Tirante suspended over the Frisian standard. His place was supplied by his brother, Thomas of Montauban, a champion of stature still more gigantic, who was, however, defeated by the young Breton knight and forced to sue for his life.

Having paid his respects to the Earl, Tirante returned to his native Brittany, but he had been only a few days in the castle of his fathers when a messenger arrived with the news that the Knights of Rhodes were closely besieged by the Genoese and the Soldan of Cairo. Accompanied by Philip, youngest son of the King of France, Tirante set out to the relief of the island, and in the course of the voyage anchored in the roads of Palermo, where he sojourned for a space. When at length he arrived at Rhodes the besiegers beat a hasty retreat, and having freed the island from their presence Tirante and his men returned to Sicily, where Prince Philip espoused the princess of that country.

But the wedding festivities had scarcely come to an end when a herald from the Emperor of Constantinople arrived at the Sicilian Court with the moving information that his master's territories had been invaded by the

Grand Turk and the Soldan of the Moors. Once more chivalric honour demanded that a Christian land should be rescued from the clutches of the paynim, and Tirante, setting sail for Constantinople, was, on his arrival there, entrusted with the supreme command of the Hellenic forces. A great part of the romance is occupied by the details of the war carried on against the Turks, who were invariably defeated in battle after battle, so that at length they called for a truce. This was granted, and the interval of repose was occupied with splendid festivals and tournaments.

At this juncture of affairs no less a personage than the celebrated Urganda arrived in Constantinople in quest of her brother, the renowned Arthur, King of Britain. The Emperor, searching among those of his prisoners who were kept in the most obscure dungeons, found the hero of heroes pining out his old age in an iron cage, reduced to the lowest level of physical debility. Restored to his ancient weapon, the good sword Excalibur, the hapless monarch was able to answer any questions put to him with address. But when the blade was withdrawn from his grasp he sank ever lower into the second childhood of senility. After giving a splendid supper, Urganda disappeared with her ancient brother, nor was anyone aware whither they had gone.

Up to this time Tirante had contrived to remain fancy-free, but at last he fell a willing victim to the bright eyes of the Emperor's daughter, the Princess Carmesina. His affair went smoothly enough until one of her attendants, Reposada, having fallen passionately in love with the young knight, succeeded in arousing his jealousy by a wretched stratagem, and, offended to the soul at what he believed to be the baseness of his mistress, he set out

Tirante the White

once more for the army without taking his leave of her. But the vessel in which he set sail was caught in a violent tempest and driven upon the coasts of Africa. Wandering disconsolate on the shore, Tirante encountered an ambassador of the King of Tormecen, who conducted him to Court and presented him to his master, whom he assisted in the wars in which that monarch was naturally engaged. On one occasion he besieged the city of Montagata, when a lady issued from its gates to sue for peace on behalf of its inhabitants. To his surprise he found her to be one of the Princess Carmesina's attendants, who told him the truth regarding the trick played upon him by the false Reposada. He at once raised the siege, and returned to Constantinople at the head of an enormous army to succour the Greek Emperor. Burning the Turkish fleet, he rendered the retreat of the Soldan's forces impracticable, and secured an advantageous peace.

Splendid preparations were now made for the wedding of Tirante and Carmesina. But while on his return to Constantinople after the conclusion of the treaty he received orders, at the distance of a day's journey from the city, to wait until the completion of those preparations before entering Constantinople. While walking on the banks of a river in conversation with the Kings of Ethiopia, Fez, and Sicily, he was seized with a deadly pleurisy, and, despite all the efforts of his attendants, expired shortly afterward. The Emperor and Princess, on learning of his demise, were unable to restrain their grief, and died on the day they heard of his death.

We have at last encountered a romance which does not end happily. In what manner such a *dénouement* was received by the Spanish public we know not, but at least they cannot but have been struck by its originality. That *Tirante the White* was a popular favourite, however, is clear from the praise lavished upon it Cervantes. "By her taking so many romances together," he says, "there fell one at the barber's feet, who had a mind to see what it was, and found it to be *Tirante the White.* 'God save me,' quoth the priest in a loud voice, 'is *Tirante the White* there? Give me him here, neighbour, for I shall find him a treasure of delight, and a mine of entertainment.'" He then advised the housewife to take it home and read it, " for though the author deserves to be sent to the gallows for writing so many foolish things seriously, yet in its way it is the best book in the world. Here the knights eat and sleep and die in their beds, and make their wills before their death, with several things which are wanting in all other books of this kind."

Is not this the essence of the revolt against the unnatural absurdities which so often characterized romance, expressed succinctly by the man who headed the mutiny?

CHAPTER VII : RODERIC, LAST OF THE GOTHS

Last night I was a King of Spain—to-day no King am I.
Last night fair castles held my train, to-night where shall I lie?
Last night a hundred pages did serve me on the knee,
To-night not one I call my own ; not one pertains to me.

LOCKHART, *Spanish Ballads*

THE tragic and tumultuous story of the manner in which Spain was delivered into the hands of the Moors is surely a theme worthy of treatment by the highest genius. But either because it offended the national pride or otherwise failed to make an appeal to the Castilian temperament, its epic remains unwritten. Few passages in history afford such an opportunity for the delineation of the deeper human passions as the episode which resulted in the betrayal of an entire country for the gratification of a private wrong. It presents such a catastrophe as urged Æschylus to compose the moving and majestic drama of *Electra*. Yet it has found no more potent expression than in the dreary parchment of the latest Spanish chronicle and the pedestrian verse of Southey's *Roderick, the Last of the Goths*, which draws its inspiration from the pseudo-history of that account.[1]

Before we examine the romantic material embedded in *The Chronicle of Don Roderic, with the Destruction of Spain*, it will be well to trace the story of the downfall of the Gothic empire in Spain by the aid of such materials as we can trust to supply us with a more or

[1] Unless the *Anseis de Carthage* be excepted—a romance which attributes the downfall of Spain to a son of Charlemagne, who acts as does Don Roderick. The *Anseis* is in French.

less accurate account of it. These are to be found in the *General Chronicle of Spain* and in the pages of the Moorish historians. Summarized, the facts relating to the incident are probably as follows :

From the period of the settlement of the Mohammedan Arabs in Mauretania their fleets had frequently ravaged the coasts of Andalusia, by which name the entire Spanish peninsula was known to them. An enmity arose between Spanish Goth and Moorish Arab which was heightened not only by the difference in their religion but by the circumstance that the fortress of Ceuta in Mauretania still remained in Gothic hands. This out-post of the Gothic empire was held by the vigilance and courage of Count Julian, a leader of experience, who retained the fortress against tremendous odds.

The ruler of Spain at this period was one Don Roderic, who does not appear to have held the throne by heredi-tary right. Witiza, his predecessor, had slain Roderic's father, the governor of a province, and, whether to gratify his revenge or purely because of his ambitions, Roderic succeeded in having the claims of Witiza's two sons set aside and in securing the crown for himself. But the monarchy among the Goths of Spain was still elective, and it may be that Roderic had been legally placed on the throne by the suffrages of his fellow-peers. It is probable that Count Julian was a member of the unsuccessful faction headed by the royal brothers, and that, in despair of displacing Roderic by force of arms, he sought the assistance of his Moorish enemies to accomplish his downfall.

But tradition, whether rightly or otherwise, disdains to accept the circumstances of a cold political issue as an adequate reason for Count Julian's defection from

Roderic, Last of the Goths

loyalty, and has a much more romantic explanation to advance for his traitorous act. Roderic, we are told, was a ruler of evil and scandalous character. He conceived a violent passion for Cava, the young and beautiful daughter of Count Julian, whom he abducted and dishonoured. Roused to fury and despair at Roderic's act, Julian instantly resolved upon a terrible revenge, and, not content with handing over the fortress which he had so long maintained against a powerful enemy, he suggested to Musa, the Moorish king or satrap, the invasion of Spain, binding himself even more closely to the infidels by accepting their religion and conforming to their customs. He impressed upon Musa the natural advantages of his native land, and laid stress upon its distracted and defenceless condition, the effeminacy and degeneracy of its warriors, and the unprotected state of its cities. Musa recognized that an opportunity offered itself to extend the Arab dominions, and sent an embassy to Walid, the Caliph, his suzerain, asking his opinion of such an enterprise. Walid encouraged him to proceed with it. But Musa, although a brave and active leader, was shrewd and cautious, and instead of launching a great armada against a country of whose defensive capacity he knew little, contented himself in the first instance by making a raid, in July A.D. 710, on the Spanish coast, as if to test the fighting qualities of its defenders. The expedition consisted of only five hundred men, who, landing at Tarifa, marched some eighteen miles through Spanish territory to the castle and town of Julian. There they were joined by the disaffected adherents of that nobleman, and, meeting with no opposition, returned to Africa with an abundance of spoil.

Encouraged by the success of their preliminary enterprise, the Saracens now levied an army of five thousand men, and in the spring of 711, under the leadership of a certain Tarik, landed upon Spanish soil at a spot which still bears the name of their commander, Gibraltar, for Gebel al Tarik signifies 'the Mountain of Tarik.' They speedily defeated a Spanish force under Edeco, but Roderic, now fully aroused to the danger by which his rule was threatened, summoned his vassals to the royal standard, their number, we are told, amounting to nearly one hundred thousand men. Tarik had by this time been reinforced, but could muster only some twelve thousand troops of Moorish race, though these were augmented by a host of Africans and disaffected Goths. The armies met near Cadiz, Roderic himself leading the Gothic host, resplendent in his princely robes of silk and gold embroidery, and reclining in a car drawn by white mules. The Gothic attack almost succeeded by sheer weight of numbers, and sixteen thousand of the Moorish army were slain in the first encounter. But Tarik encouraged his flagging forces by pointing out to them that retreat was impossible. "The enemy is before you," he said, "the sea behind you. Whither would ye fly? Follow me, my brethren. I shall trample on yon King of the Romans or perish."

Roderic's Fate

But assistance for the Moors was at hand, for the two sons of Witiza, who occupied the most important posts in the Spanish army, suddenly broke away from the main body. This brought about a general panic. Roderic, mounting his fleet charger Orelia, was drowned

Roderic's Fate

while attempting to swim the Guadalquivir, leaving his diadem and robes on the bank. At the instigation of Count Julian, Tarik pressed on to Toledo, which, however, held out for three months, and dispatched a force to reduce the kingdom of Granada. This was duly accomplished, and Toledo surrendered on the Moor's assurance that its inhabitants would be permitted to leave with their possessions, a promise which was faithfully kept. The Jews, who had especially assisted the pagan invaders, were richly rewarded by them, and, indeed, formed an alliance with them which lasted until both were eventually and happily expelled from the country. From Toledo Tarik spread his conquests over Castile and Leon, penetrating north as far as the town of Gijon in Asturias, where further progress was barred by the waters of the Bay of Biscay. In a few months practically the whole of Spain had become a Mohammedan province, and only a handful of Gothic warriors were able to hold out in the valleys of Asturias against the conquering Moor.

We may now leave the path of definite history for the more picturesque if also more uncertain road of romance. The chronicles recount Don Roderic's abandoned wickedness, and tell how the invasion of the Moors, instigated by Julian, broke as a thunderclap upon the unprincipled ruler. The strife with the Saracens is described, and Roderic's flight is painted in gloomy colours. But just as popular legend refused to credit the death of Arthur on that day at Camelot, or the fate of James IV of Scotland on Flodden Field, or the death of Harold at Hastings, so it refused to believe in that of Roderic. Racial sentiment refuses to admit the death of a popular leader, and have not legends been afloat even in our own day concerning the lamented Lord Kitchener?

Tradition [1] has it, then, that as Roderic was about to plunge into the waters of the Guadalquivir a divine light burst upon him, and a secret voice adjured him to repent of his sins and live. Acting upon the advice of this inward counsellor, he divested himself of his royal insignia, and taking from the dead the garment of a humble peasant, stole from the field. All night he fled, haunted by fearful visions of the wrath to come. On all sides he beheld the dreadful consequences of his defeat. Staggering on through scenes of misery and ruin which wrung his heart, he came at length, after seven days' travel, to the monastery of Canlin, on the banks of the river Ana, near Minda. The place was deserted, but the wretched fugitive cast himself down beside the altar to await his doom in prayer, for he fully believed that sooner or later the infidels would trace him to this retreat and dispatch him. He fed the lamps with oil, only leaving the holy shrine from time to time to see if the Saracens approached. Beneath the crucifix he lay, clasping the feet of the Redeemer's image, and weeping icy tears of penitence. As he grovelled there he became aware that some one had entered the chapel, and, raising his eyes in hope of a speedy death by the scimetar of a Moorish soldier, to his surprise he beheld a monk, who gently addressed him, and explained that he had returned to the place which for threescore years and five he had called home,

---

[1] As enshrined in the *Crónica Sarrazyna,* of Pedro de Carrel, which founds on the *Crónica General*, the *Chronicle of the Moor Rasis*, and the *Crónica Trayana*, the ballads relating to Roderic are all later than this compilation.

trusting to die there by the hand of an infidel and thus to gain the crown of a martyr.

Roderic revealed his name to the father, who, deeply impressed by the tone of penitence in his voice, knelt beside him and ministered to the stricken monarch throughout the long night hours. He assured him that he must live to work out his salvation, and when morning broke the aged priest and he who yesterday had been one of the proudest kings in Christendom quitted the chapel and went on their way.

The holy father led the crownless King to a hermitage, where he gave him further ghostly counsel, enjoining him to remain in that place so long as it should please God. "As for me," he said, "on the third day from hence I shall pass out of this world, and thou shalt bury me and take my garments and remain here for the space of a year at least, that thou mayst endure hunger and cold and thirst in the love of our Lord, that He may have compassion on thee."

On the third day, as he had prophesied, the hermit expired. Deeply grieved at his death, Roderic busied himself in carrying out his last wishes, and with an oaken staff and his bare hands dug a grave for the holy man's body. When he was in the act of laying him in the ground he found a scroll in his hand covered with writing, addressed to himself, and containing advice concerning the life he should lead while an inmate of the hermitage. This Roderic reverently perused, and resolved to follow its injunctions to the letter.

But the Father of Evil was not minded that the King should proceed undisturbed in his quest for salvation, and that night appeared to him as he was in the act of committing the hermit to the grave. He came in monkish garb, his features hooded by a great cowl, and further disguised by a beard of venerable length and silvery whiteness, supporting himself by a staff as if he were lame. Roderic took him for a friend of the dead hermit, and would have kissed his hand, but the Fiend drew back, saying: "It is not meet that a king should kiss the hand of a poor servant of God." The King, hearing his identity thus revealed, believed the Devil to be a holy man, speaking by aid of a revelation. "Alas!" he said, "I am not a king, but a miserable sinner, who had better never have been born, so much woe has visited the land through my misdoing."

"Thou hast not so much fault as thou thinkest," replied Satan, "for the calamity of which thou speakest would have occurred in any case. It was ordained, and the fault was not thine. My words are those of a spirit created by the will of God, and not mine own." The Evil One then pretended that he had journeyed all the way from Rome to help Roderic in his distress, and hearing this the King rejoiced, and listened reverently as the Devil attempted to controvert the teaching of the dead hermit by specious arguments. But when the King requested the seeming holy man to assist him in burying the anchorite's remains he was surprised to see him turn and make off at a good speed, despite his alleged lameness.

At the hour of noon next day the Devil returned with a basket full of savoury food. But the dead hermit had enjoined Roderic to eat of nothing but the rye bread which the shepherds would bring him once a week, and obedient to this, he withstood the tempter's proffered meat and wine. The argument betwixt the King and Satan is then elaborated with medieval prolixity and due regard to the hair-splitting, logic-chopping theology of the time. Even a medieval sense of decency might have prompted the writer to omit the King's interview with the Holy Ghost, as to which I will only say here that at the word of the Holy Spirit the foul fiend fled in the shape of a horrid devil, bristling with the insignia of hell.

Satan's Stratagem

But the Enemy was not yet finished with Don Roderic, for one evening at set of sun the hermit King saw one approach with a great power of armed men and every display of pomp and circumstance. As the train drew nearer, Roderic, to his amazement, beheld in its leader Count Julian, who came to him and would have kissed his hand with every sign of homage, offering himself up to the King's vengeance and justice, and freely acknowledging his treason. The seeming Julian begged him to rise up and take once more his proper place at the head of the Spanish forces, so that the infidel might be thrust out of Spain. But Roderic, suspecting another fiendish stratagem, shook his head, and requested Julian to accept the leadership of the Gothic army himself, as his vows did not permit him to engage any longer in worldly affairs. Julian turned to the great company behind him, among whom Roderic beheld many whom he had thought to have been slain in battle, and these enthusiastically seconded their leader's arguments. But when the fiendish crew saw that their pleading was without avail they withdrew to the plain below, where they formed themselves in battle array, as if awaiting the onset of an enemy. And lo! against them came a multitude of seeming pagans, so that a great and fierce carnage followed. To the anxious eyes of the King, those who represented the Christian host seemed to put the paynim to the rout, and messengers spurred to the hermitage, announcing to him that his people had gained a glorious victory. But as the cock crowed the whole pageant of battle passed away like smoke borne before the breeze, and the King knew that he had once more withstood the wiles of the Enemy.

Now for three months the Devil refrained from tormenting Don Roderic, but at the end of that time he sent upon him a more grievous trial than any that had gone before. As he was saying his prayers at the hour of vespers, he beheld a train of cavaliers ride up to the hermitage, and when they halted and alighted there came toward him a damsel in the guise of that Cava, the daughter of Count Julian, whom he had so foully wronged. At sight of her the wretched man's heart almost ceased to beat, but ere he could speak she told him that her father had turned his sword on the Moors and had conquered them, that Eliaca, his Queen, was no more, and that a holy man had told her that she must forthwith find Don Roderic and wed with him, and that she should bring forth a son called Elbersan, who should bring the whole world under the sceptre of Spain.

When Roderic heard these words he trembled exceedingly, for greatly had he loved Cava. She ordered a pavilion to be pitched near the hermitage, and her train set out a sumptuous repast. Seeing how beautiful she was, the King shook as with a palsy. But he clasped his hands and, commending himself to God, begged to be delivered from temptation. As he made the sign of the Cross the false Cava fled shrieking, and her infernal train followed

DON RODERIC IS TEMPTED BY A SEMBLANCE OF CAVA

COUNT ALARCOS MEETS HIS WIFE AND CHILDREN
AT THE GATE OF THE CASTLE

The Death of Roderic

with such a rout and noise that the whole world seemed
to be falling to pieces. Once more the Holy Spirit
admonished Roderic to guard against such stratagems
of the Devil, and far into the day the repentant but
victorious King prayed without ceasing in thanksgiving
for his deliverance from the snares of hell.

The Death of Roderic

The time now came when it was appointed that the
King should leave the retreat where he had passed
through trials so many and so terrible, and, following a
cloud appointed for his guidance, he girded up his loins
and set forth on his journey. Before nightfall of the
first day he came to another hermitage, where he lodged
during the hours of darkness. After two days' journeying
he came to a place unnamed, which was destined to be
that of his burial. The Elder of this place told him
that he must go to a fountain below the hermitage in
which he had taken up his abode, and that he should
there find a smooth stone. This he was instructed to
raise, when he would find below it three little serpents,
one having two heads. This two-headed serpent he
must place in a jar and nourish secretly, so that none
should know of its existence, and so hide it until it grew
large enough to wind its coils three times within the jar
and put its head out. Then he must place it in a tomb
and lie down himself with it, naked, for such, it pleased
God, should be his penance, according to a voice the
Elder had heard speaking in the church of that place.
Roderic scrupulously followed the Elder's injunctions,
found the reptile, and waited patiently till the two-
headed serpent had waxed great within the jar. Then,
in company with the Elder, he divested himself of his

raiment and sought the tomb, wherein he laid himself down. And when he had done so the Elder took a lever and laid a great stone upon the top. Having lain there three days, during which the Elder prayed and watched devoutly, the serpent raised its heads and began with one head to devour his sinful nature and with the other to eat his heart. In great torment did Roderic lie in that place. But at length the serpent broke through the web of the heart, so that incontinently the King gave up his spirit to God, Who by His holy mercy took him into His glory. And at the hour when he expired all the bells of the place rang of themselves, as if they had been rung by the hands of men.

So, in the strange spirit of medieval mysticism, ends the piteous legend of Don Roderic of Spain. Who shall unriddle the weird significance of its close, unless, like old Thomas Newton in his *Notable History of the Saracens*, they believe "that the serpent with two heads signifieth his sinful and gylty conscience"? *Requiescas in pace, Domine Roderice!*

CHAPTER VIII : "CALAYNOS THE MOOR" "GAYFEROS" AND "COUNT ALARCOS"

I BRACKET these three romances together in this chapter not only because they appear to have been held in the highest favour by the people of Old Spain, but for the equally good reason that they seem to me to manifest the national taste and genius more markedly than others of the same class, if, indeed, they did not belong to a class by themselves, as I have always suspected they did, for in all Castilian accounts of romantic fiction they are frequently mentioned together, and this traditional treatment of them may arise from the consciousness of their similarity of *genre*. But above and beyond this they possess and enshrine that grave and austere spirit so typical of all true Spanish literature, and at least one of them is deeply tinged with the atmosphere of fatal and remorseless tragedy which only the Latin or the Hellene knows how to evoke, for not the greatest masters of the Northern races, neither Marlowe nor Massinger, Goethe nor Shakespeare, can drape such sombre curtains around their stage as Calderon or Lope.

Calaynos

Calaynos, one of the most renowned of the Moorish knights, is the hero of more than one romance in verse. But that which is best known, and most regular in its sequence of events, is the *Coplas de Calainos*, which has been translated so successfully by Lockhart in his *Spanish Ballads*. The Moorish champion, it tells us, was enamoured of a maiden of his own nation, and in order to win her favour offered her broad estates and abundant wealth. But in her petulance she refused this comfortable homage, and demanded the heads of three of the most valiant champions of Christendom—Rinaldo, Roland, and Oliver! Bestowing on his lady a farewell kiss, Calaynos immediately set out for Paris, and when he had arrived there displayed the crescent banner of his faith before the Church of St John. He caused a blast to be blown upon his trumpet, the sound of which was well known to Charlemagne and his twelve peers, and was heard by them as they hunted in the greenwood, some miles from the city. Shortly afterward the royal train encountered a Moor, and the Emperor haughtily demanded of him how he dared to show his green turban within his dominions. He replied that he served Calaynos, who sent his defiance to Charlemagne and all his peers, whose onset he awaited at Paris.

As they rode back to encounter the bold infidel Charlemagne suggested to Roland that he should take the chastisement of Calaynos upon himself, but that haughty paladin proposed that the task should be delegated to some carpet-knight, as he considered it beneath his prowess to do battle with a single Moor. Sir Baldwin, Roland's nephew, boasted that he would bring Calaynos' green turban to the dust, and, spurring ahead, soon came face to face with the stern Moorish lord, who, with a sneer, offered to take him into the service of his lady as a page.

Right angry was Baldwin when he heard these words, and, hurling his defiance at Calaynos, bade him prepare for battle. The Moor vaulted upon his barb, and, levelling his lance, rode fiercely at Baldwin and bore him to earth, where he made him sue for mercy. But Roland, the youth's uncle, was at hand, and, winding his terrible horn, shouted to Calaynos to prepare for combat.

"Who art thou?" asked Calaynos. "Thou wearest a coronet in thy helm, but I know thee not."

"No words, base Moor!" replied Roland. "This hour shall be thy last," and, so saying, he charged his enemy at full speed. Down crashed the haughty infidel, and Roland, leaping from the saddle, stood over him, drawn sword in hand.

"Thy name, paynim," he demanded; "speak or die."

"Sir," replied Calaynos, "I serve a haughty maiden of Spain, who would have no gift of me but the heads of certain peers of Charlemagne."

"So!" laughed Roland. "Fool that thou art, she could not have loved thee when she bade thee beard our fellowship. Thou hast come here to thy death," and with these words he smote off Calaynos' head, and spurned his crescent crest in twain. "No more shall this moon rise above the meads of Seine," he cried, as he sheathed his falchion.

Thus was Calaynos fooled by a maiden's pride and by his own. The story is, of course, wildly improbable, and that a Moorish knight could have reached Paris on such a quest is unthinkable. But the tale has a very human accent, and is not without its moral.

Gayferos

Gayferos was a figure dear to Spanish romance. His story was connected with the Charlemagne cycle, and was included in the pseudo-chronicle of Archbishop Turpin, but, though a knight of France, he appears to have possessed a special attraction for the Castilian mind, owing, probably, to the circumstance of his seven years' search for his wife in Spanish territory.

Gayferos of Bordeaux was a kinsman of Roland, the invincible hero of the *chansons de gestes*, and husband of Charlemagne's daughter Melisenda. Shortly after their marriage the lady was kidnapped by the Saracens and confined in a strong tower at Saragossa. Determined to rescue her from pagan custody, Gayferos set out in search of his wife, but after spending seven long years in diligent inquiry failed to locate the place where she was imprisoned. From province to province, from castle to castle of sunny Spain he journeyed, until at length, disconsolate and dejected, he returned to Paris.

In the hope of drowning the remembrance of his loss, Gayferos plunged into the recreations of the Court. One day as he played dice with the Emperor's admiral, Charlemagne, seeing him thus employed, said to him : "How is it, Gayferos, that you waste your time on a paltry game, while your wife, my daughter, languishes in a Moorish prison? Were you as ready to handle arms as to throw dice, you would hasten to the rescue of your lady." The Emperor's speech was unmerited, for he had only just learned of the place in which Melisenda was held in durance, whereas the faithful Gayferos was not yet aware of it. But gathering from Charlemagne the name of the castle in which she was confined, he made speed to his uncle Roland, and begged him for armour and a horse.

Roland, seeing the dismay in which his nephew was plunged, pressed upon him his own famous arms and his favourite charger, and, thus equipped, Gayferos once more turned his face to the land of Spain. In due time he arrived at Saragossa, and, meeting with no opposition at its gates, he entered and rode straight to the house where his captive wife lay. Beholding him from the window, she begged him as he was a Christian knight to send the tidings of her to her husband Gayferos.

"Seven summers, seven winters have I waited in this tower,
While my lord Gayferos holdeth dalliance in hall and bower ;
Hath forgotten Melisenda, hopes that she hath wed the Moor ;
Yet the kindness of his memory shall I cherish evermore."

Stands the champion in his stirrups. "Lady, dry the useless tear,
For thy husband and thy lover, thy devoted knight is here.
Spring to saddle from the casement, leap into my fond embrace
That shall hold thee and enfold thee from the Moor and all his
  race."

Leaping from the casement into the arms of her faithful knight, Melisenda placed herself on the saddle before him, and setting spurs to his horse Gayferos made all speed to reach the gates. But a Moor who had witnessed the rescue gave the alarm, and soon the fugitives found themselves pursued by seven columns of horsemen.

The pursuers pressed hard upon them, but at the critical juncture Melisenda recognized the horse on which they rode to be Roland's, and remembered that by loosening the girth, opening the breastplate, and driving the spurs into its sides it could be made to leap across any barrier with complete safety to those it carried. She hastily informed her husband of this, and, acting as she directed, he drove the steed toward the city wall, which it cleared with ease. On seeing this the Moors very naturally gave up the chase. In due time Gayferos and his wife returned to Paris, and their future was as bright as their past had been clouded.

Legends & Romances of Spain

Count Alarcos

Gloomy with the hangings of tragedy is the grim story of *The Count Alarcos*, an anonymous romance, distinguished by great richness of composition. It has been translated into English by both Lockhart and Bowring, with but little distinction in either case, having consideration to the moving character of the original. The story opens with the simplicity which marks high tragedy. The Infanta Soliza, daughter of the King of Spain, had been secretly betrothed to Count Alarcos, but was abandoned by him for another lady, by whom he had several children. In the agony of her grief and shame at her seduction and desertion, the miserable princess shut herself off from the world, and consumed the summer of her days in sorrow and bitter disappointment. Her royal father, not conscious of the manner in which she had been betrayed, questioned her as to the meaning of her grief, and she answered him that she mourned because she was not a wife, like other ladies of her station.

"Daughter," replied the King, "this fault is none of mine. Did not the noble Prince of Hungary offer you his hand? I know of no suitable husband for you in this land of Spain, saving the Count Alarcos, and he is already wed."

"Alas!" said the Infanta, "it is the Count Alarcos who has broken my heart, for he vowed to wed me, and plighted his troth to me long ere he wedded. He is true to his new vows, but has left his earlier oaths unfulfilled. In word and deed he is my husband."

For a space the King sat silent. "Great wrong has been done, my daughter," he said at last, "for now is the royal line of Spain shamed in all men's eyes."

Count Alarcos

Then dark and murderous jealousy seized upon the soul of the Infanta. "Certes," she cried, "this Countess can die. Must I be shamed that she should live? Let it be bruited abroad that sickness cut short her life. Thus may Count Alarcos yet wed me."

Exasperated by the thought of his daughter's dishonour, the King summoned Alarcos to a banquet, and when they were alone broached the subject of his perfidy to the Infanta.

"Is it true, Don Alarcos," he asked, "that you plighted your troth to my daughter and deceived her? Now hearken: your Countess usurps my daughter's rightful place. She must die. Nay, start not! It must be reported that sickness has carried her off. Then must you wed the Infanta. You have brought your King to dishonour, and he now demands the only reparation that it is within your power to make."

"I cannot deny that I deceived the Infanta," replied Alarcos. "But I pray you, in mercy spare my innocent lady. Visit my sin upon me as heavily as you will, but not upon her."

"It may not be," replied the stern old King. "She dies, I say, and that to-night. When the escutcheon of a king is stained, it matters not whether the blood that washes the blot away be guilty or innocent. Away, and do my behest, or your life shall pay the forfeit."

Terrified at the thought of a traitor's death, for such an end was more dreaded than any other by the haughty Castilian nobles, Alarcos agreed to abide by the King's decision, and rode homeward in an agony of remorse and despair. The thought that he must be the executioner of the wife whom he dearly loved, the mother of his three beautiful children, drove him to madness, and when at last he met her at the gate of his castle, accompanied by her infants, and displaying every sign of joy at his return, he shrank from her caresses, and could only mutter that he had bad news, which he would divulge to her in her bower.

Taking her youngest babe, she led him to her apartment, where supper was laid. But the Count Alarcos neither ate nor drank, but laid his head upon the board and wept bitterly out of a breaking heart. Then, recalling his dreadful purpose, he barred the doors, and, standing with folded arms before his lady, confessed his sin.

"Long since I loved a lady," he said. "I plighted my troth to her, and vowed to love her like a husband. Her father is the King. She claims me for her own, and he demands that I make good the promise. Furthermore, alas that I should say it! the King has spoken your death, and has decreed that you die this very night."

"What!" cried the Countess, amazed. "Are these then the wages of my loyal love for you, Alarcos? Wherefore must I die? Oh, send me back to my father's house, where I can live in peace and forgetfulness, and rear my children as those of thy blood should be reared."

"It may not be," answered the wretched Count. "I have pledged mine oath."

"Friendless am I in the land," cried the miserable lady. "But at least let me kiss my children ere I die."

"Thou mayst kiss the babe upon thy breast," groaned Alarcos. "The others thou mayst not see again. Prepare thee."

The doomed Countess kissed her babe, muttered an *Ave*, and, rising from her knees, begged her merciless lord to be kind to their children. She pardoned her husband, but

Count Alarcos

laid upon the King and his daughter the awful curse known to the people of the Middle Ages as "the Assize of the Dying," so often taken advantage of by those who were falsely accused and condemned to die, and by virtue of which the victim summoned his murderers to meet him before the throne of God ere thirty days were past and answer for their crime to their Creator.

The Count strangled his wife with a silken kerchief, and when the horrid deed had been done, and she lay cold and dead, he summoned his esquires, and gave himself up to a passion of woe.

Within twelve days the revengeful Infanta perished in agony. The merciless King died on the twentieth day, and ere the moon had completed her round Alarcos too drooped and died. Cruel and inevitable as Greek tragedy is the tale of Alarcos. But while perusing it and under the spell of its tragic pathos we can scarcely regard it as of the nature of legend, and we know not whom to abhor the most—the revengeful Princess, the cruel King, or the coward husband who sacrificed his innocent and devoted wife to the shadow of that aristocratic 'honour' which has to its discredit almost as great a holocaust of victims as either superstition or fanaticism.

CHAPTER IX: THE ROMANCEROS OR BALLADS

Iliads without a Homer.
LOPE DE VEGA

THE word *romancero* in modern Spanish is more or less strictly applied to a special form of verse composition, a narrative poem written in lines of sixteen syllables which adhere to one single assonance throughout. Originally the term was applied to those dialects or languages which were the offspring of the Roman or Latin tongue—the spoken language of old Rome in its modernized forms. Later it came to imply only the written forms of those vernaculars, and lastly the poetic lyrico-narrative form alone, as above indicated. The *romancero* therefore differs from the romance in that it is written in verse, and it is plain from what has just been said that the name 'romance' was the product of the transition period when the term was intended to describe the written output of the more modern forms of Latin-Castilian, Portuguese, French, and Provençal, whether couched in prose or verse. We have seen that practically all the romances proper, as apart from the *cantares de gesta*—that is, such compositions as *Amadis*, *Palmerin*, and *Partenopex*—were written in prose. But the *romancero* was first and last a narrative in verse. Indeed, the three tales recounted in the last chapter are of the *romancero* type—a form, as we shall see, which gained quite as strong a hold upon the lower classes of the Peninsula as the romance proper did upon the affections of the *hidalgo* and the *caballero*. In a word, the *romancero* is the popular ballad of Spain.

The Romanceros

In a previous chapter I attempted to outline the several types of the Spanish ballad, or *romancero*, as follows :

(1) Those of spontaneous popular origin and early date.
(2) Those based upon passages in the chronicles or *cantares de gesta*.
(3) Folk-ballads of a relatively late date.
(4) Those later ballads which were the production of conscious art.

We can thus class Spanish ballads more broadly into :

(1) Those of popular origin.
(2) Those which have their rise in literary sources.

As regard class (1) of the first quaternion, like Sancho Panza I have no intention of indicating how old these may be. The fiercest controversy has raged round this question, but, as I have already indicated, it would be strange indeed if no vestiges of early Castilian folk-song had come down to us in an altered form. Folk-song, in my view, has as great a chance of survival as custom or legend, and we know how persistent these are in undisturbed areas, so I see no reason to doubt that a certain number of the original ballads of Spain have come down to us in such an altered form as would, perhaps, render them unrecognizable to their makers, just as the ancient Scottish romance of *Thomas the Rhymer* would not have been recognized in its later form by the singer who composed it.

All the arguments, archæological and philological, erected and advanced by mere erudition will not convince me to the contrary. To some people antiquity is a living thing, a warm and glowing environment, a world with the paths and manners of which they are better acquainted than with the streets of every day. To others it is—a museum. I have no quarrel with the curators of that museum, and I enjoy reading their books—records of a land which few of them have visited. But when they insist upon controverting the evidence supplied by senses which they do not possess they become merely tiresome. Like art, archæology has also its inspirations, its higher vision. Alas that those who do not share it should attempt to justify their conclusions by lifeless logic alone!

Therefore I shall say no more concerning the age of the ballads of Old Spain, but will only remark with Sancho that "they are too old to lie." I have clearly shown, too, that a number of them were based on passages in the chronicles and *cantares*, a circumstance which in itself vouches for their relative antiquity. With the later artificial imitations of Góngora and Lope de Vega, and others of similar stamp, we are not concerned here. After all, we can only take the ballads of Spain as we find them in the *cancioneros*. It is much too late in the day now to do anything else. Like the ballads of Scotland and Denmark, those of Spain have been collected and published for centuries, and in the pages of the *cancioneros* old and new, popular and literary, are mingled together in almost inextricable confusion. Let us glance, then, at the history of these *cancioneros*, these treasure-houses of a people's poetry, and attempt to realize their plan and scope as perhaps the best method by which to approach the subject of the Spanish ballad generally. Having done this, we can then discuss matters of origin with critics of insight and sympathy.

The Cancionero General

The " Cancionero General"

If we except the fragmentary collection of Juan Fernández de Constantina, the *Cancionero General,* or " Universal Song-book," as it might be translated, was originally brought together and published at the beginning of the sixteenth century by a certain Fernando del Castillo. The arrangement of the ballads it contains is neither chronological nor thoroughly systematic, although the productions of each author are kept distinct. Later editions of this work quickly multiplied, and as the collection extended the additions were always inserted at the end of the book. The collection consists for the most part of the ballads of authors of the fifteenth and early sixteenth centuries, such as Tallante, Nicolas Núñez, Juan de Mena, Porticarrero, and the still earlier Marquis de Santillana.

The first portion of the work is confined to the spiritual songs (*obras de devoción*). These are monotonous and informed with a rigid fanaticism. Nor are the " Moral Poems" which follow any more attractive, allegorizing virtues and vices according to the definitions of scholastic philosophy. The amatory verses in the collection are more ingenious than truly poetic ; they lack true feeling, and appear stiff and artificial in their reiteration of burning passion and the overwhelming woes of unrequited love, mingled with pseudo-philosophical appeals to reason. But gay and graceful love songs are not lacking, as, for example, the " Muy más clara que de luna" of Juan de Meux or the " Pensamienti, pues mostrays" of Diego Lopez de Haro. But these trail off into philosophical disquisition, and the tender sentiment in which they were conceived and commenced is lost in the shallows of paltry argument.

Much more promising are the *canciones*, or lyrical poems of a semi-conventional cast, which have a character and metrical form all their own. They usually consist of twelve lines, divided into two parts. The first four lines comprehend the idea on which the song is founded, and this is developed or applied in the eight succeeding lines. The *Cancionero General* contains one hundred and fifty-six of these little songs, some of which are the best poems contained in it, and perhaps they owe their excellence to the verbal restraint which their form compels. An allied form is the *villancico*, or conceit, usually of three or four lines, a fugitive piece, enshrining some fleeting emotion, and often packed with the matter of poesy.

The " Romancero General "

The title *Romancero General* was applied to many collections of Spanish songs and narrative romances in verse published during the seventeenth century and later. Of these only the older require illustration here. The first in point of date was the collection of Miguel de Madrigal, published in 1604, although another work containing upward of a thousand romances and songs was produced in the same year, and bears the same title. Another collection of primary importance is that of Pedro de Flores (1614). This is obviously a bookseller's compilation, but is none the worse for that, save that it pretends to embrace the entire sum of Spanish *romanceros*, whereas it contains not one of those appearing in the *Cancionero General*. All of these works contain numerous amatory poems of the kind so liberally exemplified in the *Cancionero General*, but with these we have little concern, and our attention may be better employed in examining the *romanceros* proper which it contains. These for the most part would seem to belong to the fifteenth century, and relate to the civil wars of Granada, the last Moorish principality in Spain, and the heroic and gallant adventures of Moorish knights. It is, indeed, in this work that we first perceive the trend toward a literary fashion in things Moorish to which we have referred in a previous chapter, but, as has been indicated, this is very far from saying that these poems owe their origin to Moorish models. But there are not wanting Castilian themes and stories, such as those relating to Roderic, Bernaldo de Carpio, Fernán González, the Infantes of Lara, and the Cid. Most of these were written by men of humble station, the true poets of the people, the late representatives of those *juglares* who had sung or recited the *cantares de gesta*.[1]

Mr James Fitzmaurice Kelly is at once the best informed and most sympathetic of modern critics on the subject of the *romancero*. In his admirable *Chapters on Spanish Literature*, a delightful series of excursions into several of the most interesting provinces of Spanish letters, he reviews the *romancero* in some forty vivid pages, remarkable alike for critical insight and the sanity of the conclusions to which they point. Taking Lockhart's *Spanish Ballads* as a basis for comment, he addresses

---

[1] Besides the collection of romances alluded to, which may be said to represent the standard sources of the subject, collections were published at Antwerp and Saragossa, in the middle of the sixteenth century, by Martin Nucio and Esteban de Nájera respectively. The reader may also consult the *Primavera y Flor de Romance*, by Wolf and Hofman, in the reprint published by Señor Menéndez y Pelayo, the collection of Depping (two vols., Leipzig, 1844), and the English translations of Lockhart and Bowring.

himself to the racy criticism of the collection of the Scottish translator. A better plan for the initiation of the English-speaking reader into the mysteries of the *romancero* could scarcely be conceived, for there are few who possess no acquaintance with Lockhart's work, one of the most persistent of the drawing-room books of Victorian days. Following Mr Kelly's admirable lead, then, though not in the spirit of base imitation, let us take Lockhart as our 'document' and examine the more interesting of his translations, not only as regards their subject-matter, but their excellences and shortcomings, comparing them also with those of Bowring and others. Following Depping, Lockhart divides his volume of ballads into three sections: Historical, Moorish, and Romantic. With the first two groups of poems, or rather with their subject-matter—those relating to King Roderic and Bernaldo de Carpio—we have dealt elsewhere.

The Maiden Tribute

The next in order, "The Maiden Tribute," deals with a demand of the Moorish monarch Abderahman that a hundred Christian virgins should annually be delivered into his hands. King Ramíro refused to comply with such a shameful custom, and marched to meet the Moor. A two days' battle was fought near Alveida, and at the conclusion of the first day's hostilities the superior discipline of the Saracens had told heavily against the Castilians. During the night, St Iago, the patron saint of Spain, appeared to the King in a vision and promised his aid in the field next day. With morning the battle was joined once more, the Saint, true to his word, led the Spanish charge, and the Saracens were cast into headlong rout. The maiden tribute was never afterward paid.

Count Fernán González

Lockhart's ballad, or rather translation, certainly does not enhance the original.

> If the Moslem must have tribute, make *men* your tribute-money,
> Send idle drones to tease them within their hives of honey,

is the commonest of crambo, and

> Must go, like all the others, the proud Moor's bed to sleep in—
> In all the rest they're useless, and nowise worth the keeping,

is reminiscent of the pantomime days of our youth. Mr Fitzmaurice Kelly contents himself by remarking about this ballad that it scarcely calls for comment.

Count Fernán González

"The Escape of the Count Fernán González, which is based on the old *Estoria del noble caballero Fernán González*," a popular arrangement of the *Crónica General* (1344), is later than two other ballads which Mr Kelly and others believe represent a lost epic which was worked into the *Crónica* in question. A wealth of legend certainly clustered round the name of this cavalier, and he has a string of *romanceros* to his credit. But are we to believe that in every case where ballads crystallize round a great name these are the broken lights of a disintegrated epic, worn down by attrition into popular songs? Is there, indeed, irrefragable proof that such a process ever took place anywhere? Or its reverse, for that matter? Practical writers of verse (if a writer of verse can be practical) do not take kindly to the hypothesis. They recognize the generic differences between the spirit of epic and that of folk-poetry, and prefer to believe that when both have fixed upon the same subject the choice was fortuitous and not necessarily evolutionary.

Fernán González of Castile owed not a little of his

romantic reputation to his wife, who delivered him from captivity on at least two occasions. On that celebrated in the ballad she played the part of a faithful lover and a true heroine. González, taken by his enemies, had been carried to a stronghold in Navarre. A Norman knight passing through that country requested the governor of the castle for an audience with the captive, and as he offered a suitable bribe the official gladly conceded the request. The interview over, the knight departed and sought the palace of King Garcia of Navarre, who held González in bondage. One of the counts against the prisoner seems to have been that he had asked Garcia for the hand of his daughter, and to this princess, who secretly loved the captive, the knight now addressed himself:

> The Moors may well be joyful, but great should be our grief,
> For Spain has lost her guardian when Castile has lost her chief.
> The Moorish host is pouring like a river o'er the land:
> Curse on the Christian fetters that bind Gonzalez' hand!

At 'mirk of night' the Infanta rose, and, proceeding alone to the castle where González was confined, proffered such a heavy bribe to the governor to set him at liberty that he permitted his prisoner to go free. But the hero was still hampered by his chains, and when the pair were stopped by a hunter-priest who threatened to reveal their whereabouts to the King's foresters unless the Infanta paid him a shameful ransom, González was unable to punish him as he deserved. But as the wretch embraced the princess she seized him by the throat, and González grasped the spear which he had let fall and drove it through his body. Shortly afterward they encountered a band of González' own men-at-arms, with which incident their night of adventure came to a close.

The Infantes of Lara

The Infantes of Lara

Few Spanish *romanceros* celebrate incidents more tragic or memorable than those which cluster round the massacre of the unfortunate Infantes or Princes of Lara by their treacherous uncle, Ruy or Roderigo Velásquez. Mr Fitzmaurice Kelly thinks that one of these originated from a lost epic written between 1268 and 1344, "or perhaps from a lost recast of this lost epic." Strange that such epics should *all* be lost! He pleads that Lockhart might have utilized other more 'energetic' ballads to illustrate this legend, but I think in this does some despite to the very fine and spirited translation entitled "The Vengeance of Mudara":

> Oh, in vain have I slaughter'd the Infants of Lara;
> There's an heir in his halls—there's the bastard Mudara,
> There's the son of the renegade—spawn of Mahoun:
> If I meet with Mudara, my spear brings him down.

As I read these lines I recall a big drawing-room, the narrow casements of which look upon a wilderness of garden woodland made magical by the yellow shadows of the hour when it is neither evening nor afternoon. Upon a table of mottled rosewood lies a copy of the *Spanish Ballads* in the embossed and fretted binding of the days when such books were given as presents and intended for exhibition. A child of ten, I had stolen into this Elysium redolent of rose-leaves and potpourri, and, opening the book at random, came upon the lines just quoted. For the first time I tasted the delights of rhythm, of music in words. The verses photographed themselves on my brain. Searching through the book until darkness fell, it seemed to me that I could find nothing so good, nothing that swung along with such a gallop. But the cup had been held to my lips, and my days and nights became a quest for words wedded to music. I had to look for some time before I encountered anything better than, or equal to, the haunting rhythm of "The Vengeance of Mudara." The years have brought discoveries beside which the first pales into insignificance, adventures in books of a spirit more subtle, carrying the thrill of a keener amazement; but none came with the force of such revelation as was vouchsafed by that page in an unforgotten book in an unforgettable room.

The first of the ballads in which Lockhart deals with the subject of the Infantes of Lara—for the one we have been discussing follows it—is entitled "The Seven Heads," and details the circumstance of the massacre of the unhappy princes. From the *Historia de España* of Juan de Marinia (1537–1624) we learn that in the year 986 Ruy Velásquez, lord of Villaren, celebrated his marriage with Donna Lombra, a lady of high birth, at Burgos. The festivities were on a scale of great splendour, and among the guests were Gustio González, lord of Salas of Lara, and his seven sons. These young men, of the blood of the Counts of Castile, were celebrated for their chivalric prowess, and had all been knighted on the selfsame day.

As evil chance would have it, a quarrel arose between González, the youngest of the seven brothers, and one Alvar Sanchez, a relation of the bride. Donna Lombra thought herself insulted, and in order to avenge herself, when the young knights rode in her train as she took her way to her lord's castle, she ordered one of her slaves to throw at González a wild cucumber soaked in blood, "a heavy insult and outrage, according to the then existing customs and opinions of Spain." What this

The Infantes of Lara

recondite insult signified does not matter. But surely, whatever its meaning, and making all allowance for the rudeness of the age of which she was an ornament, the lady did greater despite to herself than to her enemy by the perpetration of such an act of crude vulgarity. The slave, having done as he was bid, fled for protection to his mistress's side. But that availed him nothing, for the outraged Infantes slew him "within the very folds of her garment."

Ruy Velásquez, burning with Latin anger at what he deemed an insult to his bride, and therefore to himself, was determined upon a dreadful vengeance. But he studiously concealed his intention from the young noblemen, and behaved to them as if nothing of moment had occurred. Some time after these events he sent Gustio González, the father of the seven young champions, on a mission to Cordova, the ostensible object of which was to receive on his behalf a tribute of money from the Moorish king of that city. He made Gustio the bearer of a letter in Arabic, which he could not read, the purport of which was a request to the Saracen chieftain to have him executed. But the infidel displayed more humanity than the Christian, and contented himself with imprisoning the unsuspecting envoy.

In furtherance of his plans Velásquez pretended to make an incursion into the Moorish country, in which he was accompanied by the Infantes of Lara with two hundred of their followers. With fiendish ingenuity he succeeded in leading them into an ambuscade. Surrounded on all sides by the Saracen host, they resolved to sell their lives at the highest possible price rather than surrender. Back to back they stood, taking a terrible toll of Moorish lives, and one by one they fell, slain but unconquered. Their heads were dispatched to Velásquez as an earnest of a neighbourly deed by the Moorish king, and were paraded before him and in front of their stricken father, who had been released in order that Velásquez might gloat over his grief. When he had satisfied his vengeance the lord of Villaren permitted the stricken father to return to his empty home.

But Ruy Velásquez was not destined to go unpunished. While Gustio González had been imprisoned in the dungeons of the Moorish King of Cordova he had contracted an alliance with that monarch's sister, by whom he had a son, Mudarra. When this young man had attained the age of fourteen years his mother prevailed upon him to go in search of his father, and when he had found his now aged parent he learned of the act of treachery by which his brothers had been slain. Determined to avenge the cowardly deed, he bided his time, and, encountering Ruy Velásquez when on a hunting expedition, slew him out of hand. Gathering around him a band of resolute men, he attacked the castle of Villaren, and executed a fearful vengeance upon the haughty Donna Lombra, whom he stoned and burnt at the stake. In course of time he was adopted by his father's wife, Donna Sancha, who acknowledged him as heir to the estates of his father.

We have already indicated the stirring nature of the ballad in which Mudarra takes vengeance upon the slayers of his brethren. Its predecessor in Lockhart's collection, that in which the agonized father beholds the seven heads of his murdered sons, falls far short of it in power.

> " My gallant boys," quoth Lara, " it is a heavy sight
> These dogs have brought your father to look upon this night;

The Wedding of the Lady Theresa

Seven gentler boys, nor braver, were never nursed in Spain,
And blood of Moors, God rest your souls, ye shed on her like
rain."

.   .   .   .

He took their heads up one by one,—he kiss'd them o'er and o'er,
And aye ye saw the tears run down—I wot that grief was sore.
He closed the lids on their dead eyes, all with his fingers frail,
And handled all their bloody curls, and kissed their lips so pale.

"O had ye died all by my side upon some famous day,
My fair young men, no weak tears then had washed your blood
away.
The trumpet of Castile had drowned the misbeliever's horn,
And the last of all the Lara's line a Gothic spear had borne."

The Wedding of the Lady Theresa

" The Wedding of the Lady Theresa " is a semi-historical ballad which tells of the forced alliance of a Christian maiden to a noble worshipper of Mahoun. Alfonso, King of Leon, desirous of strengthening his alliance with the infidel, intended to sacrifice his sister, Donna Theresa, to his political necessities. He paved the way for this betrayal by pretending that Abdalla, King of the Moors, had become a Christian, and by indicating to her the benefits of a union with the pagan prince. Totally deceived by these representations, the lady consented to the match, was taken to Toledo, and wed to the Moor with much splendour. But on the day of the marriage she learned of her brother's perfidy, and when she found herself alone with the Moorish lord she repulsed him, telling him that she would never be a wife to him in aught but name until he and his people embraced the Christian faith. But Abdalla ridiculed her scruples, and took advantage of her unprotected state. As she had prophesied, a scourge fell upon him as the consequence of his wicked act. Terrified, he

235

sent Theresa back to her brother, with an abundance of treasure, and she entered the monastery of St Pelagius, in Leon, where she passed the remainder of her days in pious labours and devotions.

> Sad heart had fair Theresa when she their paction knew;
> With streaming tears she heard them tell she 'mong the Moors
>   must go:
> That she, a Christian damosell, a Christian firm and true,
> Must wed a Moorish husband, it well might cause her woe.
> But all her tears and all her prayers, they are of small avail;
> At length she for her fate prepares, a victim sad and pale.

This ballad is no earlier than the sixteenth century, and seems to be based upon historic fact, and, as Mr Fitzmaurice Kelly points out, ·it confuses Almanzor and the Toledan governor Abdalla on the one hand and Alfonso V of Leon with his father, Bermudo II, on the other, and introduces chronological difficulties.
Passing by the ballads of the Cid, to the subject-matter of which we have already done ample justice, we come to that of

Garcia Pérez de Vargas

This Mr Fitzmaurice Kelly dismisses in a word, although it seems to me to merit some attention. De Vargas distinguished himself greatly at the siege of Seville in the year 1248. One day, while riding by the banks of the river, accompanied only by a single companion, he was attacked by a party of seven mounted Moors. His comrade rode off, but Pérez, closing his visor, and setting his lance in rest, faced the paynim warriors. They, seeing who awaited them, made all speed back to their own lines. As he made his way back to camp Pérez noticed that he had dropped his scarf, and immediately returned to seek for it. But

Pedro the Cruel

although he rode far into the danger zone ere he found it, the Moors still avoided him, and he returned to the Spanish camp in safety. The ballad makes Pérez recover the scarf from the Moors, who had found it and "looped it on a spear."

> "Stand, stand, ye thieves and robbers, lay down my lady's pledge!"
> He cried; and ever as he cried they felt his faulchion's edge.

> That day when the Lord of Vargas came to the camp alone,
> The scarf, his lady's largess, around his breast was thrown;
> Bare was his head, his sword was red, and, from his pommel strung,
> Seven turbans green, sore hack'd, I ween, before Don Garci hung.

This last verse shows how strongly Lockhart was indebted to Scott for the spirit and style of his compositions.[1]

Pedro the Cruel

We come now to those ballads which recount the vivid but sanguinary history of Don Pedro the Cruel. Many attempts have been made to prove that Pedro was by no means such an inhuman monster as the balladeers would have us believe. But probability seems to be on the side of the singers rather than on that of the modern historians, who have done their best to remove the stain of his ferocious acts from Pedro's abhorred name. His first act of atrocity was that celebrated in the ballad entitled "The Master of St Iago," which refers to his illegitimate brother. On the death of that nobleman, his father, well aware of Pedro's vindictive temperament, fled to the city of Coimbra, in Portugal. But, believing

---

[1] If Scott wrote this verse himself (as Lockhart admits), he wrote others.

Pedro's asseverations that he had no intention of offering him violence, he accepted his invitation to the Court of Seville, where a gallant tournament was about to be held. No sooner had he arrived, however, than he was secretly put to death (1358), it is believed at the instance of the notorious Maria de Padilla, Pedro's mistress.

> "Stand off, stand off, thou traitor strong," 'twas thus he said to me.
> "Thy time on earth shall not be long—what brings thee to my knee?
> My lady craves a New Year's gift, and I will keep my word;
> Thy head, methinks, may serve the shift—Good yeoman, draw thy sword."

The ballad recounts how Pedro, relenting somewhat, imprisoned the false Maria de Padilla, but there is no evidence that she either suggested the crime or suffered for it. Mr Fitzmaurice Kelly gives it as his opinion that the dramatic power of the romance is undeniable. Had he spoken of its melodramatic power I might feel inclined to agree with him.

"That Pedro was accessory to the violent death of the young and innocent princess whom he had married, and immediately afterward deserted for ever, there can be no doubt," says Lockhart, referring to the marriage of Pedro with Blanche de Bourbon. But whether he murdered his queen or not, his paramour, Maria de Padilla, was innocent of all complicity in the affair, although the ballad makes her the instigator of the horrid deed, and it is plain that the poems which refer to her were written with a sinister political motive.

Mariana, who is sufficiently reliable, states that Pedro's conduct toward his queen had aroused the anger of many of his nobles, who presented him with a remon-

Pedro the Cruel

strance in writing. His fierce and homicidal temper aroused to fury at what he considered an unwarranted interference in his private concerns, he immediately gave the order that his unfortunate French consort should be put to death by poison in the prison where she was confined. The poem makes Pedro and his paramour plot upon the death of the unhappy Queen in the crude manner of the balladeer all the world over.

> "Maria de Padilla, be not thus of dismal mood,
> For if I twice have wedded me, it all was for thy good,"

may be good ballad-writing, but I confess the barbarous inversion in the second line appears to me to be unnecessary.

> "But if upon Queen Blanche ye will that I some scorn should
>   show,
> For a banner to Medina my messenger shall go.—
> The work shall be of Blanche's tears, of Blanche's blood the
>   ground,
> Such pennon shall they weave for thee, such sacrifice be found."

With the example of many enchanted passages of allusion no less recondite occurring in the ballads of his own country-side, Lockhart might reasonably have been expected to have done much better than the last couplet.

> Fause luve, ye've shapit a weed for me
> In simmer amang the flowers;
> I will repay thee back again
> In winter amang the showers.
>
> The snow so white shall be your weed,
> In hate you shall be drest,
> The cauld east wind shall wrap your heid
> And the sharp rain on your breist.

But I question if folk-poetry ever captured a lilt more exquisite than that of the first four lines of "The Gardener" or a sharper note of anguish than that of the last quatrain.[1] To me at least Old Scots must always remain the language of the ballad *par excellence*, by virtue of the subtlety, the finely wrought and divinely coloured wealth of expressive idiom which bursts from its treasure-chest in a profusion of begemmed and enamelled richness, more various, more magical than any Spanish gold. Much of this Lockhart filched to give his Castilian bullion a replating. But in places he falls back most wretchedly upon the poetical trickeries of his day, falls to the level of Rogers and Southey, to the miserable devices and tinsel beggary of those bravely bound annuals beloved by the dames and damsels of the day before yesterday. In places, however, he out-ballads the ballad in pure *gaucherie*.

> These words she spake, then down she knelt, and took the
> bowman's blow,
> Her tender neck was cut in twain, and out her blood did flow.

The next, and not the last of the series, as Mr Fitz-maurice Kelly has it, is obviously the handiwork of Walter Scott, than whom none could fail more miserably on occasion. We can picture him doling "The Death of Don Pedro" from out the great thesaurus of his brain (that sadly drained mint, ever at the service of a friend or a publisher), as a dinted and defaced coin. Only in the last verse does the old fire blaze up.

> Thus with mortal gasp and quiver,
> While the blood in bubbles well'd,
> Fled the fiercest soul that ever
> In a Christian bosom dwell'd.

On such a subject the composer of "Bonnie Dundee" might well have felt the blood run faster, and the pen

---

[1] I take these two quatrains from two different versions.

Pedro the Cruel

quiver in his fingers like an arrow on a tightened bow-string. Two royal brothers strive with hateful poniards for each other's lives. Pedro, a prisoner in the hands of Henry of Trastamara, his natural brother, is wantonly insulted by the victorious noble, and replies by flying at his throat in an outburst of animal courage and kingly rage. Dumbfounded at the death-struggle of monarch and usurper, Henry's allies look on, among them the great Du Guesclin. Pedro pins the lord of Trastamara to the ground. His dagger flashes upward. Du Guesclin turns to Henry's squire. "Will ye let your lord die thus, you who eat his bread?" he scoffs. The esquire throws himself upon Pedro, clings to his arms and turns him over, and, thus aided, Henry rises, searches for a joint in the King's armour, and thrusts his dagger deep into that merciless heart. The murderer, the friend of Jew and Saracen, is slain. His head is hacked off, and his proud body trampled beneath mailed feet. Surely a subject for a picture painted in the lights of armour and the red shadows of blood and hate.

> Down they go in deadly wrestle,
> Down upon the earth they go.
> Fierce King Pedro has the vantage,
> Stout Don Henry falls below.
>
> Marking then the fatal crisis,
> Up the page of Henry ran,
> By the waist he caught Don Pedro,
> Aiding thus the fallen man.

They had better have let the ballad alone, those two at Abbotsford. It does not seem to me "a very striking ballad," as Mr Fitzmaurice Kelly observes, but in its Castilian dress it is sufficiently dramatic and exciting.

Legends & Romances of Spain

Los fieros cuerpos revueltos
Entre los rubustos brazos
Está el cruel rey Don Pedro
Y Don Enrique, su hermano.

No son abrazos de amor
Los que los dos se están dando ;
Que el uno tiene una daga,
Y otro un puñal acerado.

So run the first two verses, which I leave the reader
to translate for himself, lest further damage be done
them.
The proclamation of Don Henry takes up the story
where the preceding ballad left it off. In the translation
of this, it seems to me, Lockhart has been much more
successful than his great father-in-law proved himself in
that of its companion ballad. I do not think it possible,
however, to render adequately by an English pen the
dignified rhythm of the Castilian in which this *romancero*
is dressed. But the second verse,

So dark and sullen is the glare of Pedro's lifeless eyes,
Still half he fears what slumbers there to vengeance may arise.
So stands the brother, on his brow the mark of blood is seen,
Yet had he not been Pedro's Cain, his Cain had Pedro been,

is really fine, expressive, and ascends a whole scale of
terrible thought and realization. Are these awful eyes
dead? Can the threat they hold be imaginary? My
hands are wet with brother's blood, but it is only by
virtue of a slender chance that his are not imbrued with
mine. The verse is horribly eloquent of the death-
cold atmosphere of the moment which follows murder
—simple, appalling, desperately tragic. The mad grief
of the slain King's paramour is drawn with a touch almost
as successful.

242

The Moor Reduan

In her hot cheek the blood mounts high, as she stands gazing down,
Now on proud Henry's royal stole, his robe and golden crown,
And now upon the trampled cloak that hides not from her view
The slaughtered Pedro's marble brow, and lips of livid hue.

The Moor Reduan

We may pass by "The Lord of Butrayo" and "The
King of Arragon" and come to the ballad of "The Moor
Reduan," a piece based on the siege of Granada, last
stronghold of the Moors, and the first of those in which
Lockhart deals with the *romanceros fronterizos*, or
romances of the frontier, which, as we have before
remarked, may have been influenced by Moorish ideas,
or may even represent borrowings or *données* of a kind
more or less direct. In his *critique* of this *romancero*
Mr Fitzmaurice Kelly says: "Lockhart is, of course,
not to blame for translating the ballad precisely as he
found it in the text before him. Any translator would
be bound to do the same to-day if he attempted a new
rendering of the poem ; but he would doubtless think it
advisable to state in a note the result of the critical
analysis which had scarcely been begun when Lockhart
wrote. It now seems fairly certain that Pérez de Hita
ran two *romanceros* into one, and that the verses from the
fourth stanza onward in Lockhart,

They passed the Elvira gate with banners all displayed,

are part of a ballad on Boabdil's expedition against
Lucena in 1483." This is only partially correct.
Lockhart knew perfectly well that the piece was not
homogeneous. Indeed he says, "The following is a
version of certain parts of *two ballads*," although he
seems to have been unaware that one of them was that
dealing with Boabdil's expedition. That portion,

243

indeed, provides by far the best elements in the composition.

> What caftans blue and scarlet, what turbans pleach'd of green ;
> What waving of their crescents, and plumages between ;
> What buskins and what stirrups, what rowels chased in gold,
> What handsome gentlemen, what buoyant hearts and bold !

Reduan had registered a rash vow to take the city of Jaen so that he might win the daughter of the Moorish king. The ninth verse is full of a grateful music, not too often found in the poetry of the Britain of 1823 :

> But since in hasty cheer I did my promise plight,
> (What well might cost a year) to win thee in a night,
> The pledge demands the paying, I would my soldiers brave
> Were half as sure of Jaen as I am of my grave ;

although, I confess, the internal rhyming of " paying " and " Jaen " detracts from the melody of the whole. And this is the besetting sin of Lockhart, that he mars his happiest efforts by crudities which he evidently confounded with the simplicity of the ballad form. In all British balladry, if memory serves me, there is no such vulgarism as this.

CHAPTER X : THE ROMANCEROS OR BALLADS—*continued*

> There was crying in Granada as the sun was going down,
> Some calling on the Trinity, some calling on Mahoun ;
> Here passed away the Koran, there in the Cross was borne,
> And here was heard the Christian bell, and there the Moorish horn.

IN this vivid verse, the first two lines of which seem to me especially successful, Lockhart, with a stroke or two of his pen, provides us with a moving sketch of the confusion and turmoil attending the Moorish flight from Granada, the last stronghold of the Moors in Spain, which fell to the victorious arms of Ferdinand and Isabella on the 6th of January, 1492, the year of the discovery of America. The remainder of the ballad is no better than Lorenzo de Sepúlveda's rather unmusical original. It is pity that a ballad beginning with such a spirited couplet should be lost in the shallows and the miseries of such stuff as :

> " Unhappy King, whose craven soul can brook " (she 'gan reply)
> " To leave behind Granada—who hast not heart to die—
> Now for the love I bore thy youth thee gladly could I slay,
> For what is life to leave when such a crown is cast away ? "

Here the spirit of the metre has deserted the body of the verse, which is now merely galvanized into life by an artificial current of pedantry. The striking inequalities in the work of Lockhart are surely eloquent of the tragedy of the half-talent.

Don Alonzo de Aguilar

Upon the fall of Granada the Catholic zeal of Ferdinand and Isabella insisted upon the conversion of the Moors of that province. Most of the defeated pagans concurred, outwardly at least, with the royal decree, but in the Sierra of Alpuxarra there remained a leaven of the infidel blood who refused baptism at the hands of the priests who were sent to seal them of the faith. A royal order at length went forth to carry out the ceremony by force of arms. For a season the Moors resisted with the stubborn courage of their race, but at length they were subdued and almost extirpated. But their ruin was not accomplished without severe losses on the side of their would-be proselytizers, one of the most notable of whom was Don Alonzo de Aguilar, brother of that Gonzalvo Hernández de Cordova of Aguilar who gained widespread renown as 'the Great Captain.' But the ballad does not seem to square with the facts of history. Indeed it places Aguilar's death before the surrender of Granada, whereas in reality it took place as late as 1501. Mr Fitzmaurice Kelly thinks that "this points to the conclusion that the romance was not written till long after the event, when the exact details had been forgotten." But why blame an entire people for what may have been a *lapsus memoriæ* on the part of a single balladeer? On the other hand, Mr Kelly might justly ask one to indicate *any* ballad springing from folk-sources the details of which square with the circumstances as known to history or ascertained by research.

Lockhart, as usual upon first mounting his destrier, dashes the spurs in its sides with a flourish:

Fernando, King of Arragon, before Granada lies,
With dukes and barons many a one, and champions of emprise;
With all the captains of Castile that serve his lady's crown,
He drives Boabdil from his gates, and plucks the crescent down.

So far good. Now for the conclusion:

Don Alonzo de Aguilar

The Moorish maidens, while she spoke, around her silence kept,
But her master dragged the dame away—then loud and long they
    wept :
They wash'd the blood, with many a tear, from dint of dart and
    arrow,
And buried him near the waters clear of the bank of Alpuxarra.

It will not serve to point out that this is just what one
might expect in a ballad, for it bears not the shadow
of resemblance to the original.

> Que de chiquito en la cuna
> A sus pechos le criara.
> A las palabras que dice,
> Cualquiera Mora lloraba :
>
> "Don Alonso, Don Alonso,
> Dios perdone la tu alma,
> Pues te mataron los Moros,
> Los Moros de el Alpujarra."

I am sometimes tempted to think that the weary giant
at Abbotsford wrote all Lockhart's first verses, as one
heads a copy-book for a child!
Lockhart omits from his collection the very fine ballad
beginning :

> Río verde, Río verde,
> Tinto vas en sangre viva ;
> Entre tí y Sierra Bermeja
> Murió gran caballería
>
> Murieron duques y condes,
> Señores de gran valía ;
> Allí muriera Urdiales,
> Hombre de valor y estima,

which was rather inaccurately rendered by Bishop Percy
as follows :

> Gentle river, gentle river,
> Lo, thy streams are stained with gore;
> Many a brave and noble captain
> Floats along thy willow'd shore.
>
> All beside thy limpid waters,
> All beside thy sands so bright,
> Moorish chiefs and Christian warriors
> Joined in fierce and mortal fight.

Perhaps a more accurate though less finished rendering of these opening verses might be :

> Emerald river, emerald river,
> Stained with slaughter's evil cheer,
> 'Twixt Bermeja and thy meadows
> Perished many a cavalier.
>
> Duke and count and valiant esquire
> Fell upon thy fatal shore;
> There died noble Urdiales
> Who the stainless title bore.

I have translated these two verses chiefly for the purpose of showing how very freely those English authors who have attempted to render verse from the Castilian have dealt with the originals.   And, as I have said before, I suspect that the principal reason for this looseness is a lack of idiomatic grasp.   Indeed, it is obvious from most English translations that the sense of the original has been gathered rather than fully apprehended.
We can pass over " The Departure of King Sebastian," with its daring rhythm of

> It was a Lusitanian lady, and she was lofty in degree,

recalling in some measure the irregular lilt of the old Scots ballads, and enter the division entitled by Lockhart " Moorish Ballads."

248

Moorish Ballads

Moorish Ballads

We have already discussed the question of the ' Moorishness ' (or otherwise) of these ballads. Let us now discuss them as ballads and as nothing more. The first, " The Bull-fight of Ganzul," is not only a famous piece, but in translating it Lockhart has risen to the occasion. It describes the dexterity of Ganzul, a noble Moor, in the bull-ring, and is certainly not without its quota of Moresque colour.

> King Almanzor of Granada, he hath bid the trumpet sound,
> He hath summoned all the Moorish lords, from the hills and plains
>   around,
> From Vega and Sierra, from Betis and Xenil,
> They have come with helm and cuirass of gold and twisted steel.
> .   .   .   .
>
> Eight Moorish lords of valour tried, with stalwart arm and true
> The onset of the beasts abide, as they come rushing through.
> The deeds they've done, the spoils they've won, fill all with hope
>   and trust—
> Yet ere high in heaven appears the sun they all have bit the dust.
>
> Then sounds the trumpet clearly, then clangs the loud tambour ;
> Make room, make room for Ganzul, throw wide, throw wide the
>   door—
> Blow, blow the trumpet clearer still, more loudly strike the drum,
> The Alcaydé of Agalva to fight the bull has come.

He defeats the bulls sent against him with the exception of one Harpado, a furious yet sagacious beast. The quatrain which describes him is well forged :

> Dark is his hide on either side, but the blood within doth boil,
> And the dim hide glows as if on fire, as he paws to the turmoil.
> His eyes are jet and they are set in crystal rings of snow ;
> But now they stare with one red glare of brass upon the foe.

But it is not surpassingly like the original :

Vayo en color encendido,
Y los ojos como brasa,
Arrugada frente y cuello,
La frente vellosa y ancha.

But proud as is Harpado, he must give way to the knightly Moor, regarding whom many other tales are told, especially with reference to his love affairs with a fair lady of his own race.

The Zegris' Bride

"The Zegris' Bride" tells in ballad form of the fierce feud between the two Moorish parties in Granada, the Zegris and the Abencerrages, the Montagues and Capulets of the last of the Moorish strongholds, when factious strife certainly accelerated the fall of their city. The ballad is well turned, and attractive in rhythm:

Of all the blood of Zegri, the chief is Lisaro,
To wield rejon like him is none, or javelin to throw;
From the place of his dominion, he ere the dawn doth go,
From Alcala de Henares, he rides in weeds of woe.

Such a phrase as "the place of his dominion" is not suited to ballad composition, nor is the four-line rhyming grateful to the ear, although the measure is all that could be desired. Once more I think I see the hand of Scott in this translation, his 'equestrian' rhythm, his fondness for introducing words intended to assist local colour, as

Of gold-wrought robe or turban—nor jewelled tahali,

which he must, perforce, explain in a note as 'scimitar.' The young Zegri, we are told, is attired for action, not for the cavalcade or procession. Indeed, his armour and even his horse are camouflaged to assist his passage through an enemy's country without observation.

The Bridal of Andella

The belt is black, the hilt is dim, but the sheathed blade is bright ;
They have housen'd his barb in a murky garb, but yet her hoofs
  are light.

And again :

In darkness and in swiftness rides every armed knight,
The foam on the rein ye may see it plain, but nothing else is white.

Lisaro wears on his bonnet a sprig of bay given him by
Zayda, his lady.

And ever as they rode, he looked upon his lady's boon.
"God knows," quoth he, "what fate may be—I may be slaughtered
  soon."

But he lives to win his bride, as we are told in the curt
final verse :

Young Lisaro was musing so, when onwards on the path
He well could see them riding slow ; then prick'd he in his wrath.
The raging sire, the kinsmen of Zayda's hateful house,
Fought well that day, yet in the fray the Zegri won his spouse.

The Bridal of Andella

"The Bridal of Andella" is brilliant with Oriental
colouring :

Rise up, rise up, Xarifa, lay the golden cushion down ;
Rise up, come to the window, and gaze with all the town.
From gay guitar and violin the silver notes are flowing,
And the lovely lute doth speak between the trumpet's lordly blowing,
And banners bright from lattice light are waving everywhere,
And the tall, tall plume of our cousin's bridegroom floats proudly
  in the air :
Rise up, rise up, Xarifa, lay the golden cushion down ;
Rise up, come to the window, and gaze with all the town.

Skilful weaving this. The lady would not look, however,
because Andella, who was about to wed another, had
been false to her. Ballad literature is scarcely a record
of human constancy. In Ballad-land the percentage of

faithless swains, black or white, clown or knight, is a high one. Was the law regarding breach of promise first formulated by a student of ballad lore, I wonder? Whatever else it may have effected, it seems to have put an end to ballad-writing, perhaps because it ended the conditions and circumstances which went to the making of balladeering.

Zara's Earrings

The intriguing ballad of "Zara's Earrings" bears upon it the stamp of natural folk-song. It may come from a Moorish original, but appearances are often deceptive. In any case it is worth quoting in part.

> "My earrings, my earrings, they've dropt into the well,
> And what to say to Muça, I cannot, cannot tell."
> 'Twas thus Granada's fountain by, spoke Albuharez' daughter.
> "The well is deep, far down they lie, beneath the cold, blue water.
> To me did Muça give them when he spake his sad farewell,
> And what to say when he comes back, alas! I cannot tell."

The lady resolves in the end to do the best thing she can—that is, to tell the truth. There is a sequence of romances about this Muça, who seems to have been a Saracen of worth, and the same must be remarked about Celin or Selim, his successor in the collections of Lockhart and Depping. Had Lockhart been well advised, he would have substituted the ringing and patriotic "Las soberbias torres mira," which is certainly difficult of translation, for the very sombre "Lamentation for the Death of Celin," fine though it is. Anything in the nature of a ceremony or a procession seems to have attracted him like a child. But let us have a verse of the first poem. Even should we not know Spanish its music could not fail to haunt and hold us.

Romantic Ballads

Las soberbias torres mira
Y los lejos las almenas
De su patria dulce y cara
Celin, que el rey le destierra ;
Y perdida la esperanza
De jamás volver a vella
Con suspiros tristes dice :
" Del cielo luciente estrella,
Granada bella,
Mi llanto escucha, y duélate mi pena ! "

Romantic Ballads

We now come to consider the romantic ballads, the third and last section of Lockhart's collection. "The Moor Calaynos" we have already described, and the same applies to "Gayferos" and "Melisendra," its sequel. The ballad which follows these, " Lady Alda's Dream," is alluded to by Lockhart as "one of the most admired of all the Spanish ballads." It is no favourite of mine. I may judge it wrongly, but it seems to me inferior, and I much prefer the stirring "Admiral Guarinos," which treads upon its halting heels with all the impatience of a warlike rhythm to spur it on.

Guarinos was admiral to King Charlemagne. In my boyhood days the condition of the British Navy was a newspaper topic of almost constant recurrence, and I was wont to speculate upon the awful inefficiency which must have crept into the Frankish fleet during the enforced absence of its chief in the country of the Moors, for Guarinos was captured by the Saracens at Roncesvalles. His captor, King Marlotes, treated him in a princely manner, but pressed him to become a convert to Islam, promising to give him his two daughters in marriage did he consent to the proposal. But the Admiral was adamant and refused to be bribed

or coaxed into the acceptance of the faith of Mohammed
and Termagaunt. Working himself up into one of those
passions which seem to be the especial privilege of
Oriental potentates, Marlotes commanded that Guarinos
should be incarcerated in the lowest dungeon in his
castle keep.

It was the Moorish custom to hale captives to the light
of day three times in every year for the popular edifica-
tion and amusement. On one of these occasions, the
Feast of St John, the King raised a high target beneath
which the Moorish knights rode in an attempt to pierce
it with their spears. But so lofty was it that none of
them might succeed in the task, and the King, annoyed
at their want of skill, refused to permit the banquet to
commence until the target was transfixed. Guarinos
boasted that he could accomplish the feat. The royal
permission was accorded him to try, and his grey
charger and the armour he had not worn for seven
long years were brought to him.

> They have girded on his shirt of mail, his cuisses well they've
>   clasp'd,
> And they've barred the helm on his visage pale, and his hand the
>   lance hath grasped,
> And they have caught the old grey horse, the horse he loved of
>   yore,
> And he stands pawing at the gate—caparisoned once more.

Guarinos whispered in the old horse's ear, and it recalled
the voice of its master.

> Oh! lightly did Guarinos vault into the saddle-tree,
> And slowly riding down made halt before Marlotes' knee;
> Again the heathen laughed aloud—"All hail, sir knight," quoth he,
> "Now do thy best, thou champion proud. Thy blood I look to
>   see."

With that Guarinos, lance in rest, against the scoffer rode,
Pierced at one thrust his envious breast, and down his turban
  trode.
Now ride, now ride, Guarinos—nor lance nor rowel spare—
Slay, slay, and gallop for thy life—the land of France lies *there!*

There would seem to be some connexion between this
ballad and the French romance of "Ogier the Dane,"
and Erman tells us that it was sung in Russian in
Siberia as late as 1828.

"The Lady of the Tree" tells how a princess was
stolen by the fairies, and how a knight to whom she
appealed for rescue turned a deaf ear to her request
and was afterward scorned by her when she returned
to her rightful station. "The False Queen" is a mere
fragment, but "The Avenging Childe" is both complete
and vivid. Mr Fitzmaurice Kelly declares that Gibson's
version of this ballad is superior to that of Lockhart.
Let us compare a verse of both.

Avoid that knife in battle strife, that weapon short and thin;
The dragon's gore hath bath'd it o'er, seven times 'twas steeped
  therein;
Seven times the smith hath proved its pith, it cuts a coulter
  through—
In France the blade was fashioned, from Spain the shaft it drew.

Gibson renders this:

'Tis a right good spear with a point so sharp, the toughest plough-
  share might pierce.
For seven times o'er it was tempered fine in the blood of a dragon
  fierce,
And seven times o'er it was whetted keen, till it shone with a
  deadly glance,
For its steel was wrought in the finest forge, in the realm of
  mighty France.

My preference is for Lockhart's rendering. Gibson's

first line is extraordinarily clumsy and cacophonous, and
the ugly inversions in the second line could scarcely be
tolerated outside the boundaries of the nursery. The
remaining lines are well enough, but no improvement,
I think, upon those of Lockhart, only the whole has
a better swing, a livelier lilt, even if in the first line this
is roughened by the crudity occasioned by the juxtaposition of so many sibilants and explosives. The
Avenging Childe duly accounts for his enemy.

> Right soon that knife hath quenched his life—the head is sundered
> sheer,
> Then gladsome smiled the Avenging Childe, and fix'd it on his
> spear.

Pity it is that a sense of humour seldom chimes with
a sense of the romantic. An 'avenging childe' who
could smile gladly when fixing the head of a foe on
his spear seems more fitted for a Borstal institution
than for the silken atmosphere of Courts. Yet he
married the Infanta, and was knighted and honoured
by the King. Possibly they found in him a kindred
soul, if all we read in romance regarding kings and
infantas be true.

Count Arnaldos

This very beautiful ballad, which is given in the
Cancionero of Antwerp (1555), tells how Count Arnaldos,
wandering by the seashore one morning, hears the
mystic song of a sailor in a passing galley.

> Heart may beat and eye may glisten,
> Faith is strong and Hope is free,
> But mortal ear no more may listen
> To the song that rules the sea.

Count Arnaldos

When the grey-hair'd sailor chaunted,
Every wind was hushed to sleep—
Like a virgin's bosom panted
All the wide reposing deep.

Bright in beauty rose the star-fish
From her green cave down below,
Right above the eagle poised him—
Holy music charmed them so.

.   .   .   .   .

"For the sake of God, our Maker"
(Count Arnaldos' cry was strong),
"Old man, let me be partaker
In the secret of thy song."

"Count Arnaldos! Count Arnaldos!
Hearts I read and thoughts I know—
Wouldst thou learn the ocean secret
In our galley thou must go."

Longfellow wrote a rather anæmic ballad, "The Seaside and the Fireside," on the Arnaldos episode, incorporating several of the lines. Some years ago I published an adaptation of it, altering the environment and changing the metre, and this the reader may perhaps be complacent enough to accept as an illustration of the manner in which "this sort of thing is done."

When the fleet ships stand inward to the shore
As a white tempest, 'tis then I implore
The gods not treasure of red spice to spill
Upon the marble quays beneath the hill,
Nor scintillant dust from far Arabian streams,
Nor weaves more brilliant than the hue of dreams,
Nor feathers, pearls, or such things as belong
To Eastern waters, but a wondrous song
To send perchance upon a seaman's lips
That once I heard when the departing ships
Swept from the arms of sea-bound Syracuse.

I know my evening vigil is in vain,
That never shall I hear that song again.
Some splendid sea-spell in the sailor's soul,
Swelling his heart, and bursting all control,
Some white sea-spirit chanting from his mouth
Sang the strange colours of a distant south.
Music deep-drowned within the siren sea
Art thou beyond the call of ecstasy?

The "Song for the Morning of the Day of St John the Baptist" has little to do with ballad, so we may pass it by, as we may do the "Julian" fragment, one of the Gayferos group. "The Song of the Galley," which Mr Kelly regards as "too dulcet," seems to me poorly rendered:

Ye galleys fairly built,
Like castles on the sea,
Oh, great will be your guilt
If ye bring him not to me!

This seems to me facility run mad, and great would be my guilt did I quote more. To the very fine "Wandering Knight's Song" I have already made allusion. "Minguillo" enshrines a *motif* of almost world-wide usage:

Since for kissing thee, Minguillo,
My mother scolds me all the day,
Let me have it quickly, darling;
Give me back my kiss, I pray.

A conceit current from Caithness to Capo d'Istria. "Serenade," from the *Romancero General* of 1604, is certainly not peasant work. For his translation of this Lockhart deserves high praise. Its music is reminiscent of Shelley's "Skylark," though of course it lacks the almost intolerable keenness of that song most magical.

Romantic Ballads

All the stars are glowing
　In the gorgeous sky,
In the stream scarce flowing
　Mimic lustres lie:
Blow, gentle, gentle breeze,
　But bring no cloud to hide
Their dear resplendencies;
　Nor chase from Zara's side
Dreams bright and pure as these.

It is inspired by a chaste and natural music all its own,
beyond the conscious artistry of the material man. To
do Lockhart justice, he loved the art of letters for
itself alone. His was that natural modesty which is
content to sing in the shadow; nor can one recall the
memory of that fine and upright spirit, his labour and
his sacrifice, without praise and gratitude gladly bestowed. In this poem I seem to see the real Lockhart
—a man with the heart of a child.

"Minguela's Chiding" tells of the woe of a rustic maid
who loved to her destruction. "The Captive Knight
and the Blackbird" is the prison plaint of a warrior who
knows not how the seasons pass, or the moons wax and
wane:

Woe dwells with me in spite of thee, thou gladsome month of May;
I cannot see what stars there be, I know not night from day.
There *was* a bird whose voice I heard, oh, sweet my small bird
　　sung,
I heard its tune when night was gone, and up the morning sprung.

Some cruel hand had slain the blackbird which was
wont to delight the poor prisoner's heart. But the King
heard his plaint while passing beneath his dungeon
window, and set him free.

We may pass over the rather sepulchral "Valladolid,"
which tells of the visit of a knight to the tomb of

259

his lady-love in that city. "The Ill-Married Lady" recounts the grief of a dame whose husband is faithless to her, and who consoles herself with another cavalier. They are surprised by her lord, and she artlessly asks: "Must I, must I die to-day?" and requests to be buried in the orange garden. The romance does not tell us if her last wishes were complied with, or even if her life was forfeited, but to a Spanish public of the seventeenth century it was probably a supererogation even to allude to such a sequel.

"Dragut" tells the story of a famous corsair whose ship was sunk by a vessel belonging to the Knights of Malta. Dragut saved himself by swimming ashore, but the Christian captives with whom his barque was laden were all drowned save one, to whom the Maltese threw a rope.

> It was a Spanish knight, who had long been in Algiers,
> From ladies high descended and noble cavaliers,
> But forced for a season a false Moor's slave to be,
> Upon the shore his gardener, and his galley-slave at sea.

We have already recounted the tale of the Count Alarcos, and with it Lockhart's collection comes to an end. But it is not in the pages of Lockhart alone that we should look for good translations of the Spanish *romanceros*. John Bowring in his *Ancient Poetry and Romances of Spain* (1824) has undoubtedly done much to render some of the lesser lyrics of Castilian balladeers into successful English verse. His translation of the celebrated "Fonte Frida" is, perhaps, the best version of that much-discussed poem to be met with in our language. It is clear that Ticknor's rendition of this piece is practically a paraphrase of Bowring's translation, of which I give the first two verses:

Romantic Ballads

Fount of freshness, fount of freshness,
Fount of freshness and of love,
Where the little birds of spring-time
Seek for comfort as they rove ;
All except the widow'd turtle,
Widow'd, sorrowing turtle-dove.

There the nightingale, the traitor,
Lingered on his giddy way ;
And these words of hidden treachery
To the dove I heard him say :
" I will be thy servant, lady,
I will ne'er thy love betray."

But no English translation, however fine, can possibly
do justice to this beautiful lyric :

Fonte frida, fonte frida,
Fonte frida, y con amor,
Do todas las avezicas
Van tomar consolacion,
Sino es la tortolica
Que esta viuda y con dolor,
Por ay fue a passar
El traydor del ruyseñor
Las palabras que el dezia
Llenas son de traicion :
" Si tu quisiesses, Señora,
Yo seria tu servidor."

Ticknor speaks truly when he says of the Spanish
ballads : " To feel their true value and power we must
read large numbers of them, and read them, too, in their
native language ; for there is a winning freshness in the
originals, as they lie embedded in the old *romanceros*,
that escapes in translations, however free, or however
strict."

The *romancero* entitled " Sale la estrella de Venus "
recounts a tragic story. A Moorish warrior, flying from
the city of Sidonia because of the cruelty of his lady,

who had taunted him with poverty and had bestowed her hand upon another, makes the rocks and hills re-echo with his plaints. He pronounces a terrible and bitter curse upon the proud and wanton maiden who has spurned him. Maddened, he seeks the palace of the Alcalde to whom his faithless fair one is to be espoused that night. The building is bright with torches and gay with song.

> And the crowds make way before him
> While he pays his courtesies.
> Ha! his bloody lance has traversed
> The Alcalde's fluttering breast,
> And his life-blood now is flowing,
> Flowing through his purple vest.
> O what horror! What confusion,
> Desolation and dismay!
> While the stern, unnoticed murderer,
> To Medina takes his way.

We have examined every type of Spanish ballad poetry. The general note struck, we will observe, is a grave and romantic one, the fruit of the thoughts of a proud and imaginative people. Nor can we fail to notice the national note which rings through these poems, the racial individuality which informs them. "Poor Spain!" How often do we hear the expression employed by men of Anglo-Saxon race! Let these undeceive themselves. What can material poverty signify to a people dowered with such treasures of the imagination? Poor Spain! Nay, opulent Spain; treasure-house of the minted coin of story, of the priceless jewels of romance, of drama, and of song!

CHAPTER XI : MOORISH ROMANCES
OF SPAIN

THESE are, of course, more of the nature of
romances *of* the Moors than *by* the Moors—
tales embedded in Spanish folk-lore relating to
Saracen times and themes, rather than written fictions
existing in ancient Arab manuscripts. The Arab literature of Spain was rather didactic, theological, and
philosophical than romantic. Fiction was, perhaps, the
province of the itinerant story-teller, as it still is in the
East. But that many Moorish legends and stories were
handed down among the Spanish peasantry, especially
in the more southerly parts of the Peninsula, can hardly
be doubted. These, however, have been much neglected
by compilers, and but few of them are available. Such
as exist in written form make up for their scantiness in
number by the qualities of wonder and beauty which
inform them. Perhaps no collection of the traditions of
the Moors of Spain equals that of Washington Irving
in his *Tales of the Alhambra*. These, he tells us, he
"diligently wrought into shape and form, from various
legendary scraps and hints picked up in the course of
my perambulations, in the same manner that an
antiquary works out a regular historical document from
a few scattered letters of an almost defaced inscription."
The first of our Moorish legends, therefore, I shall retell
from the enchanted pages of the great American wizard
in words, apologizing to his shade for the alterations
in verbiage which I have been forced to make in view
of the requirements of modern readers. I have, indeed,
entirely recast the tale for twentieth-century use.

Legends & Romances of Spain

The Arabian Astrologer

Aben Habuz, King of Granada, had in his old age earned the right to repose. But the young and ardent princes whose territories marched with his were in no mind that his old age should be free from the alarms of war, and although he took every precaution to ensure his possessions against the incursions of such hotheads, the constant menace of an attack from one or other of them, no less than the unrest which occasionally raised its head within his own dominions, filled his declining years with irritation and anxiety.

Harassed and perplexed, he cast about him for an adviser capable of assisting him to strengthen his position, but among the sages and nobles of his Court he experienced such a cold selfishness and lack of patriotic fervour as restrained him from adopting any of them as his confidant in high affairs of state. While he meditated upon his friendless condition it was announced to him that an Arabian sage had arrived in Granada, whose fame as a man of wisdom and understanding was proverbial throughout the East. The name of this pundit was Ibrahim Ebn Abu Ajib, and it was whispered of him that he had existed since the days of Mohammed, of one of whose personal friends he was the son. As a child he had accompanied the army of Amru, the Prophet's general, into Egypt, where he had remained for generations, employing his time in the study of those occult sciences of which the Egyptian priests were such consummate masters. Old as he was—and his appearance was most venerable—he had walked the whole way from Egypt on foot, aided only by a staff, on which were engraved hieroglyphs of deep and hidden import. His

The Arabian Astrologer

beard descended to his girdle, his piercing eyes bespoke insight and intelligence almost superhuman, and his bearing was more grave and majestic than that of the most reverend *mullah* in Granada. It was said that he possessed the secret of the elixir of life, but as he had attained this knowledge when already well on in years, he had perforce to be content with his aged exterior, although he had already succeeded in prolonging his existence for upward of two hundred years.

King Aben Habuz, gratified at being able to extend his hospitality to a visitor of such consequence, entertained him with marked distinction. But the sage refused all his offers of soft living, and established himself in a cave in the side of the hill on which the famous palace of the Alhambra was later to be erected. This cavern he caused to be altered in such a manner that it bore a resemblance to the interiors of those lofty temples of the Egyptian land in which he had passed so many years of his long life. Through the living rock which formed its roof he commanded the Court architect to drive a deep shaft, so that from the gloom of his cavernous abode he might be able to behold the stars even at midday; for Ibrahim was pre-eminent in the study of that lore of the heavenly bodies, that thrice noble science of astrology, which the truly wise of all ages have recognized as the real source of all divine knowledge, and the shallow erudition of a later day foolishly despises. But only for a day in the round of eternity shall that great and golden book be set aside; nor shall its pages, arabesqued with mysterious and awful characters, ever be wholly closed to man. The weird, serpentine script of this language of the sages ornamented the walls of the astrologer's cavern, interspersed with the no less mystic symbols of ancient Egypt, and, surrounded by these hieroglyphs and provided with the primitive telescope we have described, the wise Ibrahim busied himself in deciphering the history of events to come as written in the glittering pages of the heavens.

It was only natural that the distressed Aben Habuz should avail himself of the wisdom and foresight of the astrologer to the fullest degree. Indeed, Ibrahim became indispensable to him, and was consulted in every emergency. He responded graciously, and placed his marvellous gifts entirely at the service of the harassed monarch. On one occasion Aben Habuz complained bitterly of the constant vigilance he was forced to maintain against the attacks of his restless neighbours. For a space the astrologer was lost in thought. Then he replied : " O King, many years since I beheld a marvel in Egypt, wrought by a wise priestess of that land. Above the city of Borsa towers a lofty mountain, on which was placed the image of a ram, and above it the figure of a cock, both cast in brazen effigy and turning upon a pivot. Should the land be threatened by invasion the ram would turn in the direction of the enemy and the cock would crow, and by this means the inhabitants of Borsa were enabled to take timely measures for defence."

"Would that such a contrivance might be erected at Granada," said the King fervently. "Then might we rest in peace."

The astrologer smiled at the King's earnestness. " I have already told you, O King," he said, " that I have spent many years in Egypt mastering the hidden knowledge of that mysterious land. One day while seated

The Arabian Astrologer

on the banks of the Nile speaking with a priest of that country, my companion pointed to the mighty pyramids which cast their shadows on the place where we reclined. 'My son,' remarked the sage, 'thou beholdest these mountains in stone, the memorials of kings who died while Greece was yet in the cradle and Rome was unthought of; all the lore that we can teach thee is as a drop of water to the ocean compared with the secrets contained in those monuments. In the heart of the Great Pyramid is a death-chamber where rests the mummy of the high priest who designed and builded that stupendous pile. On his breast lies a wondrous book containing magical secrets of great potency—that book, indeed, which was given to Adam after the fall and by the aid of which Solomon built the temple at Jerusalem.' From the moment I heard those words, O King, I might not rest. I resolved to find my way into the Great Pyramid and possess myself of the magic volume. Collecting a number of the soldiers of the victorious Amru and many of the native Egyptians, I addressed myself to the task of piercing the solid masonry which concealed this ineffable treasure, until, after unheard-of labours, I came upon one of its hidden passages. Long time I searched in the labyrinths of the vasty pyramid ere I arrived at the sepulchral chamber. At length, groping in profound darkness, and haunted by the rustling of the wrappings of mummied Pharaohs, I came upon the shrine where the corpse of the high priest lay in grim state. I opened the sarcophagus, and, unwrapping the voluminous bandages, found the mystic tome lying among spices and amulets on the shrivelled breast. Seizing it, I hastened through the black corridors, nor stayed until I beheld the fierce Egyptian day and the friendly green of the languid river."

"But in what manner may all this assist me in my dilemma, O son of Abu Ajib?" asked the King querulously.

"This have I told thee, O King, because by the aid of this book most magical I can call to my assistance the spirits of earth and air—jinns, and afreets, and peris—by whose help I shall construct a talisman like that which surmounted the hill above Borsa."

The astrologer was as good as his word. With all the resources of the kingdom at his command, he built a great tower on the steeps of the hill of Albayan. At his words of power spirits conveyed great stones from the pyramids of Egypt, and of these the edifice was built. In the summit of this tower he made a circular hall with windows looking toward every point of the compass, and before each window he set a table on which was arranged, as on a chessboard, a mimic army of horse and foot, with the effigy of the potentate who ruled in that direction, carved out of wood. Along with each table there was a small lance engraved with magical characters. And this hall he closed with a gate of brass, the key of which was kept by the King. Surmounting the tower was a figure of a Moorish horseman cast in bronze and fixed on a revolving pivot. He bore a shield and spear, the latter held perpendicularly. This image looked toward the city, but when a foeman approached it the horseman would face in his direction and would level the lance as if about to charge.

Now, averse as Aben Habuz had been to war, he was all impatience to test the virtues of this talisman. He had not long to wait, for one morning he was informed that

The Arabian Astrologer

the face of the bronze horseman was turned toward the mountains of Elvira, and that his lance was directed against the pass of Lope. The trumpets were at once commanded to sound the alarm, but Ibrahim requested the King not to disturb the city nor call his troops together, but only to follow him to the secret hall in the tower.

When they entered they found the window overlooking the pass of Lope wide open. "Now, O King," said the astrologer, "behold the mystery of the table." Aben Habuz looked at the table covered with tiny effigies of horse- and foot-soldiers, and to his astonishment saw that they were all in motion, that the warriors brandished their weapons, and the steeds neighed, but these sounds were no louder than the hum which rises from a beehive.

"Your Majesty," said the astrologer, "if you desire to cause panic and confusion among your enemies, you have only to strike with the butt of the magic lance; but if you wish to bring death and destruction among them, then strike with the point."

Aben Habuz, seizing the tiny lance, thrust it into some of the figures, belabouring others with the butt. The former dropped upon the board as dead, and the rest fell upon one another in confusion. Scouts sent to confirm the destruction caused among the real invaders told how a Christian army had advanced through the pass of Lope, but had turned their weapons upon one another and had retreated across the border in great confusion.

Delighted, the King requested Ibrahim to name his own reward. "My wants are few," replied the astrologer; "if my cave be fitted up as a suitable abode for a philosopher, I crave no more."

Surprised at his moderation, the King summoned his

treasurer and commanded him to take a note of the astrologer's requirements. The sage desired that an entire suite of apartments should be hewn out of the solid rock, and this having been done, he caused them to be furnished with the most lavish magnificence. Princely ottomans and magnificent divans filled every corner, and the damp walls were hung with the luxurious silks of Damascus, while the rocky floors were carpeted with the glowing fabrics of Ispahan. Seductive baths were constructed, and provided with every kind of Oriental perfume. The apartments were hung with innumerable silver and crystal lamps, which Ibrahim filled with a fragrant and magical oil, which burned perpetually and could not be exhausted.

Amazed at the profligacy of the astrologer, the treasurer made complaint of it to the King, but as his Majesty had passed his word to the sage and had, indeed, invited his extravagance, he could not interfere, and could only hope that the furnishing of the cavern would soon come to an end. When at last the hermitage was replete with the luxuries of three continents, the treasurer inquired of the astrologer if he was satisfied.

" I have only one small request more to make," replied the sage. " I desire that several dancing women be provided for my amusement."

The treasurer, rather scandalized, carried out the sage's instructions, as he was bound to do, and Ibrahim, having all his wants supplied, enclosed himself in his retreat. Meanwhile the King occupied himself in the tower with mimic battles, and as the hand of the astrologer was not there to moderate his warlike propensities, he amused himself by scattering armies like chaff and smashing whole battalions by a stroke of the magic lance. His enemies, terrified at the fate of such expeditions as approached his territory, ceased to trouble him, and for many months the bronze horseman remained stationary. Robbed of his amusement, Aben Habuz pined and grew peevish. But one glorious morning news was brought him that the bronze cavalier had lowered his lance toward the mountains of Guadix.

The King at once repaired to the tower, but the magic table placed in the direction indicated by the horseman was placid. Not a mimic warrior stirred, not a toy charger neighed. Perplexed, Aben Habuz dispatched a scouting party, which returned after three days' absence to report that they had encountered no warlike array, nothing more formidable, indeed, than a beauteous Christian damsel, whom they had found sleeping by a fountain, and made captive.

Aben Habuz commanded that the damsel should be brought to him. Her stately bearing and the lavish ornaments she wore bespoke her of exalted station. In answer to the King, she explained that she was the daughter of a Gothic prince, whose armies had been destroyed in the mountains as if by magic.

"Beware of this woman, O King," whispered the astrologer, who stood by. "Methinks she is a sorceress who has been sent hither to work evil upon thee. Beware, I say."

"Tush, Ibrahim," replied Aben Habuz, "thou art a wise man enow, but little versed in the ways of women. Which of them, pray, is not a sorceress? The damsel finds favour in mine eyes."

"O King," said Ibrahim, "many victories have I given thee, but of all the spoil thou hast won I have received nothing. Give me then this Christian captive, who, I see, carries a silver lyre, and who will make sweet music for me in my retreat below ground. If she be a sorceress, as I suspect, I have spells that will render her harmless. But as for thee, she will speedily overcome thee if thou takest her into thy house."

"What?" cried the incensed monarch. "By the beard of the Prophet, thou art a strange hermit indeed! Know that this damsel is not for thee."

"So be it," said the sage, in wavering tones. "But I fear for thee, royal Aben Habuz. Beware, I say to thee again, beware!" And the astrologer retired to his subterranean abode.

Now Aben Habuz had fallen over head and ears in love with the fair daughter of the Goths, and in his desire to please her strained the resources of his kingdom to their utmost limits. He lavished upon her all that was most exquisite and most magnificent in his storehouses and treasuries. He devised for her pastime a hundred spectacles and festivities, pageants, bull-fights, and tournaments. All these the haughty beauty took quite as a matter of course. Indeed it almost seemed as if she urged the infatuated monarch to greater extravagance and more lavish expenditure. But no matter how profuse was his bounty, she refused to listen to a single amorous word from the lips of Aben Habuz, and whenever he essayed to speak his love she swept her fingers across the strings of her silver lyre and smiled enigmatically. When she acted thus the King invariably felt a drowsiness steal over his senses, and as the dulcet sound gained ascendancy over him he would sink into a sleep from which he usually awoke refreshed and reinvigorated.

His subjects were, however, by no means so satisfied with this condition of affairs as he was. Irritated by his

ABEN HABUZ AND THE CAPTIVE PRINCESS

THE THREE PRINCESSES WATCH THE APPROACH
OF THE WHITE-SAILED GALLEY

The Arabian Astrologer

profligate expenditure, and virtual enslavement by a woman of hostile race, they at length broke into open revolt. But, like Sardanapalus of Babylon, he roused himself from silken dalliance and, putting himself at the head of his guards, crushed the outbreak almost before it had come to a head. The episode disquieted him, however, and he recalled the words of the wise Ibrahim, how that the Gothic princess would bring him woe.

He sought the astrologer in his cavern, and requested his advice. Ibrahim assured him that his position would be insecure so long as the princess remained one of his household. To this Aben Habuz refused to listen, and begged the sage to find him some retreat where he might pass the remainder of his days in tranquillity along with the princess of whom he was so deeply enamoured.

"And my reward if I can procure thee such a retreat?" asked Ibrahim.

"That thou shalt name thyself, O Ibrahim," replied the infatuated old man.

"Thou hast heard of the garden of Irem, O King, that jewel of Arabia?"

"Aye, in fable. Dost thou mock me, astrologer?"

"No more than these eyes have mocked me, O King, for I myself have beheld that most delectable of all paradises.

"As a youth I stumbled upon it when searching for my father's camels. Once the country of the Addites, its capital was founded by Sheddad, son of Ad, great-grandson of Noah, who determined to build in it a palace surrounded by gardens that should rival Paradise itself. But the curse of heaven fell upon him for his presumption. He and his subjects were swept from the earth, and his palace and gardens were laid under an enchantment that hides them from human sight. When I had recovered the book of Solomon I revisited the garden of Irem, and wrung from the jinns who guard it the secret of the spells which render it invisible to mortal sight. By virtue of these spells I can rear for thee, O King, such a retreat even here on the mountain above thy city."

"O wise philosopher!" cried Aben Habuz, "ill was it of me to doubt thee. Do as thou dost promise, and name thy reward."

"All the reward I ask is the first beast of burden with its load that shall enter the gate of thy paradise," said Ibrahim; "a moderate request, surely."

"Moderate indeed!" cried the King, transported by the thought of joys to come, "and I grant it immediately."

The astrologer at once set to work. On the summit of the hill above his cavern he built a strong tower pierced by a great gateway, and on the keystone of this portal he wrought the figure of a great key. The gateway had also an outer guard, on which he engraved a gigantic hand. Then on a night of unexampled darkness he ascended the hill and wrought many incantations. In the morning he sought Aben Habuz and intimated that his labours were at an end, and that the paradise which should be invisible to all save him and his beloved awaited him.

On the following morning the King, accompanied by the princess, ascended the hill, the latter riding on a white palfrey. Beside them stalked the astrologer, assisted by his hieroglyph-covered staff. They came to the arch, and the sage pointed out the mystic hand and key. "No mortal power can prevail against the lord

The Arabian Astrologer

of this paradise," he said, "until yonder hand shall seize that key."

As he spoke the princess on her palfrey passed through the portal.

"Behold!" cried the astrologer. "Did we not agree that the first animal with its burden which should pass through the magic gateway should be mine?"

Aben Habuz smiled at first at what he regarded as a humorous sally on the part of the sage; but when he discovered him to be in earnest he waxed wroth.

"Presumptuous astrologer!" he cried. "Dare you raise your thoughts to her whom I have chosen from among many women?"

"Thy royal word is pledged," replied Ibrahim. "I claim the princess in virtue of thine oath."

"Dog of the desert!" cried Aben Habuz. "Thou shalt feel the weight of my anger for this, juggler though thou art."

"I laugh at thee, Aben Habuz," cried Ibrahim derisively. "Mortal hand cannot harm me. Farewell. Remain in thy fool's paradise and continue to reign over thy province. As for me, I go where thou canst not follow me." And with these words he seized the bridle of the palfrey, smote the earth with his magic staff, and sank with the princess through the centre of the barbican. The earth closed over them, and left not a trace of the aperture through which they had disappeared.

When Aben Habuz recovered from his astonishment he ordered gangs of workmen to be brought to the spot, and commanded them to dig. But the earth seemed to fill in as fast as they threw it out. The opening of the astrologer's cavern too had disappeared. Worse still, the talismans by which the astrologer had secured peace to Granada refused to work, and the old unrest recommenced.

But one morning a peasant came before Aben Habuz and told him that while wandering on the hill he had found a fissure in the rock through which he had crept until he had looked down into a subterranean hall, in which sat the astrologer on a magnificent divan, dozing, while the princess played to him on her silver lyre. The distracted monarch failed, however, to find the fissure. Nor could he enter the paradise built by his rival. The summit of the hill appeared a naked waste, and received the name of 'the Fool's Paradise.' The remainder of the wretched King's life was made a burden to him by the inroads of his warlike neighbours.

Such is the story of the hill of the Alhambra, the palace on which almost realizes the fabled delights of the garden of Irem. The enchanted gateway still exists entire, and is now known as the Gate of Justice. Under that gateway, it is said, the old astrologer remains in his subterranean hall, lulled to constant slumber by the silver lyre of the princess. They are, indeed, each other's captives, and will remain so until the magic key shall be grasped by the magic hand and the spell which lies upon this enchanted hill be dissolved.

Cleomades ana Claremond

The wonderful tale of *Cleomades and Claremond* is almost certainly of Moorish origin in a secondary sense. In his preface to Adenès' *Berte aux grans Piés* (Paris, 1832), M. Paulin Paris says : " I am strongly inclined to believe that the original of the fiction of *Cleomades* is really Spanish or Moorish. All the personages are Saracens or Spaniards ; the scene is in Spain ; the

Cleomades and Claremond

character of the fiction is akin to that of the fictions of
the East." Keightley believed that Blanche of Castile,
the wife of Louis VIII of France, had heard the tale in
Spain, and had narrated it to the French poet Adenès,
who cast it into literary form.

Ectriva, Queen of Southern Spain, held a great tournament at Seville, at which Marchabias, Prince of Sardinia,
so distinguished himself as to win her heart. She
bestowed her hand upon the youthful champion, and their
union was a happy one, being blessed in time with three
daughters and a son. To the boy they gave the name
of Cleomades, while his sisters were called Melior,
Soliadis, and Maxima.

Cleomades was dispatched upon his travels at an early
age. But after he had visited several foreign countries
he was summoned home to be present at the wedding
of his sisters, who were about to be married to three
great princes, all of whom were famous as practitioners
of the magic art. They were Melicandus, King of
Barbary; Bardagans, King of Armenia; and Croppart,
King of Hungary. The last-named monarch was so
unfortunate as to be a hunchback, and to his deformity
he added a bitter tongue and a wicked heart.

The three monarchs had encountered one another while
still some distance from Seville, and had agreed to give
such presents to the King and Queen as would necessitate a gift in return. Melicandus presented the royal
pair with the golden image of a man, holding in his right
hand a trumpet of the same metal, which he sounded if
treason came near him. Bardagans gave a hen and six
chickens of gold, so skilfully made that they picked up
grain and seemed to be alive. Every third day the hen
laid an egg of pearl. Croppart gave a large wooden

horse magnificently caparisoned, which he told his hosts could travel over land and sea at the rate of fifty leagues an hour.

The King and Queen, generous to a fault, invited the strangers to ask anything that it was in their power to bestow. Melicandus requested the hand of the Princess Melior, Bardagans that of Soliadis, while Croppart demanded that Maxima should be given him as a consort. The two elder sisters were pleased with their suitors, who were both handsome and amiable, but when Maxima beheld the hideous and deformed Croppart she ran to her brother Cleomades and begged him to deliver her from such an unsightly monster.

Cleomades represented to his father the wrong done by him in consenting to such a match. But Croppart insisted that the King's word had been passed and that he could not retire from his promise. Cleomades, casting about for an argument, told the Hungarian king that the value of the gifts of Melicandus and Bardagans had been proved, but that, so far as any one knew, his story about the wooden horse might be a mere fable. Croppart offered to test the capacity of his wooden steed. At this the golden man blew his trumpet loudly, but all were so interested in the proposed trial that no one noticed it. The prince mounted the gaudily harnessed hobby, and at the request of Croppart turned a pin of steel in its head, and was immediately carried into the air with such velocity that in a few moments he was lost to sight.

The King and Queen, filled with indignation, had Croppart seized, but he argued that the prince should have waited until he had shown him how to manage the wooden horse. Meanwhile Cleomades sped onward

Cleomades and Claremond

for miles and miles. His strange steed continued to cleave the air at a terrific speed, and at length darkness fell without any signs of its slackening its pace. All night Cleomades continued to fly, and during the hours of gloom had plenty of time to ponder upon his awkward situation. Recollecting that there were pins upon the horse's shoulders like those upon its head, he resolved to try their effect. He found that by turning one of them to right or left the horse went in either direction, and that when the other was turned the wooden hippogriff slackened speed and descended. Morning now broke, and he saw that he was over a great city. By skilful manipulation of his steed he managed to alight upon a lofty tower which stood in the garden of a great palace.

Descending through a trap-door in the roof, he entered a gorgeous sleeping apartment, and beheld a beautiful lady reclining on a sumptuous couch. At his entrance she awoke, and cried out : "Rash man, how have you presumed to enter this apartment? Are you perchance that King Liopatris to whom my father has affianced me?"

"I am that monarch," replied Cleomades. "May I not speak with you?" he continued, for on beholding the princess he had at once fallen violently in love with her.

"Retire to the garden," she said, "and I will come to you there."

The prince obeyed. In a few moments the princess joined him. But they had not been long together when the lady's father, King Cornuant of Tuscany, appeared, and at once denounced Cleomades as an impostor, condemning him to death. The prince begged that he might be permitted to meet his fate mounted upon his wooden horse. To this the King assented, and the magical steed was brought. Mounting it, he immediately turned the pin, and rose high in the air, calling out to the princess, as he did so, that he would remain faithful to her.

Shortly he arrived again in Seville, to the immense relief of his parents. Croppart was requested to quit the country. But he had no mind to do so, and in the guise of an Eastern physician remained in the city. The two elder princesses were married to Melicandus and Bardagans. As for Cleomades, he could not forget the beautiful Princess Claremond, and, once more mounting his aery steed, he set off in the direction of her father's kingdom.

On this occasion he had timed his visit so as to arrive by night at the palace of his lady-love. Alighting in the garden, he made his way to the chamber of Claremond, whom he found fast asleep. He awoke her gently, and told her his name and station, avowed his love, and placed himself at her mercy.

"What!" exclaimed the princess. "Are you indeed that Cleomades whom we regard as the very mirror of knighthood?" The prince assured her that such was the case, and taking from his arm a splendid bracelet containing his mother's portrait and his own, he presented her with it as an assurance that he spoke truly. The princess confessed her love, and at his entreaty mounted behind him on the magic horse. As they rose, Cleomades beheld the King in the gardens beneath, surrounded by his courtiers. He called to him to fear nothing for his daughter, and, setting the head of his mount toward Seville, sped onward.

Alighting at a small rural palace some distance from the

Cleomades and Claremond

Court, Cleomades left the princess there to recover from her journey, while he proceeded to acquaint his royal parents with the result of his adventure. Claremond, having refreshed herself, was walking in the garden for exercise, as she felt somewhat stiff after her aerial voyage, when, as ill-luck would have it, she was observed by Croppart, who, in the guise of an Indian physician, had entered the garden, ostensibly to cull simples for medicinal purposes, but in reality to spy out the land.

Croppart, seeing his own wooden horse, and hearing the princess murmur the name of Cleomades, speedily formed a plan to carry the damsel off. Approaching her, he offered to take her to Cleomades at once on the back of the enchanted horse, and, fearing no evil, she accepted his offer, and permitted herself to be placed on its back. Croppart immediately turned the pin, and the horse ascended with terrific velocity. At first Claremond was quite unsuspicious of the designs of her abductor, but as time passed her fears were aroused, and, looking down, she beheld, instead of populous cities, only gloomy forests and deserted mountains. She begged Croppart to return with her to the palace garden, but he merely laughed at her entreaties, and at last, worn out with grief and disappointment, she swooned away.

Descending near a fountain, Croppart sprinkled the princess with its water until she revived. Then he acquainted her with his intention to make her Queen of Hungary. But the princess did not lack wit, and told him that she was merely a slave-girl whom Cleomades had purchased from her parents. This intelligence made the ferocious Croppart treat her with even less respect than before, so that to save herself from his violence she consented to wed him at the first city to which they might chance to come.

When he had wrung this promise from Claremond, Croppart, who suffered greatly from thirst, drank deeply of the fountain. So icy cold were its waters that on quaffing them he fell to the ground, almost insensible. Claremond, overcome by fatigue and anxiety, fell fast asleep. In this condition they were discovered by Mendulus, King of Salerno, who at once conceived a strong attachment to the sleeping damsel, and had her conveyed to his palace, where he lodged her in a fair apartment. As for Croppart, so severe was the disorder which he had contracted by drinking of the icy fountain that he expired shortly afterward.

Claremond told King Mendulus that she was only a foundling whose name was Trouvée, and that she had accompanied Croppart, a travelling physician, from one place to another, seeking a precarious livelihood. This did not prevent him, however, from offering her his hand and crown. To save herself from this new danger, Claremond had recourse to feigned madness, and so convincingly did she play her part that Mendulus had perforce to confine her under the charge of ten chosen women, whose duty it was to restrain her.

Meanwhile the Court of Spain was thrown into the utmost confusion. Cleomades, returning to the summer palace with his parents, could find no trace of Claremond, and, overcome with grief, was brought back to the capital in a state bordering upon frenzy. When he recovered he set out for the kingdom of Tuscany in the hope that there he might obtain tidings of his lady. Riding alone, he came to a castle, where he encountered and overthrew two knights who

Cleomades and Claremond

refused to let him pass. From them he learned that when a prince named Liopatris, who had been betrothed to Claremond, arrived at the Court of Tuscany, three of his knights had accused three of Claremond's maids of honour of being accomplices in the abduction of their mistress. The knights whom Cleomades had worsted were suitors for the hands of two of those ladies, and had challenged their detractors, but as one of them had been wounded by Cleomades, they could not now make good their challenge. Cleomades graciously offered to take the place of the wounded man, and with his unwounded comrade set out for the Court of King Cornuant.

Next morning the combatants appeared in the lists. The three accusers were overthrown, and the maids of honour pronounced innocent, according to the laws of chivalry. Taking the damsels with them, Cleomades and his new brother-in-arms returned to the castle whence they had come, and when he had doffed his armour the prince-errant was recognized by the ladies whom he had helped to rescue. Great was their grief when they learned of the fate of Claremond. But one of them begged Cleomades to seek the assistance of a famous astrologer who dwelt at Salerno, "who saw most secret things right clear." Cleomades instantly resolved to go and consult this sage, and accordingly next morning he set out for the city of Salerno, after having taken an affectionate leave of the lovers.

Arrived at Salerno, Cleomades put up at an inn, and lost no time in inquiring of the landlord where the astrologer might be found.

"Alas, sir!" said the host, "it is now a year since he passed away. Never did we need him more. For had he been alive, he might have served our King by restoring to reason the most beautiful creature who ever lived." And he told Cleomades the story of how Mendulus had found the hunchback and the maid. At the mention of the wooden horse Cleomades started, but kept his presence of mind, and assured the inn-keeper that he possessed an infallible cure for madness. He begged the man to lead him to the King, and, on the plea that his arms might excite suspicion, donned a false beard and the dress of a physician.

He was at once admitted to the royal presence, and on hearing of his skill the King led him to the place where Claremond was confined. Cleomades had taken with him a glove belonging to his lady-love, which he had stuffed with herbs, and on the pretence that these would cure her he placed it upon her cheek. Seeing her own glove, she regarded the seeming physician earnestly, and succeeded in penetrating his disguise. But, still feigning insanity, she begged that her wooden horse might be brought, so that it could dispute with the learned doctor. It was carried into the garden where they were, and the princess pretended to have a whim that she could only be cured if she and the physician mounted the wooden steed. To this Mendulus consented, and when they bestrode the artificial hippogriff Cleomades turned the pin, and in a moment they rose like an arrow from the bow. Next morning the happy pair arrived in Seville. Their nuptials were immediately performed, and Liopatris was consoled with Princess Maxima, so that no one was left lamenting.

The Three Beautiful Princesses

Legend tells us that when Mohammed el Haygari, or 'the Left-handed,' reigned in Granada he once en-

The Three Beautiful Princesses

countered a train of horsemen riding back from a foray in Christian lands. He observed in the ranks of their captives a beautiful damsel richly attired, and learned that she was the daughter of the commander of a frontier fortress which had been taken and sacked in the course of the expedition. The lady was accompanied by a duenna, and Mohammed ordered that both women should be conveyed to his harem.

Day by day he urged the captive damsel to become his queen. But his faith as well as his age caused her family to reject his advances. In his perplexity he resolved to enlist the good graces of her duenna, who undertook to plead his cause with her young mistress. She told the lady that she was foolish to pine in a beautiful palace, who had henceforth been used only to a dull old frontier castle, and that by marrying Mohammed she could make herself mistress of all she surveyed instead of remaining a captive. At last her arguments prevailed. The Spanish lady consented to unite herself to the Moorish monarch, and even outwardly conformed to his religion, which the duenna also embraced with all the fervour of a proselyte, being re-named Kadiga.

In course of time the Spanish lady presented her lord with three daughters at a single birth. The Court astrologers cast the nativities of the infants, and with many ominous warnings cautioned their father to keep strict guard over them when they arrived at a marriageable age.

Shortly afterward his queen died, and Mohammed, with the astrologers' warning ringing in his ears, resolved to shut the princesses up in the royal castle of Salobreña, a place of great strength, overlooking the Mediterranean, where he felt certain no harm could come to them.

Years passed and at length the princesses became of marriageable age. Although they had been brought up by the discreet Kadiga with the greatest care, and had always been together, their characters were of course very different one from another. Zayda, the eldest, was of an intrepid spirit, and took the lead in everything. Zorayda, the second, had a strong sense of beauty, which probably accounted for the fact that she spent a large portion of her time gazing in the glass, or in the fountain which plashed and sang in the marble court of the castle. Zorahayda, the youngest, was soft and timid, and given to reverie. All three were surpassingly beautiful, and as she gazed upon them the shrewd old Kadiga would shake her head and sigh. When they inquired of her why she did so, she would turn the question aside with a laugh and direct the conversation to a less dangerous topic.

One day the princesses were seated at a casement which commanded a noble view of the heaven-blue Mediterranean, the dreamy waters of which whispered musically to the palm-shadowed shores which skirted the height upon which the towers of Salobreña stood. It was one of those evenings on which we feel it difficult to believe that we are not temporary sojourners in a land of vague deliciousness, where all is beautiful as it is unreal. Mists dyed in the sunset rose like incense from the urns of twilight, hiding the far distances of sea and sky. From between the curtains of sea-shadows there drifted a white-sailed galley, which glided toward the shore, where it anchored. A number of Moorish soldiers landed on the beach, conducting several Christian

The Three Beautiful Princesses

prisoners, among whom were three Spanish cavaliers richly dressed. These, though loaded with chains, carried themselves in a lofty and distinguished manner, and the princesses could not refrain from gazing upon them with intense and breathless interest. Never before had they seen such noble-looking youths, who had so far only beheld black slaves and the rude fishermen of the coast, so small wonder was it that the sight of these brave cavaliers should arouse commotion in their bosoms.

The princesses remained gazing until the prisoners were out of sight. Then with long-drawn sighs they turned from the window and sat down, musing and pensive, on their ottomans. The discreet Kadiga, finding them thus, learned from them what they had seen, and in answer to their inquiries regarding such beings related to them many a tale of cavalier life in Christian Spain, which only served to heighten the curiosity which the appearance of the captives had excited. But it did not take the sage old woman long to discover the mischief she was doing, and, full of fears for which she could scarcely account, she dispatched a slave to her royal master, with the symbolic message of a basket filled with leaves of the fig and vine, on which lay a peach, an apricot, and a nectarine, all in the early stage of tempting ripeness, which Mohammed, skilled in the Oriental language of fruits and flowers, rightly interpreted as meaning that his daughters had arrived at marriageable age.

Recalling the advice of the astrologers, he resolved to bring the princesses under his immediate guardianship, and at once commanded that a tower of the Alhambra should be prepared for their reception. He himself set out for Salobreña to conduct them thither, and on beholding them, and perceiving how beautiful they were, he felt glad that he had wasted no time in bringing them to Court. So conscious was he of the danger that three such beauties would run that he prepared for his return to Granada by sending heralds before him, commanding every one to keep out of the road by which he was to pass, on pain of death. Then, escorted by a troop of the most hideous black horsemen he could find, he set forth on the journey to his capital.

As the cavalcade was approaching Granada it chanced to overtake a small body of Moorish soldiers with a convoy of prisoners. It was too late for the soldiers to retire, so they threw themselves on their faces on the earth, ordering their captives to do likewise. Among the prisoners were the three cavaliers whom the princesses had seen from the window of the castle of Salobreña, and they, too proud to obey the order to grovel before their pagan enemy, remained standing.

The anger of the royal Mohammed was aroused by this flagrant defiance of his orders, and, drawing his scimetar, he was about to decapitate the unfortunate captives, when the princesses gathered round him and implored mercy for them. The captain of the guard, too, assured him that they could not be injured without great scandal, on account of their high rank, and described to the irate monarch the manner in which these illustrious youths had been taken captive while fighting like lions beneath the royal banner of Spain. Somewhat mollified by these representations, Mohammed sheathed his weapon. " I will spare their lives," he said, " but their rashness must meet with fitting punishment. Let them be taken to the Vermilion Towers and put to labour."

288

The Three Beautiful Princesses

In the agitation of the moment the veils of the three princesses had blown aside so that their radiant beauty was revealed. In those romantic times to see was often to love at once, and the three noble cavaliers fell sudden victims to the charms of the royal damsels who pleaded so eloquently for their lives. Singularly enough, each of them was enraptured with a separate beauty; but it would be as impertinent as illogical to ask the reason of this sleight of cunning Dame Nature, who in romance, perhaps, is represented as being more judicious than she really is.

The royal cavalcade now pressed onward, and the captives were conducted to their allotted prison in the Vermilion Towers. The residence provided for the princesses was all that imagination could ask and splendour devise. It was situated in a tower somewhat apart from the main palace of the Alhambra, and on one side was cheered by the prospect of a garden beautiful as the first step into paradise, while on the other it overlooked a deep and umbrageous ravine that separated the grounds of the Alhambra from those of the Generalife. But to the beauties of this delightful place the princesses were blind. They languished visibly, and by none was their indisposition remarked so shrewdly as by old Kadiga, who guessed its cause without any great difficulty. Taking pity upon their forlorn condition, she told them that as she was passing the Vermilion Towers on the preceding evening she heard the cavaliers singing after the day's labours to the strains of a guitar, and at the request of the princesses she arranged with their jailer that they should be set to work in the ravine, beneath the windows of the damsels' apartments.

The very next day the captives were given labour which

necessitated their presence in the ravine. During the noontide heat, while their guards were sleeping, they sang a Spanish roundelay to the accompaniment of the guitar. The princesses listened, and heard that it was a love ditty addressed to themselves. The ladies replied to the sound of a lute played by Zorayda, the burden of which was:

> The rose by the screen of her leaves is concealed,
> But the song of the nightingale pierces the shield.

Every day the cavaliers worked in the ravine, and an intercourse was maintained between them and the no less captive princesses by songs and romances which breathed the feelings of either party. In time the princesses showed themselves on the balcony when the guards were wrapped in noonday slumber. But at length this desirable condition of affairs was interrupted, for the three young nobles were ransomed by their families and repaired to Granada to commence their homeward journey. They approached the aged Kadiga, and requested her to assist them to fly with the princesses to Spain. This proposal the old dame communicated to her young mistresses, and finding that they embraced it with alacrity a plan of escape was arranged. The rugged hill on which the Alhambra is built was at that time tunnelled by many a subterranean passage leading from the fortress to various parts of the city, and Kadiga arranged to conduct the royal damsels by one of these to a sally-port beyond the walls of Granada, where the cavaliers were to be in waiting with swift horses to bear the whole party over the borders.

The appointed night arrived, and when the Alhambra

The Three Beautiful Princesses

was buried in deep sleep the princesses, accompanied by their duenna, descended from their apartments to the garden by means of a rope-ladder—all save Zorahayda, the youngest and most timorous, who at the decisive moment could not endure the idea of leaving her father. The advance of the night patrol which guarded the palace made it necessary for her sisters and Kadiga to fly without her. Groping their way through the fearful labyrinth, they succeeded in reaching the gate outside the walls. The Spanish cavaliers were waiting to receive them. The lover of Zorahayda was frantic when he learned that she had refused to leave the tower, but there was no time to waste in lamentations ; the two princesses mounted behind their lovers, Kadiga behind another rider, and, dashing the spurs into the flanks of their steeds, the party galloped off at top speed.

They had not proceeded far when they heard the noise of an alarm from the battlements of the Alhambra, while a lurid watch-fire burst into flame on its topmost turret. Lashing their horses to a frenzy of speed, they succeeded in outdistancing their pursuers, and by taking unfrequented paths and hiding in wild barrancas they were at last so fortunate as to reach the city of Cordova, where the princesses were received into the bosom of the Church and united to their respective lovers.

Mohammed was well-nigh demented at the loss of his daughters, but, rather unnecessarily, took pains to redouble his watch over the one who had remained. The unfortunate Zorahayda, thus closely guarded, repented of her vacillation, and we are told that many a night she was seen leaning on the battlements of the tower in which she was confined, looking in the direction of Cordova. Legend, never very merciful either to heroine or reader, says that she died young, and her melancholy fate gave birth to many a sad ballad, both Moorish and Castilian, so that she was at least successful in inspiring song—a celebrity to which her more fortunate sisters did not attain.

The Story of Prince Ahmed

Once again the ancient city of Granada is the scene of the legend we are about to relate. But, from considerations which we will adduce later, there is good reason to believe the story to be of Persian origin. It recounts the history of Prince Ahmed, surnamed 'al Kamel,' or 'the Perfect,' because of the beauty and equability of his temperament. At the birth of this prince of happy disposition the Court astrologers predicted that his career would be singularly fortunate, provided one difficulty could be overcome; but that difficulty was sufficiently great to daunt the heart of any monarch, so that we cannot be surprised when we learn that his royal father grew pessimistic regarding his chances of happiness when the wise men informed him that in order to circumvent a cruel fate his son must be kept from the allurements of love until he attained the age of manhood.

The perplexed King acted as most fathers in romances do—that is, he confined his son from his earliest infancy in a delightfully secluded palace which he built for the purpose on the brow of the hill above the Alhambra. This building, which is now known as the Generalife, is surrounded by lofty walls, and here the young prince grew up under the care of Eben Bonabben, an Arabian sage of wisdom and other formidable qualities, which

The Story of Prince Ahmed

made him a suitable guardian for a budding royalty in such case as Ahmed.

Under the tuition of this grave preceptor the prince attained to his twentieth year totally ignorant of the tender passion. About this time a change came over his habitual docility, and instead of listening attentively to the discourses of Eben Bonabben, he neglected his studies and took to strolling in the gardens of his abode. His instructor, who saw how it was with him, and that the latent tenderness of his nature had awakened, redoubled his care, and shut him up in the most remote tower of the Generalife. In order to interest him in something that would remove his thoughts from speculations which might prove dangerous, he instructed his pupil in the language of birds, and the Prince, taking kindly to this recondite subject, soon mastered it completely. After trying his skill upon a hawk, an owl, and a bat with indifferent success, he listened to the chorus of birds in his garden. It was spring-time, and each and every feathered songster was pouring out his heart in an ecstasy of love, repeating the word again and yet again.

"Love!" cried the prince at length. "What may this love be?" He inquired of Eben Bonabben, who at the question felt his head roll ominously on his shoulders, as if in pledge of what would happen to it did he not avert the question. He informed Ahmed that love was one of the greatest evils which poor humanity has to endure ; that it made strife between friends and brethren, and had brought about the ruin of some of the greatest of men. Then he departed in perturbation, leaving the Prince to his own thoughts.

But Ahmed observed that the birds which sang so lustily

of love were far from unhappy, and therefore doubted the arguments of his preceptor. Next morning as he lay on his couch, lost in the pursuit of the enigma which had presented itself to his thoughts, a dove, chased by a hawk, flew through the casement and fluttered to the floor. The Prince took up the terrified bird and smoothed its ruffled plumage. But it seemed disconsolate, and on his asking for what it grieved, it replied that its discontent was caused by separation from its mate, whom it loved with all its heart.

"Tell me, beautiful bird, what is this thing called love that these birds in the garden sing of so constantly?"

"Love," said the bird, "is the great mystery and principle of life. Every created being has its mate. Hast thou spent so many of the precious days of youth without experiencing it? Has no beautiful princess or lovely damsel ensnared thine heart?"

The Prince released the dove and sought out Bonabben. "Miscreant!" he cried, "why hast thou kept me in this abject ignorance—why withheld from me the great mystery and principle of life? Why am I alone debarred from the enjoyment of love?

Bonabben saw that further subterfuge was useless, so he revealed to his charge the predictions of the astrologers and the consequent necessity for the precautions with which his youth had been surrounded. He further assured the prince that did the King learn how his trust had failed his head would pay forfeit. The Prince, horrified to learn this, promised to conceal his knowledge, and this in some measure quieted the fears of the philosopher.

Some days after this episode the Prince was reclining in the garden when his friend the dove alighted fearlessly

The Story of Prince Ahmed

upon his shoulder. He asked it whence it came, and it answered that it came from a far land, where it had seen a beautiful princess, who, like himself, had been enclosed within the high walls of a secret retreat and kept in ignorance of the existence of love. The knowledge that a being of the opposite sex existed who had been brought up in like circumstances to himself acted like a spark of fire to the heart of Ahmed. He at once wrote a letter couched in the most impassioned language, which he addressed, " To the unknown beauty, from the captive Prince Ahmed," and this he entrusted to the dove, who promised to convey it to the object of his adoration without a moment's delay.

Day after day Ahmed watched for the return of the messenger of love, but in vain. At last, one evening the bird fluttered into his apartment, and falling at his feet expired. The arrow of some wanton archer had pierced its breast, yet it had struggled on to the fulfilment of its mission. Ahmed, picking up the little body, found it encircled by a chain of pearls, attached to which was a small enamelled picture representing a lovely princess in the flower of youth and beauty. The prince pressed the picture to his lips in a fervour of passion, and at once resolved upon flight, his object being to seek the original of the portrait, whatever dangers and obstacles might lie in the accomplishment of his purpose.

Seeking the advice of the wise owl, whom he had not spoken to since he had been a beginner in the study of the language of birds, he collected all his jewels, and on the same night lowered himself from the balcony, clambered over the outer walls of the Generalife, and, accompanied by the wise old bird, who had agreed to act as his cicerone, set out for Seville, his purpose being to seek a raven whom the owl knew to be a great necromancer, who might assist him in his quest. In time they arrived at the southern city, and sought the high tower in which the raven dwelt. They found the gifted bird, and were advised by it to go to Cordova and seek the palm-tree of the great Abderahman, which stood in the courtyard of the principal mosque, at the foot of which they would encounter a great traveller, who would give them information regarding the object of their search.

Following the raven's instructions, they travelled to Seville, and were annoyed to find at the foot of the tree in question an immense crowd, listening attentively to the chattering of a parrot, whose plumage was of the most brilliant green, and whose pragmatical eye held much wisdom. When the crowd had departed, the prince consulted the bird regarding his quest, and was amazed to hear it burst into cries of discordant laughter when it gazed upon the picture.

"Poor youth," it cackled, "are you another victim of love? Know that this picture you worship so devoutly is that of the Princess Aldegonda, daughter of the Christian King of Toledo."

"Help me in this matter, good bird," cried the prince, "and I shall find you a distinguished place at Court."

"With all my heart," said the parrot. "All I ask is that it be a sinecure, for we clever folk have a great dislike for hard work!"

Accompanied by the owl and the parrot, Ahmed proceeded upon his journey to Toledo in search of the Princess Aldegonda. Their progress through the stern passes of the Sierra Morena and across the sun-drenched

The Story of Prince Ahmed

plains of La Mancha and Castile was slow, but at long last they came in sight of Toledo, at the foot of whose steeps the Tagus rushed in brawling cascades. The garrulous parrot at once pointed out the abode of the Princess Aldegonda, a stately palace rising out of the bowers of a delightful garden.

"Ah, Toledo!" cried the owl in ecstasy. "Toledo, thou city of magic and mystery! What spells, what enchantments of ancient wizardry have not been recited among thy carven shadows! City of learning, of strange miracles, of a thousand profundities——"

"City of a thousand fiddlesticks!" piped the parrot. "A truce to your raptures, friend philosopher. O Toledo," he apostrophized, with wings outspread in mimicry of the owl, "city of nuts and wine, of figs and oil, of banquets, jousts, and enchanting señoritas! Now, my prince, shall I not fly to the Princess Aldegonda and acquaint her with the fact of our arrival?"

"Do so, best of birds," replied the Prince enthusiastically. "Tell her that Ahmed, the pilgrim of love, has come to Toledo in quest of her."

The parrot immediately spread his wings and flew off on his mission. He beheld the princess reclining on a couch, and, alighting, he advanced with the air of a courtier.

"Beautiful princess," he said, with a low bow, "I come as ambassador from Prince Ahmed, of Granada, who has journeyed to Toledo to bask in the light of thine eyes."

"O joyful news!" cried the princess. "I had begun to doubt the constancy of Ahmed. Hie thee back to him as fast as thy green wings will take thee, and tell him that his poetry has been the food of my soul, and that his letters are engraven on my heart. But, alas ! he must prepare to prove his love by force of arms. To-morrow is my seventeenth birthday, in honour of which the King my father is to hold a great tournament, and my hand is to be the prize of the victor."

Ahmed was delighted with the news which the parrot brought him, but his happiness at finding the princess had remained faithful was shadowed by the knowledge that he would have to do battle for her ; for he had not been trained in the exercises of chivalry. In his dilemma he turned to the wise owl, who, as usual, threw much light on the matter, for he unfolded to him that in a neighbouring mountain there was a cave where lay on an iron table a suit of magical armour and near it an enchanted steed that had been shut up there for generations. After a search the cavern was located. A lamp of everlasting oil shed a solemn light among the profound shadows of the place, and by its gleam the armour and the bespelled charger were soon found, as the owl had said. Donning the mail, Ahmed leapt upon the destrier's back, and with a loud neighing the steed awoke and bore him from the place, the owl and the parrot flying one on either side of him.

Next morning Ahmed proceeded to the lists, which were situated in a large plain near the city. They presented a scene of unparalleled brilliance, and noble knights and lovely ladies had congregated in hundreds to try their skill in arms or display their beauty. But all the latter were quite eclipsed by the Princess Aldegonda, who shone like the moon among the stars. At the appearance of Ahmed, who was announced as 'The Pilgrim of Love,' excitement ran high, for he made a most gallant and resplendent figure in his glittering armour and bejewelled,

The Story of Prince Ahmed

casque. He was informed, however, that none but princes might encounter in the tournament, and on learning this he disclosed his rank and name. On hearing that he was a Moslem a universal scoffing arose among the Christian champions, and Ahmed, incensed, challenged the knight who displayed the bitterest enmity. The course was run, and the brawny scoffer tilted out of his saddle. But the prince now found that he had to deal with a demoniac horse and armour. Once in action, nothing could control them. The Arabian steed charged into the thickest of the throng. Down went Ahmed's opponents before his levelled lance like ninepins, so that the lists were soon strewn with their recumbent forms. But at midday the spell which had been laid upon the charger resumed its power. The Arabian steed scoured across the plain, leaped the barrier, plunged into the Tagus, swam its raging current, and bore the prince, breathless yet avenged, to the cavern, where it resumed its station like a statue beside the iron table, on which the prince laid the armour.

Ahmed's feelings were most unenviable, for among those whom he had unhorsed in his wild career had been the King himself, the father of Aldegonda, who, on witnessing the overthrow of his guests, had angrily rushed to their assistance. Full of anxiety, he dispatched his winged messengers to gather tidings. The parrot returned with a world of gossip. Toledo, he said, was in consternation; the princess had been carried home senseless, and the general opinion was that the prince was either a Moorish magician or a demon such as tradition said dwelt in the mountain caverns.

It was morning when the owl came back. He had peered through the windows of the palace, and had seen the princess kiss Ahmed's letter, and give way to loud lamentations. Later, she was conveyed to the highest tower in the palace, every avenue to which was strictly guarded. But a melancholy, deep and devouring, had settled upon her, and it was thought that she was the victim of magic, so that at last a great reward—the richest jewel in the royal treasury—was offered to anyone who should effect her cure.

Now the wise owl chanced to know that in the royal treasury was deposited a certain box of sandal-wood secured by bands of steel, and inscribed with mystic characters known only to the learned few. This coffer contained the silken carpet of Solomon the Great, which had been brought to Spain by exiled Jews. All this caused the prince to ponder deeply. Next day he laid aside his rich attire, and arrayed himself in the simple garb of an Arab of the desert, dyeing his face and hands a tawny brown. Thus disguised, he repaired to the royal palace, and after some delay, was admitted. When the King asked him his business, he boldly claimed his ability to cure the princess, who, he said, was certainly possessed of a devil, which he could exorcise by the power of music alone, as the folk of his tribe were wont to do.

The King, seeing him so confident, immediately conducted him to the lofty tower where the princess lay, the windows of which opened upon a terrace commanding a view over the city and surrounding country. On this terrace the prince seated himself, and began to play on his pipe. But the princess remained insensible. Then, as if chanting an exorcism, he repeated the verses of the letter which he had sent to the princess, in which he had first declared his passion. Rousing, she recog-

The Story of Prince Ahmed

nized the words with emotion, and asked that the prince should be brought into her presence. Ahmed was conducted into her chamber, but the lovers, knowing their danger, were discreet, and contented themselves with the exchange of glances more eloquent than speech. Never was triumph of music more complete. The roses returned to the pale cheeks of the princess, and so delighted was the King that he at once requested Ahmed to select the most precious jewel in his treasury. The prince, feigning modesty, replied that he disdained jewels, and desired only an old carpet enclosed in a sandal-wood coffer, which had been handed down by the Moslems who once owned Toledo. The box was immediately brought, and the carpet spread out on the terrace.

"This carpet," said the prince, "once belonged to Solomon the Wise. It is worthy of being placed beneath the feet of beauty. Let the Princess stand upon it."

The King motioned his daughter to accede to the Arab's request, and she at once complied. Then Ahmed took his place beside her, and, turning to her astonished father, said :

"Know, O King, that your daughter and I have long loved one another. Behold in me the Pilgrim of Love."

He had scarcely spoken when the carpet rose in the air, and, to the consternation of all, the lovers were borne off, and swiftly disappeared.

The magical carpet descended at Granada, where Ahmed and the princess were espoused to one another with fitting splendour. In course of time he reigned in his father's stead long and happily. But although he had become a king he did not forget the services of his bird friends. He appointed the owl his vizier, and the parrot his master of ceremonies, and we may be sure by these tokens that in all his royal and domestic circumstances he was attended by wisdom and magnificence.

This striking tale is, of course, manufactured out of a number of original and separate elements—the lovers destined to be kept in ignorance of love because of some danger prophesied at their birth, the old theme of the language of birds, the 'helpful animal' theme, and that of the magic carpet. The latter is merely an adaptation of the idea that a magician was able to transport himself through the air in a non-natural manner, and this ability he seems to have handed on to the witches of the Middle Ages, whose broomsticks were merely magical substitutes for the 'flying horse.'[1] But the appearance of the carpet in such a tale makes it probable that it drew its inspiration from Persia, the land where carpets were first manufactured, as the wizards of more primitive folk adopted other and simpler means of supernatural flight.

The Paynim's Promise

A singular story which shows that tolerance and even generosity were occasionally to be found between Moor and Christian in ancient Spain is narrated in connexion with the exploits of Narvaez, the general who commanded the garrison of Medina Antequara, a Moorish town that had fallen into the hands of the Spaniards. Narvaez

---

[1] The witch-cult in Europe seems to me to have a connexion with the horse. Occasionally witches proceed to the sabbat on flying horses. One of the tests of a witch was to look in her eyes for the reflection of a horse. In Scotland even to-day a 'Horseman's Society' exists which has a semi-occult initiation and strange rites.

made the city a centre from which he launched a series of incursions into the neighbouring districts of Granada for the purpose of obtaining provisions and relieving the unfortunate inhabitants of any booty which might happen to be left to them.

On one of these occasions Narvaez had dispatched a large body of horse to scour the surrounding country. They had started on their raid at an early hour of the morning and while it was yet dark, so that by the hour of sunrise they had penetrated far into hostile country. The officer in command of the expedition rode a few bow-shots ahead, and to his surprise suddenly encountered a Moorish youth who had lost his way in the darkness, and who was now returning home. With great boldness the young man faced the Spanish horsemen, but was quickly overpowered, and when they learned from him that the district in which they were was little more than a desert, having been stripped of all its resources by the inhabitants who had abandoned it, they returned to Antequara, where they brought their captive before Narvaez.

The prisoner, a young man of about twenty-three years of age, was of handsome and dignified appearance. He was dressed in a flowing robe of rich mulberry-coloured silk, gorgeously decorated in the Moorish manner, and was mounted on a magnificent horse of the Arab breed. From these indications, Narvaez judged him to be a cavalier of importance. He inquired his name and lineage, and was told that his prisoner was the son of the Alcayde of Ronda, a Moor of high distinction, and an implacable enemy of the Christians. But when Narvaez questioned the young man himself, to his astonishment he found that he was unable to reply to him. Tears streamed down his face, and his utterance was choked by sobs which seemed to rise from a heart overflowing with grief.

"I marvel to see thee," said Narvaez. "That thou, being as thou art, a cavalier of good race, and the son of a noble so valiant as is thy father, should be thus cast down and weep like a woman, knowing too what are the chances of war and having all the appearance of a brave soldier and a good knight—this surpasses my understanding."

"I do not weep because I have been taken captive," replied the youth. "The tears flow from mine eyes because of a much deeper sorrow, compared with which my fallen state is as nothing."

Struck by the young man's earnestness, and pitying his position, Narvaez asked him sympathetically to confide to him the cause of his sorrow. The cavalier, touched by the general's kindness, sighed deeply, and replied:

"Lord Governor, I have long loved a lady, daughter of the Alcayde of a certain fortress. Many times have I fought in her honour against the men of your race. In time the lady came to return my affection, and declared herself willing to become my wife, and I was on my way to her when, by evil chance, I encountered your horsemen and fell into their hands. Thus I have lost not only my liberty, but all the happiness of my life, which I believed I held in my hand. If this does not seem to you to be worthy of tears, I know not for what purpose they are given to the eyes of man, or how to make you understand the misery I am suffering."

The bold Narvaez was much affected at the pitiful nature of his prisoner's story, and being a man of sympathetic instincts and generous heart, he at once resolved to do

The Paynim's Promise

what he could to lighten the captive's sorrowful predicament.

"Thou art a cavalier of good family," he said, "and if thou wilt pledge me thy word to return to this place, I will give thee permission to go to thy beloved and acquaint her with the cause of thy failure to be with her this day."

The Moor gladly availed himself of his captor's indulgence, gave Narvaez the required assurance, and that same night reached the castle wherein his lady dwelt. Entering the garden, he gave the signal by which he usually signified his presence there, and she immediately came to the trysting-place agreed upon between them. She at once expressed the greatest surprise that he had not arrived at the time he had promised to be with her, and he explained the circumstances which had attended his delay. On hearing what had occurred the lady was cast into the deepest grief, and as her lover was attempting to console her by every means in his power the hour of dawn reminded him of his pledge to Narvaez, and how he had given his word as a soldier and a cavalier to return to his captivity.

"There is nothing left but that I should return," he said. "I have lost my own liberty, and God forbid that, loving you as I do, I should bear you to a place where yours also would be in danger. We must wait patiently until the time when I can obtain my ransom, when I shall immediately return to you."

"Before this hour," replied the lady, "you have given me many proofs that you truly love me, but now you show your attachment more plainly than ever in your desire for my safety, and for that very reason I should be most ungrateful if I did not go with you to share your captivity. Therefore I shall accompany you to the Christian prison for which you are destined. If you must be a slave, so also shall I be."

The lady then commanded her waiting damsel to bring her jewel-case, and when this had been done she mounted behind her lover. All night they rode, and in the morning they arrived at Antequara, where they presented themselves to Narvaez, who was no less struck with the constancy of the lady than with the honour and fidelity of the young Moorish cavalier. He immediately gave both their liberty, and, loading them with presents and other marks of honour, accorded them permission to return to their own land, providing an escort of troops to accompany them until they had reached a place of safety.

This adventure, the love of the lady, the loyalty of the Moor, and more than all the generosity of the high-souled Christian commander, were greatly celebrated and applauded by the noble Saracens of Granada, and were sung in the lays of their most distinguished poets and chronicled by their annalists. And although this story in every way partakes of the nature of romance, it has the additional merit of being true.

The Dream of King Alfonso

A mysterious story indeed is that which tells of the manner in which Don Alfonso, King of Galicia, one of the Christian states which held out against the Moors, was haunted by a dream which came to him again and again in the watches of the night, and which no one might interpret, until at last he was forced to call to his aid the occult science of those very enemies against whom the vision warned him.

The Dream of King Alfonso

In the year 1086 the territories of Alfonso and other Christian sovereigns were invaded by a vast army of Almoravide Moors, who, sweeping over from Africa, menaced Central and Northern Spain. When he learned of their advance Alfonso was engaged in the siege of Saragossa, but in view of the danger which confronted him he joined his allies at Toledo and prepared to give battle to the invaders, who, numerous in themselves, had been reinforced by the Moors of the various Mohammedan states in Spain. Before leaving Toledo Alfonso was visited by one of those terrible visions of the night which, history tells us, have so often prophesied the fall of nations. It appeared to him that he was mounted on an elephant, and that beside him, on the flank of the great beast, was placed an atambore or Moorish drum, which he beat with his own hands. But the clamours which pealed forth from the instrument were so loud and terrifying that he instantly awoke in terror and amazement. At first he scoffed at the dream as nothing but a nightmare, but when it returned again and again on the succeeding nights of his stay at Toledo he began to feel that it must contain some element of awful warning. Night after night he awoke in great terror, drenched with perspiration, and with the echoes of the Eastern drum thundering in his ear, until at last, in great disquietude, he resolved to ask the advice of the learned men of his Court regarding what the vision might portend.

With this object in view, he summoned to his presence the scholars and sages of his retinue, as well as the bishops and priests, and even the rabbis of the Jews who were his vassals, and who were more profoundly skilled in divination and the interpretation of dreams than any of his Christian subjects. When they had come before him, he related the substance of his dream, which he described very minutely, concluding his narration by saying : "That which most amazes and alarms me in this matter is the peculiarity of the elephant which I see in my visions, and which is an animal not reared in our country nor seen therein. In like manner, the atambore is not of the form and kind which we have in use among us, nor is that either to be seen in Spain. Wherefore do ye consider what these may portend, and give me the signification thereof without delay."

The wise men thereupon retired, and having considered the dream, returned to the royal presence. "Lord King," they said, "we are of opinion that this dream of yours was sent to signify that you shall vanquish these great armies that the Moslems have brought against you, that you shall despoil their camp and plunder it of the riches it contains, and that you shall occupy their territory and return victorious, with great honour and glory. Moreover, we believe that your triumph will be made known through all parts of the East, since the elephant which you nightly appear to bestride can be no other than Juzef Aben Taxfin, King of the Moslems and lord of the far-extending lands of Africa, who, like that animal, has been reared in the deserts of that country. The strangely formed atambore which you have sounded on these many nights implies the fame which shall echo throughout the world, to every part of which it shall carry the knowledge of your illustrious victories."

Alfonso listened to this interpretation with the utmost attention, and when it concluded he said : "It appears to me that you have gone far from the true interpre-

DON ALFONSO SUMMONS HIS SAGES

TORRALVA AND THE SPIRITS

The Dream of King Alfonso

tation of my dream, seeing that the explanation which my heart gives me is of a widely different kind, for it announces to me nothing better than events of terror and dismay."

Having thus spoken, the King turned his head, and, looking toward certain Moorish knights who were his vassals, he asked them if perchance they knew of any wise man of their nation who had skill in the interpretation of dreams. They replied that they did know of one such, and that there was in Toledo at that moment a wise man who taught in one of the mosques and who would interpret the vision to the satisfaction of the King.

Alfonso at once commanded that they should bring the sage before him, and in a short space the Moorish cavaliers returned with the man of whom they had spoken, the Faki Mohammed Aben Iza, who, however, sternly refused to interpret the dream of an infidel, and when he learned for what purpose he was required would not even set foot in the palace. The Moorish knights in their dilemma told Alfonso that the Faki's religious scruples would not permit him to appear in a Christian court, and the King, who well knew the niceties of Mohammedan law, contented himself with their assurance that they would bring him the wise man's interpretation of the dream. They then entreated the Faki to consider it, and as they pressed him urgently he replied : " Go to the King Alfonso and say that the accomplishment of his vision is very near, and that its significance is after this wise. He shall be vanquished, yea, in a disgraceful defeat, and with great slaughter. He shall fly, with but few of his people, and the victory shall remain with the Sons of the Prophet. Tell him, moreover, that this declaration is derived from the Koran : ' Know ye not what your God has prepared for him of the Elephant? Hath he not brought his force to nothing and rendered his evil intentions of no avail? See ye not that he hath sent over them the vultures of Babel?' These words," continued the Faki, "foretold the downfall of Ibrahim, King of the Abbassides, when he went forth with his army against Arabia, riding on a great elephant. But God sent for his destruction the wild vultures of Babel, who cast balls of glowing fire upon that host and turned his pomp into wretchedness and the vileness of dust. As to the atambore which Alfonso described, that signifies that the hour of his desolation is approaching."

The Moorish cavaliers, as in duty bound, returned to the King and acquainted him with the prophetic words of the Faki. On hearing them he turned pale, and ejaculated : "By the God of my worship, let this your Al Faki tremble if he hath lied, for be sure that I will make of him a warning."

Shortly after this King Alfonso assembled his host, an innumerable multitude of foot-soldiers and more than eighty thousand cavalry, nearly thirty thousand of whom were Arabs. With this array he marched to the encounter with King Taxfin and his allies, and came face to face with him near Badajoz, among the groves and plains called Zalacca, about twelve miles from that city. The armies were divided by a river, and across this Taxfin sent an insulting message to Alfonso, bidding him either abjure the Christian faith or acknowledge himself his vassal. When Alfonso read this missive he cast it to the earth in great anger, and, turning haughtily to the envoy, said : "Go and bid Taxfin not to conceal himself in the battle, which if he do not, we shall see each other."

Certain circumstances affected the combat. Friday was the holy day of the Moslems, Saturday was the Sabbath of the Jews, of whom there were many in the Christian host, and Sunday that of the Christians, and Alfonso had already requested Taxfin that truce should be observed on these days, and the Moor had consented. But Alfonso considered himself justified in attacking at the hour of dawn on the Friday morning. He marshalled his host into two divisions, and set on. The Moorish King of Seville had asked his astrologer to cast a horoscope with the intention of discovering the fate of the day, and as this had been entirely unfavourable to the Moslems they were somewhat disheartened. But as they succeeded in withstanding Alfonso's first attack, the student of the stars cast another mystical diagram, and on this occasion found his prognostication more auspicious. The King of Seville, inspired by the favourable prophecy, sat down in his pavilion and, taking pen and parchment, dashed off the following verse, which he sent for the inspiration of his ally, Taxfin :

> God's anger on the Christian horde
> Sends cruel slaughter by thy sword,
> While favouring stars announce to thee
> And to thy Moslems victory !

Taxfin was greatly inspirited by these words, and rode up and down his ranks encouraging his men, but he had not much time to do so, for King Alfonso, heading a terrific charge, dashed down on him with all the mail-clad chivalry of Spanish Christendom. A sanguinary and murderous conflict ensued. The Moslems stood their ground bravely, but the heavy cavalry of the

Spaniards bore them down, and overwhelmed them on all sides. The Moorish allies of the Christian force now came into action, surrounding and hemming in the Arabs of Andalusia, and the Moslem chroniclers tell us that the darkness produced by that mass of men and horses was so great that those who fought could no longer see each other, and grappled hand to hand, as in an obscure night. At last Taxfin's forces began to retreat, and broke into disorderly rout, closely pressed by the Christian cavalry. The Moors of Seville alone stood their ground. Taxfin placed himself at the head of his reserve and, charging with great fury, threw his mounted columns directly at the pavilion of King Alfonso. This was but slightly defended, and easily fell a prey to the Moslems, with all its treasure. Alfonso, noting the advance of Taxfin, charged him in flank, and the two principal leaders were soon engaged in furious battle. The Moorish monarch rode among his men, exhorting them to constancy, and crying out that the reward of their valour would be the crown of paradise. As the result of his repeated charges the Christian host began to give way, and on the renewed attack of Taxfin's allies, who had before been beaten, fled in precipitate rout. Alfonso, seeing that all was lost, and accompanied by five hundred followers only, rode fast before the conquering Moors. It was with difficulty that he made his escape to the city of Toledo, where he arrived with only a hundred men.

From that day King Alfonso never regained heart, and some years later, on learning of the death of his son and the defeat of his people in battle with the infidel, he fell sick and died. So was the prophecy of the Faki fulfilled.

The Prince who Changed Crowns

The Prince who Changed Crowns

During the age-long struggle between the Gothic and Arab races in Spain many small kingdoms on both sides rose and fell, the names of which have long since been forgotten. Perhaps two hundred years after the infidels had gained a footing in the Peninsula, it chanced that in the central portion of the country there existed side by side two diminutive kingdoms, or rather principalities, the more northerly of which preserved its Spanish nationality with the most jealous care, while that which existed upon its borders was equally conservative in its Moslem prejudices. At this period the Spanish principality had at the head of its fortunes a prince of exceptional enlightenment and ability, Don Fernando. His training had naturally been of a kind which had led him to regard his Moslem neighbours with the profoundest distrust and dislike. They were, he was told by his instructors, a race of men lost to all humanity, deficient in honour, cruel, malicious, and revengeful—in short, it is not to be wondered at that, having the demerits of his Saracen neighbours so constantly dinned into his ears, the young Fernando began to regard them with the utmost repugnance.

The low range of hills which divided the two principalities rather assisted than hindered the constant raids which Moslem and Christian made upon each other's territory, as they constituted a description of No Man's Land, where the forces of either might be carefully marshalled for a lightning foray. In these raids Fernando himself occasionally took part, as it was thought necessary that the prince of a state which lived in a condition of almost constant warfare should be well acquainted with the practical side of military affairs. During one of these constantly recurring miniature invasions, the company which Fernando commanded had ridden far into Moorish territory without encountering any resistance, and, advancing in loose formation and without sufficient care, suddenly encountered an ambuscade of the enemy, who, taking it in flank, succeeded in penetrating its ranks and cutting them in two. The little band of Spaniards, thus separated, fled in opposite directions, and Fernando, accompanied by only a handful of followers, turned his horse's head in the direction of his own country and galloped out of the range of immediate danger.

The route which he was now forced to take to regain his own dominions necessitated his following a wide *détour*, and as he and his companions had already ridden far that day their horses shortly became so jaded that further progress was almost impossible. They also became aware, to their dismay, that the foremost of the enemy were now not far distant. In the dilemma in which they found themselves they resolved to sell their lives dearly, as befitted Christian knights, and they were about to dismount from their horses to seek a spot which might afford them some advantage in such a struggle when they beheld, some little way off, a building of rough stone standing on a little eminence. "There, if anywhere," said Fernando, "we shall be able to make a good defence. Let us secure that position and take full advantage of the shelter it offers us."

Spurring their beaten horses to a last effort, they soon gained the summit of the little hill. Dismounting, Fernando sought for the entrance to the rather dilapidated building, and having found it, was about to make his way inside, when he was surprised to see a man

The Prince who Changed Crowns

kneeling on its flagstones, engaged in earnest prayer. His long beard, his patched clothing, and his general appearance signified that he was a Moslem hermit, one of those who had retired from the haunts of men to practise his religious austerities in peace. Fernando was about to address him roughly and bid him begone, when the holy man, hearing the ring of his mailed foot upon the pavement, looked up and asked him what he required.

"Get you gone," said Fernando, "for we are about to defend this place to the last extremity against your infidel brethren."

The hermit smiled. "Young man," he said, "what possible defence can you hope to make in this poor place against the numbers which will shortly surround you? Your sword and that of your companions will be of little more avail than these poor walls, which, almost ruined as they are, would soon be beaten down. Trust me, there is a much better defence against the violence of man than either stone or steel."

"I know not of what you speak, old man," said Fernando, "but in those things which you deride, I, as a soldier, have been accustomed to place my trust."

"Alas," said the hermit, "that it should be so! Have you not been taught, young man, in your own country that God is a surer defence to those who trust Him than those vain material bulwarks which men of blood erect against one another's rage? Put your trust in God, I say, and He will be able to succour you, even through the least of His servants."

"Were it the God of the Christians of whom you speak," replied Fernando, "I would agree that your words were those of wisdom, but in the mouth of an unbeliever they have naught but a blasphemous ring."

"Sir Knight," said the hermit, "you are yet a young man, but as you grow older it will be given you to understand that God is the same in all lands, and that division of His personality is one of the fictions with which the Father of Lies seeks to make enmity between the righteous. Argue no longer, I pray you, but take heed to what I say. This remnant of stone is the last remaining turret of an ancient fortalice, beneath which extends a labyrinth of dungeons. Secrete yourselves speedily in the darkness of this labyrinth, I beg you, so that you may evade your pursuers and regain your own country after nightfall."

"Have a care, Don Fernando," cried one of the prince's comrades. "This infidel seeks to beguile us into a trap, where his countrymen will be able to murder us at their leisure."

"Not so," replied the prince, "for I can see that the mind of this good and holy man holds a better purpose toward us, and I willingly yield myself to his care. Lead the way, good father, to the hiding-place of which you speak." The hermit immediately requested the cavaliers to enter the building, and indicated to them a dark and sloping passage, down which they led their horses. They had scarcely had time to conceal themselves in the gloomy recesses to which it led when with a loud clamour the infidels who had been pursuing them rode up. Their leader challenged the hermit and asked him if he had observed any Christian knights pass that way. "Assuredly no Christian knights have *passed* this way, my son," replied the man of God; "go in peace." The Moslem captain with a grave salutation immediately remounted his horse, and the band swept on.

The hermit having entertained the Christian knights to

The Prince who Changed Crowns

the best of his poor resources, returned to them within a few hours and told them that darkness had now fallen. "You will now be able," he said, "to make a safe return to your own land."

"How can I reward you?" cried Fernando, whose generous heart had been deeply stirred by the old man's unaffected kindness.

"There is one way in which you can do so, young cavalier," said the recluse, "and that is by trying to form a better opinion of the men of my race."

"You ask a difficult thing," said the prince sadly, "for truth compels me to say that I have heard great evil of the Moors, and but little good."

"That is not surprising," said the hermit, with a smile, "since you will readily admit that you have not encountered them otherwise than with sword in hand or as prisoners whose hearts are burning with the bitterness of defeat. Open your mind, young man, or rather pray that its doors, until now closed, should be thrown wide to admit the rays of celestial wisdom. Seek for the best in your enemies, and believe me you will not fail to find it."

As he spoke, Fernando indeed felt as if the doors of his spirit, until now rusty with prejudice, had been unbarred. "I shall not forget your advice," he said, "for surely nothing evil can come from one so good and noble," and with a respectful gesture of farewell he mounted his horse and, followed by his companions, rode away.

He arrived safely in his capital in the early hours of the morning, and having bathed and refreshed himself, sought his audience chamber, where, surrounded by his anxious ministers, he told them of the adventure which had befallen him.

"Great has been your good fortune, your Majesty," said one of his advisers. "But for the services of this good man you would certainly now have been a captive in the citadel of your enemies. Surely few such spirits can reside in Moorish bodies."

"How so, señor?" replied the prince. "May it not be otherwise? When all is said and done, what do we know of the Moors, save that knowledge which is gained by constant strife with them? Would it not be well for us to strive to know them better?"

"What!" cried another councillor, "do we not know them for dogs and infidels, for perjured blasphemers and worshippers of false gods? Heaven forbid that we should have further converse with them than that of the herald, which serves to call us into the same field as they, so that we may bring our lances to bear upon their infidel bodies."

"These words seem to me neither good nor wise," said Fernando gently; "and I tell you, señors, that while riding home this morning I made a resolution to know those Moors better, even to travel into their country, study their institutions and their faith, and meet them as men rather than as enemies."

"Madness!" cried the Chancellor. "The rash vow of a young and inexperienced prince."

"That is not my opinion," replied Fernando, "but in order to avoid all unnecessary risks I have resolved to disguise myself as a Moslem. As you are aware, I have a perfect acquaintance with the Moorish tongue, and the manners and religious customs of our neighbours I know by report. I have taken this resolve, and am not to be dissuaded from it."

"Your Majesty's word is law," replied the Chancellor,

318

The Prince who Changed Crowns

who saw in the prince's resolve an opportunity for the extension of his personal power. Others of his suite did their best to turn aside Fernando's resolution by every argument in their power, but to no avail. His preparations were speedily made, and within three days of announcing his determination the prince, disguised as a Moslem of rank, set out by night for the frontiers of his enemies.

On entering their country he resolved to make in the first place for the capital, a town of considerable importance, on reaching which he dismounted from his Arab steed and put up at a *khan*, or public hostelry. Here he found himself in the company of travellers of all sorts and conditions. The merchant sat at the same table with the *mullah*, or priest, and the soldier shared his meal with the pilgrim. The first thing that Fernando noticed regarding these people was their great abstemiousness. They ate but little food, and drank not at all, unless of milk or water. The atmosphere of gravity prevalent in the inn surprised him. These sober, sallow-faced men sat, for the most part, with downcast eyes, speaking rarely, and without gesticulation, and in a low and decorous tone of voice. If asked a question, they did not answer at once, but appeared to cogitate upon their reply, which was invariably courteous and couched in formal but agreeable language. All their conduct seemed to be subservient to decency and dignity. Fernando noticed that they were spotless in their cleanliness. Not only was this so as regards their garments, but they were constantly performing ablutions, either in the inn itself during the stipulated hours of prayer, or in the magnificent public baths of the city.

On the other hand, the disguised prince could not but

see that these men were one and all within the grip of a powerful formalism, which had the effect of cramping and limiting their ideas, and which was only too painfully evident in their speech and manners. There seemed to be no room for individuality in their system of life. He entered into conversation with one of the shaven *mullahs*, who had retired into a corner the better to read his copy of the Koran. At first he evinced but little inclination to talk, but seeing that the prince wished to exchange ideas with him, he soon brought the conversation round to the especial point of Moslem law he was studying, upon which he split so many hairs that the hapless Fernando deeply regretted that he had ever approached him.

Fernando Makes Comparison

That night as Fernando lay in bed he summed up his impressions of the day.

"These people seem to me exceedingly formal and conventional," he thought, "but against that we have to place the garrulity and boisterousness of men of European race, their frequent lack of dignity and too great familiarity of manner. That *mullah*, too, was terribly long-winded, but have we not bores of our own, and in plenty? Is it not the case that in all parts of the world selfish introspection and scholarly pride frequently turn a man into a public nuisance? It seems to me that the great bulk of mankind merely acts in imitation of its fellows, and that only here and there does one meet with a person of any outstanding individuality."

When he arose next morning Fernando paid a visit to the great mosque of the city. It was the first time he

Fernando Makes Comparison

had entered a Moorish place of worship, and he was struck by the circumstance that the atmosphere which prevailed within it closely resembled that to be found in a Christian cathedral. The same hushed silence was distinctly noticeable. Here and there stood a *mullah*, or teacher, instructing his disciples in Mohammedan law and ritual, and this Fernando was rather pleased than otherwise to notice, as direct instruction in the tenets of the Christian faith was but seldom to be procured in the churches of his own country. Another thing he could not but observe was the manifest learning and erudition of the speakers. This seemed to him far in advance of the monkish accomplishments of his own priestly subjects, whose learning was of the most slender description, and but few of whom were able to write, and he was deeply interested to find that in an annexe to the mosque, which was fitted as a scrivenry or writing-room, a number of *mullahs*, old and young, sat at desks writing swiftly in the Arabic script and engaged in the multiplication of copies of the Koran and other works of a religious nature.

From the mosque Fernando speedily found his way to the university, and was soon lost in wonder at the rich intellectual life which flourished there. In one room a white-robed teacher was lecturing upon the practice of medicine with an acumen and ability he had never heard equalled. His knowledge of drugs and chemistry and of the properties of plants and herbs appeared to be both wide and exact, and when Fernando thought upon the wretched leeches to whom so many of the lives of his subjects annually paid forfeit he experienced a deep feeling of shame that these swarthy yet studious foreigners were so easily able to eclipse them in both theory and application. But he was acute enough to discern that the lecturer spoke of the medical art as a thing the principles of which were already fixed beyond the power of expansion. He spoke of experiment in the past tense, and all his references were to the great teachers of the old world, to Galen and Hippocrates, to Avicenna and to Rhazes. If he did chance to allude to the teachers of his own day, it was in rather an apologetic manner, and by no means in a complimentary sense. Antiquity was everything to him, and the tenets of the old masters of medicine appeared to him quite as sacred in their way as the words of the Prophet himself.

In an adjoining classroom Fernando lingered some time to listen to a professor of astrology. This ancient art had always held a certain fascination for him, and he was well aware that the Moors were among its greatest interpreters. The lecturer described at length the influences which the various planets had upon the destinies of man, the manner in which their conjunctions and oppositions affected human affairs, and the characters of persons born under certain astrological conditions. This science too appeared to him incapable of extension or fresh effort, and while hearkening to the speaker he found that though he heard much that his common sense told him was incapable of definite proof, he gleaned nothing of the nature of those planets themselves, their physical movement, or their scientific relation to the earth. In the geography classroom he found that instruction was based upon more modern lines. The works of Arab travellers who had journeyed extensively in Asia and Africa were touched upon. The conditions of life in distant countries of the world were discussed,

Fernando Makes Comparison

and as a general rule with much greater exactitude than in the European schools which he had visited, where fact was often subordinated to fancy and where the extraordinary was prized at a much higher rate than the probable.

Leaving the university, the court of which was filled to overflowing with scholars who appeared to be disputing on various phases of erudition, Fernando walked to the crowded market-place, a portion of which, he observed, was given over to the sale of manuscripts, and this part, he could not help noticing, was much better patronized than those where food-stuffs and wearing apparel were for sale. In the more open spaces jugglers and mountebanks, usually accompanied by performing animals, went through all sorts of gambols and antics. Here and there small knots of men discussed the more obscure points of the Koran or of Mohammedan law, while others sat in shady corners, lazily drinking sherbet or drowsing away the hot morning hours. In the booths which surrounded the market-place he saw various tradesmen at work—carpenters, smiths, sandal-makers, tailors—but he noticed that the efforts of these were of the most leisurely description, and that their tools were of a type much more antiquated than those in use among the tradesmen of his own country. The hand of time was indeed heavy upon the whole race. In some things it appeared to have made great advances, while in others it seemed to have retained the primitive ideas of the Dark Ages. Its progress seemed to have been made in the realm of thought alone, but even here everything was derivative and had reference to the experiments of an older age.

Strangely enough, however, Fernando felt that much

of this conservatism touched a responsive chord within his own nature.

"Are these people not right," he argued with himself, "when they let well alone, as the proverb says? If they have brought about a condition of things which suits them as a race, would it not be folly in them to embark upon a career of experiment which might prove wholly unsuitable to them? They seem reasonably happy and contented. Suppose a condition of affairs such as obtains within my own principality were suddenly to be forced upon them, would their happiness not be changed into wretchedness? It must be that long experience has taught them that their present manner of life is by far the most convenient for them. Can it be that their dislike of us arises from the great differences between our institutions and theirs? But, again, is it not possible that these things are very much on the surface? Their real natural sympathies and antipathies are, after all, very similar to our own. They are entirely dependent upon the changes of the seasons and upon the tillage of the earth for their food; they live constantly in fear of warfare; the same private troubles between man and man, between neighbour and neighbour, arise among them as among ourselves; they are subject to the rule of authority precisely as we are. The modifications of all these things are, after all, those of place and circumstance, nor is it possible for any one individual among them to break away from established custom, any more than it is in Spain. We do not differ from them in the salient things of life, but only in its surface details. Their religion teaches that the good are rewarded and the bad punished, that a man must be constant in his patriotic and domestic affections. After

Fernando Makes Comparison

all, had one of these brown men been reared in Spain, at the age of twenty years he would have been moved by the same prejudices as myself, and have become so like me in every particular as to be indistinguishable from an ordinary Spaniard."

Passing through one of the gates of the city, Fernando walked into the country. It very much resembled the rural portions of his own principality, except that it was cultivated with greater care. Here and there tiny, snow-white farm-steadings nestled in hollows, and from these streams of reapers and gleaners spread across the fields in every direction, for it was harvest-time. Fernando joined one of these groups, and was surprised to find that there was little difference between it and a similar party in Christian Spain. At intervals the work of garnering the grain was relaxed, and the reapers sat in a circle and listened to the music made by one of their number on the pipe, which possessed a strange melancholy of its own. Fernando found in them the same simple and easily satisfied disposition that he had discovered among his own peasantry. They shared their bread and cheese with him, and tendered him a draught of goat's milk from a large skin bottle, which he made shift to swallow with rather a wry face, for princes as a rule do not accustom themselves to the pungent odours of such a beverage. Thus refreshed, he passed on, walking slowly through the heat of the day, which was now well advanced, and resting every now and then beneath the shadows of the roadside trees.

He had advanced perhaps a mile and a half farther on when he came to a wide, open plain upon which he beheld a large body of Moorish cavalry performing military evolutions. His soldier's eye took in the scene with interest, and he was quick to see that the rapid movements of these lightly armed horsemen were greatly superior to those of his own heavily accoutred warriors. At the word of command the squadrons wheeled and charged with surprising unanimity and rapidity, and when the word was given to halt they did so on the instant, without scattering or losing the alignment of their ranks. The evolutions of one of the squadrons brought it quite close to where the prince was standing, and the officer in command, evidently regarding him as a pilgrim of sanctity, gave him a courteous salutation.

"I take it, reverend sir," he said, "from the evident pleasure with which you regard this scene, that you have once been a soldier yourself?"

"That is quite true," replied Fernando; "I was a soldier for many years, and saw a good deal of service in another part of the country; but war is no longer my business, and I do not, as I once did, cherish it for itself alone."

"But surely," said the soldier, "war is the only career to which a noble mind can turn? You are young, and have evidently left its ranks too early."

"Nay," rejoined the prince, "I am ready, if necessity enjoins, to take up the sword once more, but only in case of unrighteous invasion or to settle a grievous wrong. As I have said, I no longer desire war for its own sake."

"But," said the soldier, smiling, "you do not mean that we should be unprepared for attack? We know not the moment at which the rude and savage Christians from the north may send a multitude of warriors against us."

"Nor do they know, my friend, when we shall take it into our heads to make a foray into their lands," said Fernando.

Fernando Meets his ' Double '

" But," said the officer, "if we were to do so, it would only be as a protective measure after all, for we are well aware that they will never become reconciled to us."

" Have we ever tried to discover that ? " asked Fernando.

" I fear not. We have certainly made treaties with them, but these seem to have been made for the very purpose of being broken."

"Yes," said the officer, his lip curling, "they are treacherous dogs, these Spaniards, upon whose word no honest man can rely. They have broken treaty after treaty."

" If I'm not mistaken," said Fernando, "we have done the same, only our rulers take extraordinary care that the people shall not be acquainted with the full measure of our national dishonesties, but shall be told that it was necessary to act in such and such a manner because of the untrustworthy nature of our enemies. May I ask, sir, if you have ever travelled in Christian Spain, or have known other Christians than those whom you may have chanced to take as prisoners ? "

The cavalryman shook his head. "Now I come to think of it," he said, " I have crossed swords with more Spaniards than I have bandied words with, but I do not doubt, as you imply, that there are noble spirits among that people, for I know out of my own experience that they are stout men of war, and a brave soldier can scarcely be other than an honourable man. But you will excuse me, sir ; I can remain no longer. In the name of God, I wish you a pleasant journey."

Fernndo Meets his " Double "

Fernando passed on his way, and this day in his wanderings may be taken as representative of many another. For three months he wandered through the Moorish land, studying its institutions and its people at first hand, and gleaning a practical insight into the national characteristics. At the end of that time he had conceived such a high opinion of his one-time foes that it was with heartfelt sorrow that he turned his steps northward to the borders of his own principality. Loath to cross them, he resolved to spend the night at a small *khan* on the Moorish side of the hills. It was a poor place, but beautifully situated at the entrance to a peaceful little valley. Giving his horse to the white-robed ostler, he entered. To his utter amazement, the first person he encountered was a young man who so closely resembled himself that he started back in surprise and dismay, for there was not a lineament in the stranger's countenance which was not mirrored in his own. The young man thus confronted also halted abruptly, and stared at his living counterpart; then a smile broke over his pleasant face, and he said, with a laugh: "I see, sir, you are as surprised as myself, but I hope you are not angry that God has made us so alike, for I have heard that people who closely resemble one another are apt to cherish a mutual distrust."

"There is small danger of that, friend," said Fernando, "for if God has made our minds as like each other as He has fashioned our bodies, I am convinced that you are of a liberal and unconventional disposition," and, laughing heartily, he indicated a table. "It would be fitting," he continued, "that we should break bread together."

"Agreed!" cried the other; "I accept your invitation with all the goodwill in the world." And, seating themselves at the rough board, the two young men were soon engaged in an animated conversation. Much as they had been surprised at the physical resemblance between them, they were even more astonished at the close similarity they bore to one another in taste and disposition. For hours they sat in close discussion. At last the stranger said : "I feel as if we had known each other for a lifetime, and as I am certain that I can trust you thoroughly, I will reveal to you my secret. Know then that I am Muza, the prince of this country, and that I am even now returned from a prolonged journey in the land of the Christians, whose character and customs it had long been my desire to study."

"I am indeed honoured by your Majesty's condescension and confidence," replied Fernando, "and you may rest assured that your secret will remain inviolate with me. But may I ask what opinion you formed of the inhabitants of Christian Spain during your sojourn among them ?"

"Such a high opinion," replied Muza, "that it is with the greatest regret that I quit their country, for I find among them a spirit so much more in consonance with my own than that of my native subjects that I solemnly assure you I had much rather rule over them than over my own people."

"Have then your wish, noble Muza," said Fernando, rising, "for I am none other than Fernando, prince of the Christians, who, impelled by a similar desire, has been travelling in your dominions, and who has conceived such a strong predilection for the character and customs of its people that he asks nothing better than to be permitted to guide their destinies. That I am what I represent myself to be you may know by this token," and, searching beneath his burnous, Fernando drew out a gold chain, from which was suspended his royal signet. "There is, so far as I can see," he continued, "but one possible bar to our compact, and that is the difference between our religions."

"Nay, Fernando," said Muza, with uplifted hands, "I find no difficulty in that, for, as I understand the matter, the difference is merely one of exteriors. The inward spirit of our faiths is the same, and it is only in their outward manifestations that they present any divergency. Both spring from the one God, Who designed them for the uses of differently constituted races, and if you agree with me that this is so, there should be no greater difficulty in our embracing the religions of each other's people than in accepting their customs."

"I heartily agree," replied Fernando, "but what I fear is that we shall not be able to convince our respective peoples of the purity of our motives. They certainly must not share our secret."

"Our great safeguard," said Muza, "is the extraordinary resemblance between us, but it will be necessary that we should instruct each other in our past histories, and in the intricacies of our personal affairs, in order that ignorance of these may not give rise to suspicion."

"You speak like a wise man," rejoined Fernando; "let us address ourselves to this business at once."

Far into the night the two young princes sat initiating each other into the intimacies of their respective national diplomacies and personal relationships, and at last, when morning broke, they parted with every mark of mutual esteem, mounted their horses, and rode off, Fernando to the capital of the Moor, Muza to that of the Christian. But ere they parted they agreed to meet at the inn where they had first forgathered at least once in three months, in order to discuss any eventualities which might arise.

Three months passed rapidly, and, prompt to the day, the two young rulers met once more at the inn. There was a noticeable stiffness in the manner of their greeting.

" And how fare you, noble Muza, in the kingdom of my fathers?" asked Fernando.

" Alas! your Majesty," replied Muza, " I am constrained to say that I fare but ill. Every day your advisers present to me new schemes of aggression against my late kingdom to which I can give no manner of countenance, and they upbraid me bitterly with what they are pleased to call my disloyalty."

" Precisely the same thing has happened to myself," said Fernando, "and may I say, with all due regard to the race from which you spring, that they do not compare in liberality of outlook with my own, that they are extremely conservative, and difficult of comprehension!"

" On the other hand," said Muza, " I find your people much too active and unruly, and I do not encounter the same implicit obedience to which I have hitherto been accustomed. If I may say so, there is a want of dignity——"

" I find some of my personal relations awkward too," groaned Fernando; "your matrimonial arrangements, for example."

" And your lack of the same," replied Muza.

" On the whole I think——" said Fernando.

" I fully agree," replied Muza.

" If we put the matter in a nutshell," remarked Fernando, " it is better for a man—even a liberal-minded one—

to remain in the bosom of his own people, for no matter how broad his views may be, among strangers he must constantly be doomed to encounter much which will tend to strengthen his prejudices against them and create odious comparisons and regrets."

"Once more I agree," said Muza. "When once the novelty wears off——"

"Exactly," responded Fernando. "After all, what country can compare with that in which one has been born?"

So the two princes parted, each to take his way to his native land. But, despite the threats and entreaties of their advisers, neither of them would ever again consent to make war upon the dominions of the other, and it was even hinted by disgruntled and badly disposed persons that Fernando and Muza met occasionally on their common frontiers for the sole purpose of settling difficulties which had arisen between their respective states—an unnatural proceeding which they avowed was bound sooner or later to end in political disaster.

CHAPTER XII : TALES OF SPANISH MAGIC AND SORCERY

SPAIN seems to have been regarded by the other countries of Western Europe as the special abode of superstition, sorcery, and magic, probably because of the notoriety given to the discoveries of the Moorish alchemists, the first scientists in Europe. But with the coming of the Inquisition a marked and natural falling off is noticeable in the prevalence of occult belief, for anything which in the least tended to heresy was repressed in the most rigid manner by that illiberal institution. In this way much of the folk-lore and peasant belief of Spain, many fascinating legends, and many a curious custom have been lost, never to be recovered. The Brothers, in their zeal for the purity of their Church, banished not only the witch, the sorcerer, and the demon from Spain, but also the innocent fairy, the spirits of wood and wold, and those household familiars which harm no one, but assist the housewife and the dairymaid.

The first information we receive that the authorities intended a campaign against the whole demonhood, good and evil, of Spain is contained in a work by Alfonso de Speria, a Castilian Franciscan, who wrote, about 1458 or 1460, a work specially directed against heretics and unbelievers, in which he gives a chapter on those popular beliefs which were derived from ancient pagan practices. The belief in witches, whom he calls *xurguine* (*jurguia*) or *bruxe*, seems to have been imported from Dauphiné or Gascony, where, he tells us, they abounded. They were, he says, wont to assemble at night in great numbers on a high tableland, carrying candles with them, for the purpose of worshipping Satan, who appeared to them in the form of a boar, rather than in that of the he-goat in which he so frequently manifested himself in other localities.

Llorente, in his *History of the Inquisition in Spain*, states that the first *auto-de-fé* against sorcery was held at Calabarra in 1507, when thirty women charged with witchcraft by the Inquisition were burnt. In the first treatise on Spanish sorcery, that of Martin de Castanaga, a Franciscan monk (1529), we learn that Navarre was regarded as the motherland of Spanish witchcraft, and that that province sent many 'missionaries' to Aragon to convert its women to sorcery. But we find that the Spanish theologians of the sixteenth century were so much more enlightened than those of other countries that they admitted that witchcraft was merely a delusion, and the punishment they meted out to those who believed in it was inflicted in respect that the belief, erroneous though it was, was contrary to the tenets of the Church. Pedro de Valentin, in a treatise on the subject (1610), entirely adopts the opinion that the acts confessed to by the witches were imaginary. He attributed them partly to the manner in which the examinations were carried out, and to the desire of the ignorant people examined to escape by saying what seemed to please their persecutors, and partly to the effect of the ointments and draughts which they had been taught to use, which were composed of ingredients that produced sleep and acted upon the imagination and the mental faculties.

The Religion of Witchcraft

This view is very generally held at the present time as accounting for the phenomena of witchcraft. But the researches of Charles Godfrey Leland, Miss M. A. Murray, and others, seem to indicate that the cult of witchcraft is by no means a thing of the imagination. The last-named writer, indeed, claims that it is the detritus of an ancient pagan faith surviving into modern times, having a priesthood and well-defined ritual of its own, and in a measure conserving the practice of child-sacrifice.

There can be little doubt that this conception of witch-craft is the correct one. In the records of the caste there are numerous proofs that it had a definite ritual and an established priesthood, and that imagination played but a small part in shaping the belief of the adherents of the cult.[1]

The Story of Dr Torralva

Spain had not in the sixteenth century ceased to be celebrated for its magicians, who still retained a modicum of the occult philosophy of the Moorish doctors of Toledo and Granada. Perhaps the most celebrated of these comparatively modern masters of magic was Doctor Eugenio Torralva, physician to the family of the Admiral of Castile. Educated at Rome, he early became a pronounced sceptic, and formed an intimacy with a certain Master Alfonso, a man who, after changing his Jewish faith for Islam, and that again for Christianity, had at last become a free-thinker. Another evil companion was a Dominican monk called Brother Pietro, who told Torralva that he had in his service a good angel called Zequiel, who had no equal in the spiritual world as a seer, and was besides of such a disinterested

[1] The reader who wishes to follow this phase of the subject further should consult Miss M. A. Murray's recent articles in *Man*.

temperament that he served only those who had complete confidence in him and deserved his attachment.

All this excited Torralva's curiosity to an unbounded degree. He was one of those people, fortunate or otherwise, in whom the love of mystery has been deeply implanted, and when Pietro generously proposed to resign his familiar spirit to his friend's keeping he eagerly accepted the offer. Nor did Zequiel himself offer any opposition to this change of master, and, appearing at the summons of Pietro, assured Torralva that he would follow his service as long as he lived, and wherever he was obliged to go. There was nothing very startling in the appearance of the spirit, who was dressed in a flesh-coloured habit and black cloak, and had the appearance of a young man with an abundance of fair hair.

From this time onward Zequiel appeared to Torralva at every change of the moon, and as often as the physician required his services, which was generally for the purpose of transporting him in a short space of time to distant places. Sometimes the spirit assumed the appearance of a hermit, at others that of a traveller, and even accompanied his master to church, from which circumstance Torralva concluded that he was a beneficent and Christian-minded spirit. But, alas! Dr Torralva was to find, like many another, that attendance at the sacred edifice is not necessarily a guarantee of piety.

For many years Torralva continued to reside in Italy, but in the year 1502 he felt a strong desire to return to the land of his birth. He did so, but seems to have made Rome his headquarters once more in the following year, placing himself under the protection of his old patron, the Bishop of Volterra, now become a cardinal. The influence this connexion brought him proved of the greatest service to him, and he soon rose to high repute for his skill in medicine. But neither the pious cardinal nor any of the other distinguished patients who sought his aid knew that he drew practically all his medical knowledge from his unseen famulus, who taught him the secret virtues of young plants, with which other physicians were not acquainted. Zequiel, however, was untainted by the love of lucre ; for when his master pocketed those 'thumping' fees to which all good physicians aspire the spirit rebuked him, telling him that since he had received his knowledge for nothing he ought to impart it gratuitously. On the other hand, did the doctor require funds, he never failed to find a supply of money in his private apartment, which he knew implicitly must have been placed there by his familiar.

Torralva returned to Spain in 1510, and lived for some time at the Court of Ferdinand the Catholic. One day Zequiel confided to him that the King would shortly receive some very disagreeable news. Torralva at once communicated this piece of intelligence to Ximenes de Cisneros, Archbishop of Toledo, and to the Grande Capitan, Gonzalvo Hernández de Cordova. On the same day a courier arrived from Africa bearing dispatches which informed his Majesty that an expedition against the Moors had met with disaster, and that its commander, Don Garcia de Toledo, son of the Duke of Alva, had been slain.

When in Rome it appears that Torralva had been so indiscreet as to summon Zequiel to appear before his patron, Cardinal Volterra, who now, hearing of the manner in which his *protégé* had 'prophesied' the disaster to the Spanish arms, acquainted the Archbishop of Toledo with the means by which the doctor had received intelligence of the defeat. Torralva, ignorant of this, continued in his forecasts of political and other events, and soon found his reputation as a seer greatly enhanced. Among others who consulted him was the Cardinal of Santa Cruz, to whom a certain Donna Rosales had complained that her nights were disturbed by a frightful phantom, which appeared in the form of a murdered man. Her physician, Morales, had watched at night with the lady, but although she had pointed out the precise spot where the grisly vision took its stand, he could discern nothing.

Torralva accompanied Morales to the lady's house, and, seated in an ante-chamber, they heard her cry of alarm about an hour after midnight. Entering her apartment, Morales again confessed his inability to see the apparition, but Torralva, who was better acquainted with the spiritual world, perceived a figure resembling a dead man, behind which appeared a shadowy female form. "What dost thou seek here?" he inquired, in a firm voice, whereupon the foremost spirit replied: "I seek a treasure," and immediately vanished. Torralva consulted Zequiel upon the subject, and upon his advice the cellars of the house were dug up, whereupon the corpse of a man who had been stabbed to death with a poignard was discovered, and upon its receiving Christian burial the visitations ceased.

Among Torralva's intimate friends was one Don Diego de Zuñiga, a relative of the Duke of Bejar, and brother of Don Antonio, Grand Prior of the Order of St John in Castile. Zuñiga had consulted the learned doctor as

The Story of Dr Torralva

to how he could gain money at play by magical means, and Torralva informed him that this could be accomplished by writing certain characters on paper, using for ink the blood of a bat. This charm Torralva advised him to wear about his neck, so that he might experience good luck at the gaming-table.

In 1520 Torralva went once more to Rome. Ere he left Spain he told Zuñiga that he would be able to travel there astride a broomstick, the course of which would be guided by a cloud of fire. On his arrival at Rome he interviewed Cardinal Volterra, and the Grand Prior of the Order of St John, who earnestly begged him to abandon all commerce with his familiar spirit. Because of their exhortations, Torralva requested Zequiel to leave his service, but met with a stern refusal. The spirit, however, advised him to return to Spain, assuring him that he would obtain the place of physician to the Infanta Eleanora, Queen-Dowager of Portugal, and later consort of Francis I of France. Acting upon this counsel, Torralva sailed once more for the land of his birth, and obtained the promised appointment.

In 1525 an incident occurred which greatly enhanced Torralva's celebrity as a seer. On the 5th of May of that year Zequiel assured him that the troops of the Emperor would take Rome on the following day. Torralva desired the spirit to carry him to Rome so that he might witness this great event with his own eyes. Zequiel gave him a stick full of knots, and commanded him to shut his eyes. Torralva obeyed the request of the famulus, and when after a space the spirit told him to open his eyes once more, he found himself in Rome, standing on a high tower. The hour was midnight, and when day dawned he duly witnessed the terrible events which followed—the death of the Constable of Bourbon, the flight of the Pope into the Castle of St Angelo, the slaughter of the citizens, and the wild riot of the conquerors. Returning to Valladolid by the same means as that by which he had come, Torralva immediately made public all he had seen, and when, a week or so later, news arrived of the capture and sack of Rome, the Court of Spain was very naturally filled with unbounded surprise.

Many persons of high rank had been accomplices of the gifted doctor in his practice of the black art, and one of these, in a fit of remorse, notified the Holy Inquisition of his dealings with the supernatural. Zuñiga too, who had benefited so greatly by the occult knowledge of Torralva, now turned against him, and denounced him to the Holy Office of Cuença, which had him arrested and cast into prison. The terrified magician immediately confessed all his doings with Zequiel, whom he persisted in regarding as a beneficent spirit, and penned no less than eight declarations of his dealings with the supernatural, some of which contradicted statements made in others in a most ludicrous manner. In view of their unsatisfactory nature, the unhappy necromancer was put to the torture, and an admission of the demonic nature of his familiar was quickly extracted from him. In March 1529 the Inquisitors suspended his process for a year, a common practice of the Inquisition, which thus attempted to wear its victims down. But, to the dismay of Torralva, a new witness made his appearance, who testified that in his early days at Rome the imprisoned medico was prone to indulgence in occult arts, so that in January 1530 Torralva was once more put upon his

Moorish Magic

trial. The Inquisition appointed two learned theologians to labour for his conversion, to whom Torralva promised amendment in everything, except the renunciation of the evil spirit with whom he had been associated for so long, assuring his mentors that he had not the power to dismiss Zequiel. At length, on his making a pretence to cast off his familiar and abjure his heresies, he was released, and entered the service of the Admiral of Castile, who had employed all his influence to obtain a pardon for him. Immortalized in the pages of *Don Quixote*, he remains for all time the archetype of the Spanish magician of the sixteenth century.

Moorish Magic

By no race was the practice of the occult arts studied with such perseverance as by the Moors of Spain, and it is strange indeed that only fragmentary notices of their works in this respect remain to us. The statement that they were famous for magical and alchemical studies is reiterated by numerous European historians, but the majority of these have refrained from any description of their methods, and the Moors themselves have left so few undoubted memorials of their labours in this direction that we remain in considerable ignorance of the trend of their efforts, so that if we desire any knowledge upon this most recondite subject we must perforce collect it painfully from the fragmentary notices of it in contemporary European and Arabic literature.

The first name of importance which we encounter in the broken annals of Moorish occultism is a great one—that of the famous Geber, who flourished about 720–750, and who is reported to have penned upward of five hundred works upon the philosopher's stone and the elixir of life. In common with his fellow-alchemists, he appears to have failed signally in his search for those marvellous elements, but if he was unable to point the way to immortal life and boundless wealth, he is said to have given mankind the nitrate of silver, corrosive sublimate, and nitric acid. He believed that a preparation of gold would heal all diseases in both animals and plants, as well as in human beings, and that all metals were in a condition of chronic sickness in so far that they had departed from their natural and original state of gold. His works, all of which are in Latin, are not considered authentic, but his *Summa Perfectionis*, a manual for the alchemical student, has frequently been translated.

The Moorish alchemists taught that all metals are composed of varying proportions of mercury and sulphur. They laboured strenuously to multiply drugs out of the various mixtures and reactions of the few chemicals at their disposal, but although they believed in the theory of transmutation of metals they did not strive to effect it. It belonged to their creed rather than to their practice. They were a school of scientific artisans and experimentalists, first and last. They probably owed their alchemical knowledge to Byzantium, which in turn had received it from Egypt; or it may be that the Arabs drew their scientific inspiration at first hand from the land of the Nile, where the 'great art' of alchemy undoubtedly had its birth.

Astrology

Astrology was also an important branch of occult study with the Moors of Spain, whose consideration of it greatly assisted the science of mathematics, especially

The Moors and Astrology

that branch of it which still retains its Arabic name—
algebra (*al* = the, *jabara* = to set, compute). It is probable that the Arabs first received an insight into the
practice of foretelling events by the position of the planets
at a given time from the Chaldeans, who undoubtedly
were its earliest students. References to astrology are
plentifully encountered in Spanish story, as the reader
will have observed. But high as it stood in the estima-
tion of the Moorish sages, it was still subservient to the
grander and more mysterious art of magic, whereby
the spirits of the air could be forced to do the will of
the magus, and carry out his behests in four elements.
Most unfortunately, we are almost entirely ignorant of
the tenets of Moorish magic, owing probably to the
circumstance that it was averse to the spirit of Islam.
But we know that it was founded upon Alexandrian
magic, and therefore recognized the principles of that
art as laid down by the great Hermes Trismegistus,
who was none other than the Egyptian Thoth, the god
of writing, computation, and wisdom.

About the end of the tenth century the learned men of
Europe began to resort to Spain for the purpose of
studying the arts, occult and otherwise. Among the
first to do so was Gerbert, afterward Pope Sylvester II,
who spent several years in Cordova, and who introduced
into Christendom the knowledge of the Arabic numerals
and the no less useful art of clock-making. Strange
that he did not apply his knowledge of the one
to the other, and that even to-day our timepieces are
burdened with the old and cumbrous Roman numerals!
William of Malmesbury assures us that Gerbert made
many discoveries of treasure through the art of necromancy, and relates how he visited a magnificent

343

subterranean palace, which, though dazzling to the sight, would not remain when its splendours were subjected to the test of human touch. Ignorant Europe took Gerbert's mathematical diagrams for magical signs, and his occult reputation increased as his moral character withered. It was said that the Devil had promised him that he should not die until he had celebrated high mass at Jerusalem. One day Gerbert celebrated his office in the Church of the Holy Cross of Jerusalem at Rome, and, feeling ill, asked where he was, observed the *double entendre* of the Evil One, and expired. Such was the tale that benighted ignorance cast round the memory of this single-minded and enlightened man, much in the same spirit as it bedevilled the recollections of our own Michael Scot and Roger Bacon.

The Dean of Santiago

In the *Conde Lucanor*, a Spanish collection of tales and homilies of the fourteenth century, already alluded to, is a story of the Dean of Santiago, who went to Illan, a magician of Toledo, to be instructed in necromancy. The magus raised a difficulty, saying that as the Dean was a man of influence, and would attain a high position, he would probably forget all past obligations. The Dean, however, protested that no matter to what eminence he attained he would not fail to remember and assist his former friends, and particularly his tutor in things supernatural. Satisfied with the churchman's promises, the necromancer led his pupil to a remote apartment, first requesting his housekeeper to purchase some partridges for supper, but not to cook them until she had definite orders to do so.

The Dean of Santiago

When the Dean and his instructor had settled themselves to the business before them, they were interrupted in their labours by a messenger, who came to inform the Dean that his uncle, the Archbishop, had summoned him to his death-bed. Being unwilling, however, to forgo the instruction he was about to receive, he excused himself from the duty. Four days later, another messenger arrived, informing the Dean of the Archbishop's death, and later he learned that he had been appointed Archbishop in his uncle's place. On hearing this, Illan requested the vacant deanery for his son. But the new Archbishop preferred his own brother, inviting, however, Illan and his son to accompany him to his see. Later the deanery became vacant once more, and once again the magician begged that his son might be appointed to it. But the Archbishop refused his suit, in favour of one of his own uncles. Two years later the Archbishop became a cardinal, and was summoned to Rome, with liberty to appoint his successor in the see. Once more Illan was disappointed. At length the Cardinal was elected Pope, and Illan, who had accompanied him to Rome, reminded him that he had now no excuse for not fulfilling the promises he had so often made to him. The Pope, in anger, threatened to have Illan cast into prison and starved as a heretic and sorcerer. "Ingrate!" cried the incensed magician, "since you would thus starve me, I must perforce fall back upon the partridges I ordered for to-night's supper."

With these words he waved his wand, and called to his housekeeper to prepare the birds. Instantly the Dean found himself once more in Toledo, still Dean of Santiago, for, indeed, the years he had spent as Archbishop, Cardinal, and Pope were illusory, and had existed only in his imagination at the suggestion of the magus. This was the means the sage had taken to test his character, before committing himself to his hands, and so crestfallen was the churchman that he had nothing to reply to the reproaches of Illan, who sent him off without permitting him to sup upon the partridges!

It is strange that physicians and priests figure most notably as the heroes of Spanish magical story—strange, until we reflect upon the manner in which the learned classes were regarded by an illiterate and illiberal commonalty. Torquemada tells a story of a youth of his acquaintance, a young man of great ability, who was afterward physician to the Emperor Charles V. When he was a student at Guadalupe, and was travelling to Granada, he was invited by a traveller, dressed in the garments of a churchman, whom he had obliged in some manner, to mount behind him on his horse, and he would carry him to his destination. The horse seemed a sorry jade, unable to carry the weight of two able-bodied men, and at first the student refused the mount, but, on pressure, at length accepted a seat behind the seeming ecclesiastic. The horseman requested his companion not to fall asleep in the saddle, and they jogged on, without any appearance of their going at an extraordinary rate. At daybreak, to the student's surprise, he found himself near the city of Granada, where the horseman left him, marvelling that the distance between two places so widely separated could have been covered in a single night.

Spectres and Apparitions

As might be imagined, the strong vein of superstition in the Spanish character, if subdued to some extent by

Spectres and Apparitions

the harsh dictates of the Holy Office, yet rose triumphant in other spheres of occult belief. We find, for example, a widely diffused belief in the power of the dead to return to the scenes of previous existence, and this superstition is well illustrated by a weird passage in the thrilling and mysterious pages of Goulart, who in his *Trésor des Histoires admirables*[1] knows well how to mingle shadows with the colours on his palette.

He tells us how Juan Vasquez Ayala and two other young Spaniards, on their way to a French university, were unable to find suitable accommodation at a certain village where they had halted for the night, and were obliged to take shelter in a deserted house, the reputation of which as a haunted vicinity had flourished for a considerable time among the villagers.

The young men made the best of matters, borrowed articles of furniture from several neighbouring houses, and resolved to give a warm reception to any supernatural visitant who should have a mind to pay them a call. But on the first night of their occupancy they had scarcely fallen asleep when they were awakened by a noise as of clanking chains, which seemed to proceed from the lower regions of their temporary dwelling.

Absolutely fearless, young Ayala leaped from his bed and, donning his clothes, sallied downstairs in search of the cause of the clamour which had awakened himself and his comrades. In one hand he carried his drawn sword, in the other a lighted candle, and on coming to a door which led to the courtyard of the house he perceived a dreadful spectre—a grisly skeleton, standing in the entrance. The grim apparition which confronted him was loaded with chains, which clanked with a doom-

[1] T. i, p. 543.

ful and melancholy sound on the ears of the gallant young student, who, however, undismayed by the spectacle before him, advanced the point of his sword and demanded the intruder's reason for disturbing his rest. The phantom waved its arms, shook its bony head, and beckoned with its hand, as if asking Ayala to follow it. The student expressed his willingness to do so, on which the ghost commenced to descend a flight of steps, dragging its legs as it went like a man whose limbs were weighted with iron shackles. Ayala followed fearlessly, but as he advanced his candle suddenly flickered and went out, a circumstance which did little to reinforce his courage. "Hold!" he called to the phantom. "You perceive my candle has gone out. If you will wait till I relight it, I shall return in a moment."

Rushing to a light which burned in the hall, he relit his candle, and returned to the spot where he had left the apparition. He entered the garden, where he saw a well, close by which he perceived the ghost, which signed to him to continue his progress, and having gone a little way forward, vanished.

Puzzled, the student returned to his apartment, and told his comrades to accompany him to the garden, but search as they might, nothing could they find. Next day they reported what had occurred to the *alcalde* of the village, who had the garden examined, with the result that immediately beneath the spot where the phantom had disappeared a skeleton was exhumed, loaded with chains. When proper burial had been given to the remains the noises in the house abruptly ceased, but the adventure proved too much for the superstitious Spaniards, who returned home abruptly, without fulfilling the object of their journey.

Spectres and Apparitions

This tale is a capital example of the typical ghost story in its earliest phase. I will not descant upon it here, as a book on Spanish romance and legend is scarcely the place for a disquisition on the occult. But we are learning, slowly and painfully perhaps, to regard these matters from another point of view than our Victorian grandfathers, whose materialism pooh-poohed the supernatural without trying to account for it. In any case I am one of those who believe in it and who desire to believe in it, so that the reflections of such a biased person are perhaps better dispensed with.

Torquemada tells a gruesome story of one Antonio Costilla, a Spanish gentleman, who one day left his mansion, well mounted, on a matter of personal business. When he had ridden several leagues, night suddenly fell, and he resolved to return to his home, but to his dismay he was overtaken by the darkness, and seeing a light ahead rode his horse at a walk in its direction. He saw that it proceeded from a small hermitage, and, dismounting, he entered the little chapel and engaged in prayer. As his eyes became accustomed to the darkness, he saw that he was not alone, for the hermitage was occupied by three persons, who lay upon the ground, wrapped in black mantles. They did not address him, but lay regarding him with wild, melancholy eyes. Terrified, he knew not by what, he leaped into the saddle and rode off. In a little while the moon shone out, and showed him the three men whom he thought he had left in the chapel riding a little in front of him on black horses. In order to avoid them, he turned down a by-path, but to his horror still observed them riding a few paces ahead. Spurring madly on, yet always preceded by those whom he desired to avoid, he came in time to the gate of his own house, where he dismounted, and led his horse into the courtyard—only to find there the three cloaked figures awaiting him. He rushed into the house, and entered his wife's apartment, calling for help. Instantly the entire household came to his assistance, but although he screamed loudly that the three fiends or apparitions stood by the couch on which he had thrown himself, they were invisible to all others. A few days later the wretched Costilla died, maintaining to the last that three forms with glaring eyes stood over his bed, menacing him with frightful gestures.

Pity it is that our knowledge of the supernatural as manifested in Spain is so slight and fragmentary. But the dread of the sorcerer's fate was heavy upon the people, and the fear of torture by rack or fire successfully banished witch, wizard, fay, and phantom from the fields and cities of the Peninsula.

CHAPTER XIII : HUMOROUS ROMANCES OF SPAIN

Cervantes, the bold metal of thy lance
Shatters the crystal turrets of Romance ;
Down falls the wreck in ruin most immense
Upon the dreary plains of common sense.

L. S.

Cervantes' "Don Quixote"

CERVANTES was one of the world's great satirists, a man gifted with a keen and peculiar sense of the ridiculous. He would himself have been the first to laugh at those modern critics who professed to see in him a great poet, and indeed, at the end of his days, when he assessed his life's work in his mock-heroic *Voyage to Parnassus*, he admitted that he had not the poetic gift. That he had a golden imagination is obvious to anyone who cares to read his *Galatea*, imitative as it is, and *Don Quixote* overflows with imagination and invention, although certain later passages of the wondrous satire are extremely reminiscent of some of its earlier pages.

To me *Don Quixote* has always seemed one of the most precious and curious of books, but probably for very different reasons from those by which it makes its appeal to the majority of people, for it is because of the information it affords concerning romantic literature and customs that I treasure it most. Where the satire is really legitimate I revel in the fun as much as it is possible for anyone to do, but I feel that many of its passages are rather shabbily iconoclastic, and that some of its strictures are levelled not only against the absurdities of chivalric extravagance, but against the whole spirit and structure of romance. It had been well, too,

351

for Cervantes had he confined himself entirely to the satiric vein, for when he essays to employ the very literary vehicle at which he chiefly scoffed he frequently becomes more maudlin—that is the only word for it—than the most sentimental writers against whom he girds. His shepherds and shepherdesses and his runaway nuns are long-winded and pedantic, and he was indeed badly bitten by that tiresome Arcadian phase in European literature which culminated in the prose pastoral, which had its roots in false conventions and employed as its *mise en scène* an atmosphere of sham rural felicity. Sannazaro, in his *Arcadia*, had indeed piped the tune to which Cervantes danced for many a day ere his own strong common sense showed him the fatuity of the models which he followed. The author of the *Pastor de Filida*, Luiz Galvez de Montalvo, was his own close friend, and there is every evidence that he made wholesale raids upon the distinctly minor efforts of such poetasters as Hebrao and Alonso Perez. The works of the men who composed this school of pseudo-Arcadianism had none of the charm of the delightful canvases of Watteau and Fragonard, silk-coated and satin-gowned though their shepherds and shepherdesses be. The country of the Spanish pastoral had a background of pasteboard scenery, and theatrical effects of lighting flashed across its stage. It was peopled by bores of the most intolerable description, who, instead of looking after their live stock, as they were paid to do, wearied each other and the wretched traveller who was unhappy enough to encounter them with their amorous bellowings and interminable tales of misfortune. Little wonder that the native good sense of Cervantes recoiled later from this unworthy and unmanly nonsense. But it is extraordinary that although he meted out such merciless treatment to chivalric romance, he still retained a weakness for the follies of Arcady, from which, to the last, he was unable to free himself.

The circumstances of Cervantes' career undoubtedly assisted him to discipline his ideas. As a collector of taxes he had, perforce, to come into contact with the seamy side of life, and much of his time was spent in the Bohemian atmosphere of inns, where he was compelled to lodge while he worked the district allotted to him. In these circumstances and in these places he encountered men and women of flesh and blood, and came up against the iron wall of hard, solid reality. Such an experience is undoubtedly most valuable to a man of romantic or imaginative temperament, gifted with creative ability. It tempers his natural capacities and enlarges his views. Doubtless Cervantes, when he first went his rounds, had been in the habit of regaling his fellow-travellers in the *posadas* in which he sojourned with high-falutin stories of errant shepherds and wandering shepherdesses. We can imagine the degree of amusement with which the rough muleteer, the blunt soldier, and the travelling quack would greet those sallies. The criticism of such people is not strained—it is annihilating! Can we doubt that the laughter with which his earlier rhapsodies were received in company of this sort blew away the fantastic cobwebs from Cervantes' brain?

I have already indicated that in the age in which he lived the romance proper had fallen into considerable popular disfavour. This was due partly to the circumstances of a changed environment, and partly to the type of literary opinion which had recently been fostered by the rise of the Spanish drama, which had brought about an entirely new literary ideal. Can it be that Cervantes, finding that his audiences regarded the Arcadian type of tale with disfavour, attributed this to the circumstance that it was fashionable in high circles, and fell back upon the romance, only to find that it too was greeted with guffaws and laughed out of the inn parlour? Was it in the quips and sneers of such audiences, the very antithesis of the romantic personages of whom he had dreamed, that the idea of *Don Quixote* took shape in his brain, and that in the laughter of clowns and men of the hard world, of the struggling lower middle class, he perceived the certain popularity which a caricature of chivalry would enjoy? So, it seems to me, it may have been.

For many a year the sham romance of chivalry had been regarded as a pest. Serious and responsible writers had thundered against it, and there is every evidence that in a measure it stood between a certain section of the people of Spain and anything like mental advancement. It had, indeed, turned the heads of that portion of the nation unaccustomed to think for itself, and unable to form a rational opinion regarding its demerits. In all countries and at all times, this class, usually impressionable and easily led, falls an easy prey to the blandishments of the hack writer of sensational proclivities. It is not too much to say that unhealthy sensationalism in literature constitutes a real and active danger to national well-being. It seduces the people from their duties, unfits them for the serious business of life, renders them pretentious rather than independent, and leads them to the belief that they reflect the virtues or vices of the absurd heroes and heroines of their favourite tales. The one weapon which the more sensible portion of the community can bring to bear against such a pernicious condition of affairs is healthy ridicule, which it usually meets with from the rational and the well-balanced. But the danger exists that in the revulsion of public feeling against literary extravagance not only the absurdities which have obsessed the thoughtless and irritated the sensible will undergo destruction and banishment, but those higher virtues and graces of which they are the distorted reflection will not be discriminated against, but will be demolished along with them. Such, indeed, was the fate which befell the greater romances, those jewels of human imagination, which, although Cervantes himself made an effort to save them, shared in the general wreck and ruin of the fiction of which they were the flower, until the taste and insight of a later day excavated them from the superincumbent mass under which they lay buried.

The Figure of Don Quixote

Don Quixote, the central figure of the mighty satire which gave its death-blow to chivalry, is perhaps typical of the romance reader of Cervantes' day. Crack-brained and imaginative to the verge of madness, he is entirely lost to the uses of everyday existence. He lives in a world of his own, and has nothing in common with that of his time, to the spirit of which he cannot adapt himself. In this gentleman of La Mancha the vices of the imagination are well portrayed, but they are unaccompanied by those gifts through which imagination can be rendered of utility to the community. Don Quixote dwells on the heights of a chivalric Parnassus, a land of magic peopled by the spectres and shadows which he has encountered in the books with which his library is so well furnished. His imagination is thus not even creative, but derivative; reliance upon the "idols he has loved so long" has "done his credit in men's eyes much wrong," and he is regarded by his neighbours as an amiable lunatic of no importance. But the dreamer, when roused to action, can be a very terrible person if his visions chance to direct him astray, and if he attempt to realize a nightmare. Thus it was with Don Quixote. Scarcely mad enough for confinement, but yet sufficiently crazy to become a public nuisance, if not a public menace, he justly typifies the kind of person in whom romance runs mad, and is thus of the same class as the small boy who is incited to acts of petty larceny by the perusal of detective stories, or the young lady behind the ribbon-counter who is under the impression that she is the long-lost daughter of a mysterious peer.

It is symptomatic of such craziness that it craves companionship. It is indeed a species of vanity which must have an audience, however small or however unsuited to its purposes. Again, the element of conspiracy is as the apple of its eye, and it must confide its ideas and aspirations to one sympathetic ear at least. In Sancho Panza, Don Quixote finds a strange confidant. The luckless peasant is completely unable to comprehend his master's point of view, but is carried away by his rodomontades and the glib and gorgeous promises of preferment and prosperity which the crack-brained knight holds out to him. To his participation in the wild scheme of the visionary Don, Sancho's shrewd spouse violently objects, but when dreamer and dunce get together common sense may hold its tongue and content itself with the knowledge that it is not until

The Adventure at the Inn

windmills have been tilted at and sound trouncings have
been received that its advice will be listened to.

But though he begins his travels as a dunce, Sancho by
no means remains one. He profits from his experiences,
and almost every page shows him increasing in judgment and in that humour which is the salt of good
judgment. As his master grows madder, Sancho grows
wiser, until at last he becomes capable of direction and
guidance toward the rueful knight. As we proceed we
begin to suspect that the peasant-squire exists as a kind
of chorus to illustrate the excesses of his master and
criticize his absurdities. But apart altogether from Don
Quixote, Sancho Panza is a striking and arresting figure
in modern fiction, possessing a philosophy of his own,
rich in worldly wisdom and abounding with practical
ability. On the humorous side he is equal to Falstaff,
only whereas Falstaff's humour is typically English that
of Sancho Panza is universal. He is a world-clown,
with the outlook of a philosopher and the unconscious
humour of a Handy Andy.

The Adventure at the Inn

The true measure of the character of Don Quixote is
perhaps met with in that chapter which recounts what
occurred to him in the inn which he took for a castle.
The place seems to have been a very ordinary Spanish
posada. The host and hostess were kindly folk whom
the knight at once exalted to the rank of a castellan
and châtelaine, and in the dowdy maidservant, who has
been immortalized under the name of Maritornes, he saw
a great lady who dwelt in their company. After the
terrible trouncing he had received from the Yanguesian
carriers the wretched knight was glad to rest his battered

limbs in a miserable garret of the place, while Sancho explained to the inn-folk the nature of a knight-errant and the vicissitudes of errantry, which one day compelled its adherents to undergo such hardship as the Don now suffered from, and the next exalted them to the heights of sovereignty over many empires. These explanations were seconded by the Knight of the Rueful Countenance himself, who, sitting up in bed, entertained the hostess and maidservant to a speech so grandiloquent that, lost in wonder at his eloquence, "they admired him as a man of another world." But Don Quixote, anxious to recover from his injuries, begged his squire to procure from "the governor of the castle" the ingredients of a magical balm of which he had read in some book of chivalry. These he obtained, and Don Quixote busied himself by concocting the enchanted liquor over the fire, saying over it many credos and paternosters. Then he drank deeply of the awful compound, with distressing effect, and Sancho, following his example, underwent a similar but more violent experience, and was assured by his master that the balsam disagreed with him because he had not received the order of knighthood!

Saddling his horse, the knight was about to proceed on his journey, but before he set out he assured "the lord governor of the castle" how deeply grateful he was for the honours he had received while under his roof. The innkeeper suggested that the time for paying his reckoning had come, but Don Quixote retorted that it was impossible for him to do so, as no knight-errant of whom he had ever read was wont to pay for board and lodging. The innkeeper protested loudly, whereupon, clapping spurs to Rozinante, the knight rode out at the gate. The innkeeper then attempted to extort his dues from

Don Quixote's Love-Madness

Sancho Panza, but without avail, as the squire quoted the same authorities as his master, whereupon some of those who sojourned at the inn seized him and tossed him in a blanket. Don Quixote, hearing his cries, rode back, but although he stormed loudly the travellers still continued to toss Sancho in the blanket, until at length, tired of the exercise, they let him go.

Don Quixote's Love-Madness

In the space at our disposal it would be impossible to follow Don Quixote step by step through the land of false romance which he had created for himself. We will recall how Amadis on the Firm Island bemoaned his separation from his lady-love, and how, when he came to a locality known as the Black Mountain, Don Quixote resolved to follow the example of the great hero of chivalry. Before he left his native village he had placed his affections upon a country wench, to whom he gave the romantic name of Dulcinea del Toboso, and now that he had come to the Black Mountain he resolved to spend his time in meditation upon the virtues and beauties of this super-excellent damsel. After lecturing Sancho Panza upon the duty of a knight-errant in meditation upon his lady, he became irritated with the squire because he could not understand the reason for his amorous fury.

" Pray, sir," quoth Sancho, "what is it that you mean to do in this fag-end of the world ? "

" Have I not already told thee," answered Don Quixote, "that I intend to copy Amadis in his madness, despair and fury ? Nay, at the same time I will imitate the valiant Orlando Furioso's extravagance when he ran mad, at which time in his frantic despair he tore up trees by the roots, troubled the waters of the clear fountains, slew the shepherds, destroyed their flocks, and committed a hundred thousand other extravagances worthy to be recorded in the eternal register of fame."

"Sir," quoth Sancho, "I dare say the knight who did these penances had some reason to be mad. But what lady has sent you a-packing, or even so much as slighted you?"

"That is the point," cried Don Quixote, "for in this consists the singular perfection of my undertaking. It is neither strange nor meritorious for a knight to run mad upon any just occasion. No, the rarity is to run mad without a cause, without the least constraint or necessity, for thus my mistress must needs have a vast idea of my love. Waste no more time, therefore, in trying to divert me from so rare, so happy, and so singular an imitation. I am mad and will be mad until you return with an answer to the letter which you must carry from me to the Lady Dulcinea. If it be favourable, my penance shall end, but if not, then shall I be emphatically mad."

"Body o' me!" quoth Sancho, "why run you on at such a rate, Sir Knight? All these tales of yours of the winning of kingdoms and bestowing of islands rather appear to me as so much braggartry, and now this latest mood of yours——"

"Now as I love bright arms," cried the Don, "I swear that thou art an addle-pated ass. Know you not that all the actions and adventures of a knight-errant seem to be mere chimæras and follies? Not that they are so, but merely have that appearance through the malice and envy of powerful enchanters."

As they talked they came near to a high rock, round

DON QUIXOTE'S LOVE-MADNESS

The Army of Sheep

which the wild trees, plants, and flowers grew in profusion, and here the Knight of the Woeful Figure
resolved to perform his amorous penance. Throwing
himself on the ground, he broke into a loud frenzy of grief.
"Go not yet," he cried to Sancho, "for I desire that thou
shalt be a witness of what I will do for my lady's sake,
that thou mayst give her an account of it."

"Bless us," cried Sancho, "what can I see more that I
have not seen already?"

"Nothing as yet," replied Don Quixote. "Thou must
see me throw away mine armour, tear my clothes, knock
my head against the rocks, and do a thousand other
things of that kind that will fill thee with astonishment."

"Beware, sir," cried the squire. "If you needs must
knock your noddle, do so gently, I pray you."

The Army of Sheep

But surely the most mirth-provoking of all the adventures of Don Quixote is that in which he takes a flock
of sheep for an army. He and Sancho were riding at
bridle-pace over a wide plain, when they perceived a
thick cloud of dust in the distance.

"The day is come," cried the knight, "the happy day
that fortune has reserved for me, and in which the
strength of my arm shall be signalized by such exploits
as shall be transmitted even to the latest posterity.
Seest thou yonder cloud of dust? Know then that it
is raised by a prodigious army marching this way and
composed of an infinite number of nations."

The wretched Don's brain was of course full to overflowing of the accounts of those stupendous battles of myriads
of paynims which, as we have seen, are so frequently
encountered in the old romances, and he was delighted

when Sancho pointed out that two separate hosts seemed
to be approaching from different points of the compass.

" Ha, so! " cried Don Quixote, flourishing his lance,
"then shall we assist the weaker side.   Know, Sancho,
that the host which now confronts us is commanded
by the great Alifanfaron, Emperor of the Island of
Taprobana.   The other that advances behind us is his
sworn enemy, Pentapolin of the Naked Arm, King of
the Garamantians."

" Pray, sir," quoth Sancho, "what is the cause of this
quarrel between two such great men?"

" It is a simple matter," answered Don Quixote.   " The
pagan Alifanfaron dares to make his addresses to the
daughter of Pentapolin, who has told him that he will
have naught of him unless he abjure his false beliefs."

" If a battle be at hand," said Sancho nervously, " where
shall I place my ass, for I fear he will not prove of much
avail in the charge."

" True," answered Don Quixote.   " We will soon provide
a destrier for thee when the knights begin to fall from
their saddles.   But let us scan their ranks.   He who
wears the gilded arms and bears on his shield a crowned
lion couchant at the feet of a lady is the valiant Lord
Luarcalco, Lord of the Silver Bridge.   Yonder is the
formidable Micocolembo, the great Duke of Quiracia,
wearing armour powdered with flowers of gold.   The
gigantic form upon his right is the dauntless Brandabar-
baran, sovereign of the Three Arabias, whose armour
is made of serpents' skins, and who carries for a shield
the gate of the temple which Samson pulled down at his
death.   But our allies also advance.   Yonder marches
Timonel of Carcaxona, Prince of New Biscay, who
bears on his shield a cat *or* in a field *gules*, with the

The Army of Sheep

motto 'Miau.' Beside him rides Espartafilardo of the Wood, whose blue shield is powdered with asparagus plants. But the pagans press on. To the right cluster those who drink the pleasant stream of the Xanthus, there the rude mountaineers of Massilia, behind them those who gather gold from the sands of Arabia Felix, the treacherous Numidians, the bowmen of Persia, the Medes and Parthians who fight flying, the houseless Arabians, and the sooty Ethiopians."

"Upon my soul," cried Sancho, "surely thy magicians are at work again, for not a single knight, giant or man can I see of all those you talk of now."

"Blockhead!" cried Don Quixote. "Hark to the neighing of countless horses, the fanfare of the trumpets, and the thunder of many drums."

"Surely this is sorcery," replied the puzzled Sancho, "for I hear nothing but the bleating of sheep."

"Retreat, if thou fearest the engagement," replied the Don, with a haughty sneer, "for I with my single arm am sufficient to give the victory to that side which I shall favour with my assistance," and with a loud and warlike cry he couched his lance, clapped spurs to the lean side of Rozinante, and charged like a thunderbolt into the plain, crying : "Courage, brave knights! Woe upon that great infidel Alifanfaron of Taprobana."

In another moment he was among the flock of sheep, charging through and through it, and piercing an animal at each thrust of his lance. The shepherds, in great dismay, unloosed their slings and began to ply him with stones as big as their fists. But, disdainful of this petty artillery, he cried upon Alifanfaron, whom in imagination he was about to engage, when a stone as big as a good-sized pippin struck him heavily upon the short ribs. Thinking himself desperately wounded, he pulled out the earthen flask which contained his magic balsam ; but just as he was in the act of raising this to his lips, a stone from the sling of a shepherd struck it so forcibly as to shiver it to atoms, and passing through it broke three of his teeth and tumbled him from the saddle. The shepherds, fearing that they had killed him, picked up the dead sheep and made off, leaving him more dead than alive.

Mambrino's Helmet

No less notable is Cervantes' account of the adventure in which Don Quixote succeeded in obtaining the helmet of Mambrino. At a distance he espied a horseman who wore upon his head something that glittered like gold. Turning to Sancho, he said :

" Behold, yonder comes he who wears upon his head the helmet of Mambrino, which I have sworn to make mine own."

" Now the truth of the story," says Cervantes, " was this : there were in that part of the country two villages, one of which was so little that it had not so much as a shop in it, nor any barber ; so that the barber of the greater village served also the smaller. And thus a person happening to have occasion to be let blood, and another to be shaved, the barber was going thither with his brass basin, which he had clapped upon his head to keep his hat, that chanced to be a new one, from being spoiled by the rain ; and as the basin was new scoured, it made a glittering show a great way off. As Sancho had well observed, he rode upon a grey ass, which Don Quixote as easily took for a dapple-grey steed as he took the barber for a knight, and his brass basin for a golden helmet ; his distracted brain easily applying every object to his romantic ideas.   Therefore, when he saw the poor imaginary knight draw near, he fixed his lance, or javelin, to his thigh, and without staying to hold a parley with his thoughtless adversary, flew at him as fiercely as Rozinante would gallop, resolved to pierce him through and through ; crying out in the midst of his career : 'Caitiff ! wretch ! defend thyself, or immediately surrender that which is so justly my due.'"

The barber, seeing this awful apparition come thundering down upon him, and in terror lest he should be run through by Don Quixote's lance, threw himself off his ass on to the ground and, hastily rising, ran off at the top of his speed, leaving both his ass and his basin behind him.

"Of a truth," said Don Quixote, "the miscreant who has left this helmet has shown himself as prudent as the beaver, who, finding himself hotly pursued by the hunters, to save his life cuts off with his teeth that for which his natural instinct tells him he was followed."

"Upon my word," cried Sancho, "it is a right good basin, and worth at least a piece of eight."

Don Quixote at once placed it on his head, but could find no visor, and when he perceived that it had none, "Doubtless," said he, "the pagan for whom this famous helmet was first made had a head of a prodigious size, but unfortunately part of it is wanting."

At this Sancho laughed outright.

"I fancy," continued Don Quixote, "that this enchanted helmet has fallen by some strange accident into the hands of some one who for the lucre of a little money, and finding it to be of pure gold, melted one half of it

365

and of the other made this headpiece, which as thou sayest has some resemblance to a barber's basin."

The Adventure of the Windmills

The most celebrated, if not the most amusing of Don Quixote's adventures is certainly that of the windmills. Indeed "tilting at windmills" has passed into a proverb. The dismal Don and his squire had entered a certain plain where stood thirty or forty windmills, and as soon as the knight espied them he cried: "Fortune directs our affairs better than we ourselves could have wished. See, Sancho, there are at least thirty outrageous giants whom I intend to encounter, and with whose spoils we shall enrich ourselves."

"What giants?" quoth Sancho Panza.

"Those whom thou seest yonder," answered Don Quixote, "with their long, extended arms."

"By your leave, sir," said the squire, "those things yonder are no giants, but windmills."

"Alas, Sancho," said Don Quixote, "thou art but little acquainted with adventures. I tell thee they are giants, and therefore if thou art afraid, turn aside and say thy prayers, for I am resolved to engage in an unequal combat against them all." Without another word he clapped spurs to his horse, crying out: "Stand your ground, ignoble creatures, and fly not basely from a single knight who dares encounter you all!" At that moment the wind rose and the mill-sails began to move, at which the Don cried aloud: "Base miscreants! though you move more arms than the giant Briareus, you shall pay for your arrogance." Then, devoutly recommending himself to his lady, he bore down upon the first windmill, and running his lance into the sail, transfixed it. The sail, however, continued to rise, drawing up both knight and horse along with it, until at last the lance broke into shivers and Rozinante and his master fell a good distance to the ground.

Sancho Panza at once ran up to the dismounted knight, who seemed to have fared badly. "Alas, your worship," he cried, "did not I tell you they were windmills, and that nobody could think otherwise unless he had windmills in his head."

"Peace!" replied Don Quixote, who had been badly shaken by the fall. "I am verily persuaded that the cursed necromancer Freston, who continues to persecute me, has transformed these giants into windmills. But, mark you, in the end all his pernicious wiles and stratagems shall prove ineffectual against the prevailing edge of my sword."

The Story of the Captive

One of the most remarkable of the tales which are interspersed throughout the history of Don Quixote is that of the captive which the hero encounters at a certain inn, and which, if it is not actually based upon the facts of Cervantes' own personal captivity among the Moorish pirates, certainly draws much of its substance and colour therefrom. On 26th September, 1575, the Spanish vessel *Sol*, on which Cervantes served as a private soldier, was separated from the rest of the Spanish squadron in the neighbourhood of Marseilles, and, falling in with a flotilla of Moorish pirates, was captured after a desperate resistance. Cervantes himself was sold as a slave to one Dali Mami, a Greek renegade, who found upon his prisoner certain highly eulogistic letters from Don John of Austria and the Duke of Sessa. These flattering credentials led his new master to suppose that Cervantes was a man of consequence, and that he would presumably be able to draw a large ransom for him. But although the great are often quite ready to provide genius with grandiloquent testimonials which cost them only the expense of a little ink and paper, they are by no means prone to back their assertions of ability by tabling large sums of money, and Cervantes continued to languish in captivity. In 1576 he attempted to escape with other prisoners, but their Moorish guide played them false, and, threatened by hunger, the party was forced to return to Algiers. In the following year Cervantes' brother was ransomed, and he undertook to send a vessel to carry off Miguel and his friends. Meanwhile the author of *Don Quixote* enlisted the sympathies of a Spanish renegade, a Navarrese gardener named Juan. Between them they dug a cave in a garden near the sea, and secreted in it, one by one, fourteen Christian slaves, who were secretly fed during several months by the help of another renegade known as El Dorador. The vessel sent by Rodrigo de Cervantes stood in to the shore, and was on the point of embarking those hidden in the cave when a Moorish fishing-boat passed by, and so alarmed the rescuers that they put to sea again. Meanwhile the treacherous El Dorador had revealed the plan to Hassan Pasha, the Dey of Algiers, and when several of the crew of rescuers landed on a second occasion to convey the fugitives on board, the Dey's troops surrounded the garden, and the entire band of Christians was captured. Cervantes, with that true nobility which characterized him throughout life, took the entire blame of the conspiracy upon himself. Dragged bound before Hassan, he adhered to his statement, and although the unfortunate

The Story of the Captive

gardener was hanged, Hassan decided to spare Cervantes'
life, and for some reason known to himself purchased the
poet from Dali Mami for five hundred crowns.   Perhaps
the tyrant expected an immense ransom from a man
whose nobility of bearing must have impressed him.
But be that as it may, Cervantes at once began to set on
foot a third scheme of escape.   He sent a letter to the
Spanish Governor of Oran, asking for assistance, but
this was intercepted, and the poet was sentenced to two
thousand blows, which, however, were never inflicted.
Cervantes now conceived the idea of inducing the
Christian population of Algiers to rise and capture the
city.   In this project he was assisted by some Valencian
traders, but the scheme was revealed to Hassan by a
Dominican monk, and the Valencians, hearing of the
priest's treachery, and fearing lest they might be impli-
cated, begged Cervantes to make his escape on a ship
which was about to start for Spain.   But Cervantes
refused to desert his friends, and when he was once more
dragged before Hassan with a hangman's rope round
his neck, and threatened with instant death unless he
revealed the names of his accomplices, he obstinately
refused to betray them.
Meanwhile his family were doing their utmost to procure
his release, and in order that they might collect his
ransom, his mother, the better to inspire pity, actually
passed herself off as a widow, though her husband, a
medical practitioner of great age, was still alive.   By
tremendous exertions they succeeded in collecting two
hundred and fifty ducats, which they paid to a certain
monk who went regularly to Algiers, but this Hassan
refused to accept, asking for one prisoner of distinction,
called Palafox, the sum of one thousand ducats.   The

monk seems to have acted as an official ransomer to the Spaniards, and when Hassan found that he would pay no more than five hundred ducats for Palafox, he offered to ransom Cervantes for that sum by way of making a bargain. So after five years of slavery the author of *Don Quixote* was set free, and returned to his native soil. But the Dominican monk who had revealed to Hassan his attempted escape, and who was probably afraid that Cervantes would charge him with this treachery, no sooner heard that he had landed in Spain than he spread false reports regarding his conduct. These, however, Cervantes was easily able to rebut, and his character as a heroic leader among the captives was amply vindicated. The captive's story, for which Cervantes had had the mournful privilege of collecting so much 'local colour,' is recounted to Don Quixote by an escaped slave, who, with his Moorish lady-love, has come to the inn where the woeful knight is sojourning. I shall adhere to Cervantes' manner of recounting it in the first person, but as it occupies a considerable portion of the first part of his famous history, considerations of space will necessitate its condensation.

"My family had its origin in the mountains of Leon, and although my father had considerable substance, he had by no means been prudent in his expenditure, and at an early age my brothers and myself were faced with the necessity for carving out our own fortunes. One of my brothers resolved to go to the Indies, the youngest embraced Holy Orders, and I concluded that for my part I would be a soldier. With a thousand ducats in my pocket I travelled to Alicant, whence I took ship to Genoa. From that city I went to Milan, where I joined the forces of the great Duke of Alva and saw

The Story of the Captive

service in Flanders. Some time after my arrival in that country there came news of the league concluded by Pope Pius V in conjunction with Spain against the Turks, who had at that time taken the island of Cyprus from the Venetians. Hearing that Don John of Austria had been given the conduct of this expedition, I returned to Italy, enrolled myself in his service, and was present at the great battle of Lepanto, on which glorious day the fable that the Turk was invincible, which had so long deluded Christendom, was dissipated. But instead of participating in this victory, I was so unfortunate as to be made a prisoner in the course of the engagement. Vehali, the bold pirate king of Algiers, having boarded and taken the galley *Capitana* of Malta, the vessel of Andrea Doria, to which I had been commissioned, bore up to assist it. I leaped on board the enemy's ship, which, however, succeeded in casting off the grappling-irons thrown upon it, and I found myself surrounded by enemies who quickly bore me down. I was carried to Constantinople, and was made a slave in the captured *Capitana* at Navarino.

"As I did not wish to burden my father with the collection of a ransom, I refrained from letting him know of my circumstances. My master Vehali dying, I fell to the share of a Venetian renegade called Azanaga, who sailed for Algiers, where I was shut up in prison. As it was thought that I might be ransomed, the Moors placed me in a *bagnio*, and I was not forced to labour like those captives who had no hope of redemption. Upon the courtyard of this place there opened the windows of the house of a wealthy Moor, and it chanced one day that I was standing underneath one of these, when there appeared from it a long cane, to which was attached a piece of linen. This was moved up and down, as if it was expected that some of us should lay hold upon it, and one of our number stood immediately beneath it to see if it would be lowered. But just as he came to it, the cane was drawn up and shaken to and fro sideways, as if in denial. Another of my comrades advanced, and had the same success as the former. Seeing this, I resolved to try my fortune also, and as I came under the cane, it fell at my feet. I untied the linen, and found wrapped up in it about ten gold coins called *zianins*. I took the money, broke the cane, and looking upward, beheld a white hand close the window in haste. Shortly afterward there appeared out of the same casement a little cross made of cane, and by this token we concluded that some Christian woman was a slave in that house. But the whiteness of the hand and the richness of the bracelets upon the arm made us think that perhaps we had to deal with a Christian lady who had turned Mohammedan.

" For more than fifteen days we received no other token of the lady's presence, although we watched carefully for the same, but we learned that the house belonged to a Moor of high rank, called Agimorato. At the end of this time the cane appeared once more, and on this occasion I found that the linen bundle contained no less than forty crowns of Spanish gold, with a paper written in Arabic, at the top of which was a great cross. But none of us understood Arabic, and it was with difficulty that we could find an interpreter. At last I resolved to trust a renegade of Murcia, who had shown me great proofs of his kindness. He agreed to translate it, and I found the contents were as follow :

" ' As a child I had a Christian nurse who taught me

much of your religion, and especially of Lela Marien, whom you call the Virgin. When this good slave died, she appeared to me in a vision and bid me go to the land of the Christians to see the Virgin, who had a great kindness for me. I have seen many Christians out of this window, but none has appeared to me so much of a gentleman as thyself. I am young and handsome and can carry with me a great deal of money and other riches. Pray consider how we may escape together, and thou shalt be my husband in thine own country, if thou art willing. But if not, it does not matter, for the Virgin will provide me a husband. Trust no Moor with this letter, for they are all treacherous.'

" The renegade to whom I had given the letter for translation promised to assist us in every way in his power, should we venture upon making our escape, and indeed the hearts of all of us rose high, for we argued that the influence and means of the lady who had befriended me might greatly help us in our efforts for freedom. I dictated a reply to the renegade, who translated it into the Arabic tongue, offering the lady my services and those of my companions, and promising on the word of a Christian to make her my wife. Soon the cane was let down from the window once more. I attached the note to it and it was drawn up. That night we prisoners discussed the best means of effecting our escape, and at last we agreed to wait for the answer of Zoraida (for such we discovered was the lady's name), feeling assured that she could best advise us how to proceed.

For some days the *bagnio* was full of people, during which time the cane was invisible, but when we were once more left to ourselves it was thrust through the window, and on this occasion the bundle which depended from it contained a letter and a hundred crowns in gold. The renegade speedily translated the missive, which stated that although the writer could not contrive the manner of our escape, she could still furnish us with sufficient money to enable us to buy our ransoms. She suggested that having done this one of us should proceed to Spain, purchase a ship there, and return for the others. She concluded by saying that she was now about to proceed to the country with her father, and that she would pass all the summer in a place near the seaside, which she closely described.

" Every one of our company offered to be the man who should go to Spain and purchase the ship which was to deliver the rest, but the renegade, who was experienced in such matters, strongly opposed this proposal, saying that he had seen too many such enterprises wrecked by placing trust in a single individual. He offered to purchase a ship in Algiers, and pretend to turn merchant, by which means, he said, he could contrive to get us out of the *bagnio* and the country. Meanwhile I answered Zoraida, assuring her that we would do all she advised, and in reply to this she gave us, by means of the cane, two thousand crowns in gold. Of this sum we gave the renegade five hundred crowns to buy the ship, and through the good offices of a merchant of Valencia, then in Algiers, I effected my own ransom with another eight hundred crowns. But on the advice of this trader the money was not paid down to the Dey at once, lest his suspicions should be aroused, but he was informed that it would shortly be forthcoming from Spain, and meanwhile I remained in the Valencian's house upon parole. Before Zoraida finally departed for her father's

The Flight from Algiers

summer residence she gave us another thousand crowns,
explaining, by letter, that she kept the keys of her
father's treasury, and on this occasion I made arrangements for ransoming three of my friends.

The Flight from Algiers

" Soon after this the renegade purchased a vessel capable
of carrying above thirty people, in which he pretended
to make several voyages in company with a Moorish
partner whom he took in order to avoid suspicion. Each
time he passed along the coast he cast anchor in a little
bay close to the house where Zoraida lived, so that the
people of the place should get used to his doing so. He
even landed on several occasions and begged fruit from
Zoraida's father, which he always received, for the old
Moor was of a liberal spirit. But he could never succeed
in having speech with Zoraida herself. Our plan was
now upon such a footing that he asked me to fix a day
upon which we might make the great effort upon which
everything depended. So I collected twelve Spaniards
known to be good oarsmen and whose comings and
goings were not very closely watched. It was arranged
among us that we should steal out of the town upon the
evening of the next Friday, and rendezvous at a certain
spot near Agimorato's dwelling. But it was necessary
that Zoraida herself should be apprised of our intention,
and with this object in view I entered her garden one
day upon pretence of gathering a few herbs. Almost at
once I encountered her father, who asked me what I did
there. I told him I was a slave of Arnaut Mami, who I
knew was a friend of his, and that I wanted a few herbs
to make up a salad. While we spoke Zoraida came out
of the garden house, and as it was quite the custom for

375

the Moorish women to be seen before Christian slaves, her father called her to come to him. She was most richly dressed and wore a profusion of jewels, and now that I beheld her for the first time I was astounded by her beauty. Her father told her for what purpose I was there, and she asked me if I were about to be ransomed. Speaking in *lingua franca*, I replied that I had already been ransomed, and that I intended to embark on the morrow upon a French ship.

"At that juncture the old Moor was called away upon business, and I at once assured Zoraida that I would come for her on the morrow. She immediately threw her arms around my neck and began to walk toward the house, but her father returning at that moment espied us, and came running to us in some alarm. Immediately Zoraida pretended to be in a fainting condition, and explained to Agimorato that she had suddenly felt indisposed. I yielded her up to him and they retired into the house.

"Next evening we embarked and dropped anchor opposite Zoraida's dwelling. When darkness had come we walked boldly into the garden, and finding the gate of the house open entered the courtyard. Zoraida immediately emerged from the house carrying a small trunk full of treasure, and told us that her father was asleep, but as misfortune would have it, some slight noise that we made awakened him and he came to a window calling out, 'Thieves, thieves! Christians, Christians!' The renegade at once rushed upstairs aud secured him, and we carried father and daughter on board. We also made prisoners of the few Moors who remained on the vessel, bent to the oars, and set out to sea.

The Flight from Algiers

"At first we endeavoured to make for Majorca, but a strong wind arising, we were driven along the coast. We were in great fear that we might encounter some of the Moorish cruisers which we knew to be in the vicinity. I made every effort in my power to assure Agimorato that we would give him his liberty on the very first occasion, and told him that his daughter had become a Christian and desired to live the rest of her life in a Christian land. On hearing this the old man behaved as if suddenly seized with a frenzy, and rising cast himself into the sea, whence we succeeded with difficulty in rescuing him. Shortly afterward we drove into a small bay, where we set Agimorato ashore. I shall never forget his curses and imprecations upon his daughter, but as we sailed away he called out, begging her to return. However, she hid her face in her hands and commended him to the Virgin.

"We had proceeded some little distance from the coast when the light of the moon became obscured. All at once we nearly collided with a large vessel, which hailed us in French, bidding us to heave to. Perceiving that it was a French pirate, we made no answer, but pressed onward, whereupon its crew launched a boat, boarded us and dragged us on board, stripping Zoraida of all her jewels and throwing us into the hold. As we neared the Spanish shore next morning they placed us in their long-boat with two barrels of water and a small quantity of biscuits, and the captain, touched with some remorse for the lovely Zoraida, gave her at parting about forty crowns in gold. We rowed on through the early dawn, and after some hours of plying the oars landed. After proceeding some miles inland we came upon a shepherd, who on seeing our Moorish dresses, made off and gave the alarm. Soon we encountered a company of horsemen, one of whom chanced to be related to one of our number. They placed us on their horses and we soon reached the city of Velez Malaga. There we went straight to church to thank God for His great mercy to us, and there for the first time Zoraida saw and recognized a picture of the Virgin. With some of the money the pirate had given Zoraida I bought an ass and resolved to discover whether or no my father and brothers were still alive. That is, gentlemen, the sum of our adventures."

The escaped Christian had scarcely finished his narration when a splendid coach drove up to the door of the inn. From this equipage there alighted a richly dressed gentleman and lady, who entered the *posada* and were met with great courtesy by Don Quixote. The Christian refugee recognized the gentleman as his brother, now a judge of the Court of Mexico, who greeted him affectionately and introduced the lady as his daughter. The man of many adventures with his Moorish bride resolved to return with the judge to Seville, whence they intended to advise their father of these strange happenings, that he might come to see the baptism and marriage of Zoraida, for whose future, and that of his sorely tried brother, the grandee resolved to make ample provision.

The Growth of Cervantes

It is in such a tale as the above that we observe how Cervantes' style grows more supple and adaptable as his work proceeds. It is clear that he has made an effort to shake off the literary trammels of his time, and that he has succeeded. No longer does he find it necessary

The Growth of Cervantes

to imitate such writers as Antonio de Guevara, as in the passage in which Don Quixote describes the Age of Gold. He has shaken off the rather recondite euphuism of some of the earlier passages, and has become more human and familiar. His speeches are appropriate to his characters ; his dialogue is full of life and his narrative of incident. But although in these pages we behold the evolution of a realist, Cervantes never altogether throws off the cloak of academic eloquence—only it becomes a carefully restrained eloquence which has left affectation far behind.

The great and immediate success of *Don Quixote* was, however, principally due to its large humour, and to its faithful portraiture of the Spanish types of Cervantes' day. Into juxtaposition with figures that were familiar to all he brought the extraordinary character of the Knight of the Rueful Countenance, a burlesque original out of another age, and yet not lacking in the dignity and greater qualities of the times whose spirit he strove to imitate. Into the environment of seventeenth-century Spain stalked the antiquated figure of Don Quixote, disturbing its ordinary routine and quarrelling with its conventions, carrying the days of chivalry in his head, and projecting their phantasms on the landscape by means of the all too powerful light of his imagination. But if the incongruity of the Don in a modern setting roused grave and sober Spain to inextinguishable laughter, his character and that of Sancho Panza were still recognized as triumphs of creative fiction — the representatives of imagination run mad and of the grossest common sense.

The perfection and finish of *Don Quixote*, and the consummate craftsmanship with which it is conceived, cannot fail to commend themselves to readers of discretion. It is full of the knowledge of the man of the world; it breathes leisure and urbanity, its spirit is that which stamps the work of the great master. Here there are no loose ends, no clumsy constructions, no weaknesses of diction. It does not seem to me that Cervantes wrote with any great facility, and herein probably lies the measure of his great literary excellence. On the other hand, no drudgery is apparent in his composition. He strikes the happy medium between brilliant facility and that meticulous and often nervously apprehensive mode which so frequently disgraces the work of modern stylists. He is precise and wonderfully sure-footed, and we cannot imagine him grasping in alarm at every projection in the course of his ascent. Whatever the secret of his style, it succeeded in producing a wonderfully equable yet varied narrative, just and appropriate in expression. His entire canvas is filled in and completed with a masterly eye to the smallest detail.

The Second Part of "Don Quixote"

We can see by the time which he permitted to elapse between the first and second parts of his great romance how careful Cervantes was not to hazard his well-won reputation upon an unfortunate sequel, and the fictioneer of our own time, harassed by a public greedy for sensation and flushed by momentary success, might well turn to him for an example in this respect. It is often alleged that the circumstances of modern literature do not permit of that leisure which is necessary to the excogitation of a carefully developed technique or a sound style. This, alas! is only too true. The

The Second Part of " Don Quixote "

successful author of to-day can scarcely permit ten months, much less ten years, to elapse between one effort and another, and to this feverish condition of things we undoubtedly owe those disappointing sequels to great novels with which all of us must be only too familiar. Ours is emphatically not an age of connoisseurs. We eat, drink, and read pretty much what is given us, and if we grumble a little at the quality thereof, we feel that no complaints will alter the conditions which produce the things against which we inveigh. The Spain of Cervantes' day offered a much more critical environment. Bad or hastily conceived work it would not tolerate. But there were elements within it which frequently did much to hasten the publication of a sequel, and the chief of these was undoubtedly literary piracy. Cervantes appears to have been spurred on in the publication of the second part of *Don Quixote* by the appearance in 1614 of a book by Alonso Fernández de Avellaneda, a spurious sequel to the first portion of his great work, the preface of which is filled with personalities of the most insolent kind. That he resented the piracy is shown by the circumstance that he put all his other work aside and brought *Don Quixote* to a hurried conclusion.

In the last chapters of *Don Quixote* he was forced to write hastily because his rival had stolen his plan, and it was necessary for him to recast it as well as to bring out his novel with all speed. But, these blemishes notwithstanding, much of the sequel is truly epical in its grandeur. Don Quixote, if less amusing, is greatly more thought-provoking, and Sancho Panza becomes even richer in common sense and clear-sightedness. The portraiture of the remaining characters, too, is sharper in outline than in the first part. The sequel, indeed, is a great mirror in which the Spanish society of Cervantes' day is reflected with all the thaumaturgy of genius. The immense success which followed it must have afforded the greatest gratification to the dying novelist, and must in great measure have consoled him for the disappointments of a career spent in the shallows of exile and poverty.

Lazarillo de Tormes

The greatest humorous romance which Spain had produced prior to *Don Quixote* was the *Lazarillo de Tormes* of Diego Hurtado de Mendoza, a many-sided man and once Spanish Ambassador to England. He was of noble extraction on both sides, and was born in Granada in 1503. As a younger son he was destined for the Church, and studied at the university of Salamanca, where, while still a student, he wrote the novel which rendered him famous. Its graphic descriptions, its penetration into character, and its vivacity and humour instantly gained for it a high place in contemporary Spanish literature. But Mendoza soon exchanged the clerical for the political sphere of activity, and Charles V created him Captain-General of Siena, a small Italian republic which had been brought beneath Spanish rule. Haughty and unfeeling, Mendoza exercised a most tyrannical sway over the wretched people committed to his care. They complained bitterly to the Emperor regarding his conduct, and when this remained without effect, his life was attempted by assassination. On one occasion, indeed, his horse was killed under him by a musket-shot aimed at himself. During his absence Siena was captured by a French army, and as

Lazarillo de Tormes

the weakness of the city was attributed to his withdrawal of certain troops he was recalled to Spain in 1554.

But while thus employed in Italy as a statesman and a soldier Mendoza had not been idle in a literary sense, for he had written his political commentaries, a paraphrase of Aristotle, a treatise on mechanics, and other notable works, none of which, however, have achieved for him a tithe of the popularity of his first literary effort.

Lazaro, or, to give him his diminutive name, Lazarillo, was the son of a miller who plied his trade by the banks of the river Tormes, from which he took his name. When he was only ten years old his father was killed in a campaign against the Moors, and as his mother was unable to support him she gave him into the charge of a blind man who wandered about the country as a beggar. While at the bridge of Salamanca the boy noticed an animal carved in stone in the form of a bull, and was told by his master that if he placed his ear to the effigy he would hear it roar. He did so, when the old man gave his head such a violent thump against it as almost to bereave him of sense, and, laughing brutally, told him that a blind man's boy must needs have his wits about him. "I have no silver or gold to give you," said he, "but what is far better, I can impart to you the result of my experiences, which will always enable you to live."

The little Lazarillo had much difficulty in getting enough food to keep body and soul together. The old beggar kept his bread and meat in a linen knapsack, the neck of which was tightly secured. But the boy made a small rent in one of the seams of the bag, and thus helped himself to the choicest pieces of meat, bacon, and sausage. It was his task also to receive the alms which charitable people bestowed on the blind man, and part of this he secreted in his mouth, until, by dint of practice, he was able to hide a goodly treasure of copper money in that receptacle. It irked him on a hot day to watch the beggar drinking his wine while he himself went thirsty. The wine was kept in a large jar, and from time to time he managed to get a sip of the cooling liquor. But his master soon discovered the practice and kept the jar between his knees, with his hand on its mouth. Lazarillo therefore bored a small hole in the bottom of the jar, which he closed with wax. At dinner-time, when the blind beggar sat over the fire, the wax melted, and Lazarillo, putting his mouth to the hole, absorbed the wine. His master was enraged and surprised when he found that the liquor had vanished, and attributed its disappearance to magical means. But the next time his charge attempted the feat the crafty old mendicant seized the jar with both hands and dealt him such a blow on the face with it as to break the vessel and wound the boy severely. From that day Lazarillo bore a grudge against the sightless old tyrant, and took a sly revenge by guiding him over the worst roads he could find and through the deepest mud.

Resolving to quit a service the perquisites of which were all kicks and no halfpence, Lazarillo led his master to the Arcade at Escalona, beside which a brook ran rather swiftly. In order to cross this it was necessary either to jump or to wade almost up to the neck in water, and when this was explained to him the old beggar chose the former method of negotiating it. The crafty Lazarillo told him that the narrowest place was opposite a great stone pillar, and the wretched mendicant, taking

Lazarillo de Tormes

a step or two backward to give him impetus, leapt with such force that he crashed into the pillar, at the bottom of which he immediately fell unconscious. With a shout of triumph Lazarillo ran off, and from that day never set eyes upon the blind man again.

The next master whose service he entered was a priest, and if his experiences with the beggar had been unhappy, they were as nothing to what he now had to bear, for the holy man was a miser of the most pitiful description, and starved him in a shameful manner. He kept his bread in a large wooden chest, to which Lazarillo got a travelling tinker to fit a key during the priest's absence, and was thus able to regale himself daily, until his miserly master discovered the shortage. This he attributed to rats, and as there were several holes in the box he carefully mended it with small pieces of wood; but still the bread disappeared, and as one of the neighbours had seen a snake in the priest's domicile the padre concluded that this reptile was the cause of the depredations. To avoid discovery, Lazarillo slept with the key of the chest in his mouth, but one night his breathing caused a whistling sound upon the orifice of the implement, and the old priest, taking this for the hissing of the snake, delivered such a shrewd blow in the direction of the noise as to render the unfortunate Lazarillo an invalid for some considerable time. When he had recovered, the old priest took him by the hand and, leading him into the street, said to him : " Lazarillo my son, thou hast great natural gifts; thou art indeed far too clever for an old man like me, and I assure thee that I do not wish to see thee more. Farewell."

Lazarillo, however, was not long in attaching himself to another master, who appeared to be a gentleman of birth and breeding. But now he found that he was in worse straits than ever, as though his master seemed a cavalier of family, he had not a penny in the world, and was entirely dependent for his daily bread upon what the boy could beg from charitably disposed persons. One day the landlord called for the rent, and the gentleman, assuring him that he would fetch it from his banker's, sallied forth and never returned, so that once more the wretched urchin was without a master.

He next succeeded in obtaining the patronage of a pardoner who travelled from place to place selling indulgences and relics. On one occasion they stayed at an inn, where his master struck up a friendship with an *alguazil*, or constable. One night the pair sat late carousing, when a quarrel arose between them, and next day, as the pardoner was preaching in the church preparatory to selling his wares, the *alguazil* entered and denounced him as an impostor. The pardoner, with a great show of piety, prayed loudly that the heavenly powers would vindicate his character and would punish the *alguazil*, who immediately fell to the ground in the most dreadful convulsions. Some of the congregation prayed the pardoner that he would attempt some mitigation of the wrath of heaven upon his traducer, and the holy man stepped from the pulpit and laid a bull which he pretended he had received from the Pope upon the sufferer's forehead. The man instantly rose as if cured, and the people, convinced that a miracle had occurred, at once bought up the pardoner's entire stock. But the acute Lazarillo soon discovered that the pair had been in league with one another.

The last master to whose service Lazarillo attached himself was the Arch-priest of Salvador, in whose

Guzman de Alfarache

service he flourished exceedingly, and one of whose servants he married. But scandal crept into his household, and with the death of his wife he found himself as poor as ever.

Here the tale ends. It is impossible in such a brief sketch as this to do justice to the great degree of insight into the workings of the human heart which characterizes the authorship of this little novel, the first of its kind. *Lazarillo de Tormes* was the forerunner and exemplar of the entire school of the Picaresque novel, which at a later date became almost typical of Spanish fiction, and which gave rise to such masterpieces as *Guzman de Alfarache*, the *Gil Blas* of Le Sage, and the novels of Scarron, and the spirit of which to some extent was mirrored in our own Laurence Sterne; nor is its influence by any means defunct, as can readily be seen by reference to certain of the works of Mr Maurice Hewlett and Mr Jeffery Farnol.

Guzman de Alfarache

Mateo Aleman, the author of the great Picaresque romance of *Guzman de Alfarache*, was a native of Seville. Throwing up a Government appointment in early life, he crossed the sea to Mexico, where in 1609 he published a work on Spanish orthography and several treatises in Latin. But the effort which has gained for him the title of novelist was his *Vita del Picaro Guzman de Alfarache*, a work which has been translated into every European language from the date of its first appearance in 1599. Although written in the most correct and approved literary style, it is yet easy and familiar in manner, and is unrivalled in the picture it presents not only of the lowest grades of Castilian society, but of the more exclusive orders of life at the period in which he wrote.

"My ancestors," he says, "were originally from the Levant, but settled in Genoa and employed themselves in the mercantile life of that city in such a manner that they were accused of usury."

Thus the stock from which the lively adventurer came was of such a character as to bring him at an early age into contact with the realities of roguery. But if his relations were by no means particular in trade, they concealed their ignominious conduct under the cloak of hypocrisy and social correctness. They never failed to be present at Mass, and the finger of reproach could not be pointed against their family life. Before Guzman was born his father learned that one of his correspondents at Seville had become bankrupt, and setting out for Spain in order to investigate his affairs on the spot, he was captured by an Algerine pirate, adopted the religion of Mohammed, and married a Moorish lady. His agent at Seville, having heard of what had happened to his principal creditor, adjusted his affairs without him, and was soon in a better condition than ever. But the elder de Alfarache succeeded in making his escape, and, coming to Seville, demanded a reckoning from his rascally business *confrère*, from whom he succeeded in extorting a considerable sum. He set himself up in business at Seville, and bought an estate, which he named St Juan de Alfarache. Here he lived right royally, and, having married the wealthy widow of an old knight, he found himself in a fortunate position. Soon after this his son Guzman was born. But de Alfarache was unfortunately prone to the distractions of company, splendour, and show, and having dissipated most of his means, ere long became himself bankrupt, and shortly afterward paid the debt of nature.

His widow and the little Guzman were only indifferently provided for, and when the boy had entered his fourteenth year he resolved to seek his fortune, and set out for Genoa, in the hope that his father's relations would extend their assistance to him. Soon he arrived at a miserable tavern, where he asked for something to eat, and was given an omelet, which, he says, might more properly have been called an "egg poultice," but which he attacked "as hogs do acorns." Leaving the inn, he soon felt very ill, and in a condition bordering upon collapse he encountered a muleteer, to whom he described the unsavoury meal he had just eaten, and who laughed heartily at his story. The kindly fellow told him to jump on one of his mules, and soon they were trotting nimbly eastward. Shortly after this they met two friars, and arrived at an inn, where they were given another indifferent meal, which the host extolled so much that the simple boy was fain to swallow the mess without making any great ado. But to his horror he later discovered that it had been made from the flesh of a young mule. On being challenged with this the innkeeper drew a long sword, whereupon the muleteer seized a pitchfork, and murder would have been done had not the town police separated the parties. The dishonest landlord was taken to prison, but although he confessed to passing off the mule for veal he would not admit that he had stolen Guzman's cloak, which had gone amissing, and the boy had perforce to leave the place minus this article of apparel.

Riding on their way, Guzman and the muleteer were soon overtaken on the road by two persons on mules, who examined them with the greatest attention, and then quite suddenly threw themselves upon the unfortunate lad, asserting that he had stolen some jewels of value. The muleteer interfered, but only to receive a rough handling, and the strangers tied the comrades to their mules with cords. At this juncture the party was joined once more by the friars, who amused themselves by telling tales, the morals of which hinged upon the mutability of human affairs; but these are much too long and too slightly connected with the thread of our story to be repeated here. The party then arrived at the gates of Cazalla, and the officers of the law, finding that they had made a mistake in arresting Guzman, gave him his liberty. He put up at the best inn that the place afforded, and on the following morning took the direct road to Madrid on foot. At an inn on the outskirts of the capital he met with a beneficent priest, who shared his meal with him, but in the morning the landlord attempted to overcharge him, and was about to take his coat in payment of his bill when the muleteer, who had rejoined him, interfered, and gave it as his opinion that Guzman had run away from home. The villainous landlord, seeing in this some hope of enriching himself, offered to take the lad into his service as a kind of stable-boy, his duty being to hand out straw and oats to the muleteers who put up at the place. Here the young Guzman was initiated into habits of dishonesty and sharp practice, for when a cavalier or person of consequence visited the inn he usually doled out a mere handful of provender to his horses or mules, while charging him the usual sum for it. The place was, indeed, a regular sink of iniquity, and for Guzman life became so miserable that, relying upon the little money he had saved, and selling his coat and waistcoat, he absconded, and joined a passing company of beggars. These people lived right royally on what they begged and what they poached. They were inveterate gamblers, and in the evening Guzman found every opportunity of picking up tricks with playing-cards. Soon after, however, he took employment as scullion to a cook in the service of a nobleman.

Guzman as Scullion

In this situation Guzman passed a jovial time, for there was no lack of good cheer in the knight's establishment. Albeit the lad did his work to admiration. But the vice of gambling seized upon him, and every day he joined the lackeys and pages at cards, often sitting up all night to indulge in this pastime. In this way he soon got rid of the money he received in gratuities, and being short of funds wherewith to gratify his passion for gaming, began to pilfer such small articles as he could find about the house, excusing himself by saying that he only did as others did. One day his master had given a great carouse to some friends, and Guzman entered the room where they had been drinking to find them fast asleep. On the table he observed a large silver goblet, and this he purloined. The cook's wife soon missed the article, and inquiries with regard to it were set afoot, whereupon the cunning youngster, taking the cup to a jeweller, had it cleaned in such a manner that it resembled a new one. Carrying it back to the woman, who was in great fear that her master would hear of the loss, he told her that he had found a similar goblet at a jeweller's, which he could procure for fifty-six *reales*, and, anxious to avert trouble, she at once gave him the sum to purchase it. The money thus dishonestly won was instantly thrown in gaming, and Guzman was no better off than before.

About this time the cook was requested to prepare a splendid dinner for a foreign nobleman who had newly arrived at Madrid. A large sack containing game was entrusted to the lad, and this he carried home, but as it was late he took it up to his own garret. In the middle of the night he was wakened by cats, who fought over one of the hares which he had brought home. Seeing that this was not missed, and that his brother lackeys stole the provisions right and left, Guzman presently slipped half a dozen eggs into his pocket. But the head cook observed him do so, and dealt him such a furious kick that he fell, and the broken eggs gushed from his pocket, to the amusement of all present. Guzman, however, managed to embezzle a couple of partridges and some quails. These he took to sell to another cook, but his master, suspecting him, followed and discovered what he was about, and immediately dismissed him after thrashing him soundly.

After this nothing was left for the young adventurer but to return to his old trade of running errands. He soon heard that certain troops were about to be embarked for Genoa, and resolved to follow them and enlist. A certain old apothecary, who had always found him honest in his dealings, sent him to a foreign merchant with a large quantity of silver, and this Guzman secreted in a large hole by the riverside. In the morning he returned to the place, and, digging up the bags of money, found that they contained two thousand five hundred *reales* in silver and thirty *pistoles* in gold. Slinging the bags on his back, to resemble a traveller's pack, he set off in the direction of Toledo, making his way across the fields and carefully avoiding the high road.

Arriving within two leagues of Toledo, he entered a wood, where he intended to rest the whole of the day, as he did not wish to approach the city till nightfall. His plan was to betake himself to Genoa and introduce himself to his relations, and he was thinking of the best way to lay out his money in order to reach them and make a good appearance before them, when he heard a noise and, turning hastily, beheld a young man of about his own age reclining on the ground, with his head against a tree. Guzman shared his wine with him, and the youth informed him that he was penniless. Guzman offered to buy some of the clothes he carried with him in a bundle, and, opening one of his money-bags, reassured him as to his ability to pay. For a hundred *reales* a handsome suit changed hands, and, taking leave of the stranger, Guzman entered Toledo, where he at once put up at the best inn. Next day he fitted himself out with such articles of attire as he required, but his vanity got the better of him, and he ordered a most magnificent suit, which cost him a long price. On Sunday he betook himself to the cathedral, where he met a very fine lady, who asked him to accompany her home to supper. For this occasion Guzman ordered a magnificent feast, but the pair had hardly sat down to partake of it when a loud knocking was heard at the door, and the lady cried out in alarm that her brother had returned and that he had better conceal himself. The only place in which he could do so with advantage was inside a great inverted bath, and from this place of concealment he had the mortification of beholding the gentleman who entered devour the gorgeous supper which he had provided and drink every drop of the four bottles of wine he had purchased for his own use. Soon the gentleman, having eaten and drunk thus sumptuously, fell sound asleep, and Guzman took the opportunity of stealing from the house, a sadder but a wiser lad.

Hearing that an *alguazil* had been inquiring very particularly regarding him, Guzman hurriedly left Toledo, and, arriving at the town of Almagro, joined the company of soldiers who were bound for Genoa. Their captain, taken with his distinguished appearance, hailed him as a brother in arms, and treated him as an equal. Guzman had engaged the services of a page at Toledo, and this little rascal assisted him greatly in his new sphere by spreading the report that he was a gentleman of consequence. But our hero's purse was now sadly depleted, although he had still about half of his ill-gotten gains left. Instead of embarking at once the company remained at Barcelona for three months, so that his resources soon gave out, and he was neglected by the officers, and even avoided by the soldiers. His captain, indeed, condoled with him, and offered him a place in his household at the servants' table, assuring him that this was all he could do for him, as he himself was compelled to dine out from his utter incapacity to receive his friends at home. Guzman assured him of his gratitude, and hinted that he might in turn be able to assist him. The soldiers were billeted in the village, and Guzman commenced a system of imposing a larger number of men upon each house than was necessary, or at least threatening to do so, so that the anxious inhabitants were only too glad to buy him off. In this manner he completely re-established the captain's finances, and as presents of provisions poured in from the frightened villagers the young rascal and his chief lived well. But he now grew bolder, and, selecting half a dozen of the most desperate men in the company, began to rob passengers on the high road. His captain, learning of this, however, immediately put a stop to such dangerous proceedings.

One day Guzman observed that among the few jewels the captain still had left to him there was a very handsome gold reliquary set with diamonds, and this he begged his superior to lend him for a few days. The audacious stripling at once took it to a jeweller's, to whom he offered it for two hundred crowns. But the man would only tender him a hundred and twenty, and this Guzman refused. The jeweller called upon him next day to renew his offer, which the lad accepted. Guzman handed him the purse in which the reliquary was kept, receiving the hundred and twenty crowns in exchange. But the old fellow had scarcely left the house when the young adventurer raised a cry of "Stop thief! Stop thief!" Some soldiers immediately arrested the jeweller, and Guzman cried out that he had robbed him of the captain's reliquary. The jeweller assured the arquebusiers that he had paid a hundred and twenty crowns for the article, but this Guzman denied. The wretched goldsmith was haled before a magistrate, and, as he had a bad reputation for usury, was forced to disgorge the reliquary. But although the captain was glad enough to get the money thus scurvily gained, he feared that further association with such a rascal as de Alfarache would ruin him. In a few days the company set sail for Genoa, and when they had arrived there his superior intimated that they must part, at the same time thrusting a *pistole* into his hand.

Tormented by Devils

The young adventurer now began to make inquiries about his relations, and was informed that they were the most rich and powerful persons in the republic. He inquired the way to their mansion, where he was but ill received, all the more so as his appearance was shabby in the extreme. But as he had taken care to make his relationship to them public property, they could not very well repulse him. One evening he met a venerable-looking old man, who told him that he had known his father, and that he felt quite indignant at the behaviour of his relations toward him, and offered him an asylum at his own house. Without giving him anything to eat, he at once sent him to bed, where the wretched lad lay tormented by the pangs of hunger. Before he went to sleep the old man informed him that the room he occupied had the reputation of being haunted by evil spirits. Famished and restless, Guzman lay awake, when to his horror four figures in the shape of devils entered the chamber and dragged him out of bed. Throwing him into a blanket, they tossed him in the air with such violence that he struck the ceiling again and again, until, exhausted by the exercise, they placed him in bed once more and departed. In the early morning, stiff, sore, and dejected, Guzman crawled from the mansion, but he registered an oath never to forget the detestable manner in which his acquaintance had treated him, and resolved to be avenged upon him at the first opportunity.

Guzman Joins the Beggars of Rome

Leaving Genoa in this miserable plight, in which he compares himself to one of those who escaped from the

Guzman de Alfarache

battle of Roncesvalles, Guzman resolved to make his way to Rome. Italy, he says, is the most charitable country in the world, and anyone who can beg can travel within its bounds without concerning himself about his next meal. In a few weeks he found himself in the Roman Catholic capital, with money enough in his pocket to buy a new suit of clothes, but he resisted the temptation to do so, and wandered about the streets of the Imperial city seeking alms. He soon fell in with a comrade in distress, who enlightened him regarding the manners and customs of the beggars of Rome and who gave him such good instructions that he soon received more money than he could spend. In a short time Guzman was a perfect master of the trade of begging. After spending some weeks in this kind of life he fell in with one of the master-beggars of the city, who instructed him in the laws of begging, which he sets forth at length in his autobiography. These laws Guzman got by heart. The beggars lived together, and met in the evening to practise and invent new exclamations to excite pity. In the morning there was usually a scramble among them to see who could get nearest the holy water at the entrance to the churches, for there it was that the greatest harvest was reaped, and in the evening the beggars usually made a round of the country seats in the neighbourhood of Rome, whence they returned laden with provisions. Nearly all of the beggars were adepts at simulating bodily malformations or loathsome diseases. On one occasion, in the town of Gaeta, Guzman simulated a terrible disease of the head, and the Governor, who was passing, gave him alms. Next day he sat at the porch of a church with what appeared to be a grievous affection of the leg, and much money was flowing in upon him, when unhappily the Governor chanced to pass, and recognizing him, told him that he would give him some cast-off clothing if he would follow him home. Arrived there the Governor asked him by what singular remedy he had contrived to cure himself of his former complaint within the short space of one day, and without waiting for an answer sent for a surgeon, who, on examining the leg, assured the Governor that it was perfectly sound. The Governor then handed Guzman over to his lackeys, who trounced him severely and thrust him forth from the town.

One morning our rascally hero had posted himself at the gate of a certain Cardinal celebrated for his compassionate disposition, who, on passing and hearing his plaint, told his domestics to convey the seeming sufferer to a chamber in his mansion and attend to his wants. Guzman had once more simulated a terrible disease of the leg, and the Cardinal, observing this, sent for two of the most celebrated surgeons in Rome. Their preparations were of such a nature that Guzman feared they were about to amputate his leg, so when they consulted together in an adjoining room he went to the door to listen to what they were saying. One of them gave it as his opinion that the disorder was merely a bogus one, but the other as warmly maintained that it was genuine. At length they agreed to lay their deliberations before the Cardinal, and were about to do so when Guzman, entering the room where they consulted, admitted his fraud, and proposed that they should combine in deceiving the Cardinal. To this the surgeons agreed, and when his Eminence appeared they made the most alarming and touching report regarding Guzman's sham disorder. The Cardinal, who was a man of lofty character and unsuspicious nature, begged them to take as much time as they thought proper in effecting a cure, and to neglect nothing that might contribute to the patient's recovery. So anxious were the surgeons to pile up their fees that they compelled Guzman to keep his bed for three months, which appeared three ages to him, so keen was his desire to return to the gaming which had become second nature to him. At the end of this time they presented their bill to the Cardinal, telling him that a complete cure had been effected, and so pleased was the churchman at having assisted in so remarkable a case, and so keen his appreciation of Guzman's native wit, that he ended by taking the youthful charlatan into his service as one of his pages.

Guzman was, however, not very well satisfied with his new life, which in great measure consisted in waiting in ante-chambers and serving at table. The discipline was rigorous, and all that he could purloin was a few candle-ends. But he found that a large quantity of very fine preserved fruit was kept in a certain chest, and to this he applied himself. The Cardinal discovered the peculation, yet failed to trace it to its source; but when Guzman was rifling the chest on a second occasion his Eminence entered and caught him in the act. He received a thorough castigation at the hands of the major-domo, which put an end to his knaveries for some considerable time.

Guzman Cheats a Banker

But Guzman played so many tricks in the Cardinal's palace that at length this excellent prelate had to dispense with his services. He then entered the service of the Spanish Ambassador, who was a friend of the Cardinal's, and who knew all about our hero's capacities. After some considerable time spent in the service of this dignitary, Guzman resolved to leave Rome for a tour through Italy. Shortly before this he had encountered a Spaniard called Sayavedra, with whom he became very friendly. Provided with about three hundred *pistoles* and some jewels, which he had purloined from the ambassador, Guzman set out on his travels. But Sayavedra had taken a wax impression of Guzman's keys, and pilfered his luggage before he left, so that if it had not been for the generosity of the ambassador he could not have left Rome. At Siena, however, Guzman fell in with Sayavedra once more, who entreated him to pardon his perfidy, and offered to become his servant. Guzman, who was sorry for his miserable condition, agreed to the proposal, and the pair, going to Florence, began to concert measures for improving their position. It was bruited abroad that Guzman was a nephew of the Spanish Ambassador, and he even had the insolence to present himself at Court, where he was received by the Grand Duke in that capacity. Here he met a charming widow of great wealth, with whom he fell violently in love. But her relatives, making inquiries about him, discovered that he had once begged in the streets of Rome, and he was forced to leave the city. At Bologna he gained a good deal of money at play, and on arriving at Milan he and Sayavedra took apartments in that city and cast about for some means of putting their newly acquired funds to use. Here they soon fell in with a rascally friend employed as clerk in a banker's house, and concerted with him as to how they should relieve his master of his surplus wealth. Guzman called upon the banker and told him he wished to deposit with him about twelve thousand francs in gold. He was well received, and the financier entered his name and other particulars in his daybook. On his way home he bought a gilt casket, which he filled with pieces of lead, and, giving this to Sayavedra, along with a bag of real money, enjoined that he should get into conversation with the landlord of the inn where they were staying, and tell him that he was taking the cash to the banker's house—which of course he was not to do. The banker's clerk got false keys made to fit his master's coffer, and, when the latter was at Mass on Sunday, he opened it and placed therein the gilt casket, which, instead of lead, now contained ten quadruples, thirty Roman crowns, and a written account of its contents. He then counterfeited his master's handwriting, and completed the entry in the daybook which he had begun, making it appear that not only the casket, but all the money in the coffer, had been credited to Guzman.

On the Monday Guzman called at the banker's and asked him very politely to return the cash that had been sent to him a few days before. The man naturally denied that any sum had been lodged with him at all, whereupon Guzman made so great an outcry that a large crowd collected, and the quarrel assumed such a serious aspect that a constable appeared on the scene, accompanied by the landlord of the inn at which Guzman was staying. Guzman asserted that if the banker's books were examined the sum he mentioned would be found noted in them, and on the daybook being produced this was proved to be the case. The wretched banker admitted that part of the writing was in his own hand, and this was sufficient to incense the crowd, with whom he had a very bad reputation for usury and sharp practice. Guzman, too, was able to give a most circumstantial account of the contents of the coffer, which, on being opened, was found, to the banker's amazement, to contain the gilt casket he spoke of and the exact sum named by him, including even the various coinages he had enumerated and the written note of its contents. The landlord was able to corroborate Guzman's ownership of the casket, and as the evidence seemed conclusive the local magistrate awarded him the money, which he divided with his confederates.

Guzman now resolved to return to Genoa for the purpose of being revenged upon the relatives who had treated him so scurvily upon his previous visit to that city. Disguising himself as a Spanish abbot of consequence, he put up at the best inn of the place, and his relatives, learning of his arrival, and of the pomp he displayed, hastened to pay their respects to him. They failed to identify him with the ragged and friendless urchin who had sought their assistance some years before, and his uncle even retailed the adventure of the devils to him as if it had been played upon an impostor. Guzman completely gained their confidence, and as he had plenty of money to spare they readily entrusted to his keeping a valuable collection of jewels, which he told them a friend desired to borrow for his wedding ceremony. With these he and Sayavedra made off to Spain, but on the way the latter fell ill of a fever, and, rushing on the deck of the galley, threw himself overboard and was drowned.

Guzman, reaching his native country, after a number

Guzman de Alfarache

of adventures arrived in Madrid, where he sold his jewels to a rich merchant, who, believing him to be a person of consequence, gave him his daughter in marriage. The merchant relied upon Guzman's supposed wealth to further his financial operations, Guzman relied upon his father-in-law's equally supposititious resources, and as the extravagant young wife relied on both, all were soon plunged into bankruptcy. The shock was too much for the lady, and she expired, but her cunning parent succeeded in saving sufficient from the wreck to commence business once more.

Guzman, however, was tired of the world of finance, and decided to invest the remainder of his ill-gotten gains in studying for the Church. With this object in view, he betook himself to the university of Alcalà de Henares, where he took his Bachelor of Arts degree, and after four years' hard reading at divinity only awaited a benefice to permit him to graduate as a full-fledged priest, when evil influences once more began to beset him. He made the acquaintance of a lady who had a family of daughters, with one of whom he became infatuated, and whom he married. The pair betook themselves to Madrid, where they embarked upon an adventurous career, after some years of which the lady eloped, taking with her everything of value which she could lay hands upon. By this time Guzman had presented himself to his mother, who, so far from dissuading him from his evil courses, assisted him in his schemes of roguery, so that shortly, going from bad to worse, he found himself doomed to a long period of servitude in the royal galleys. But here he was able to assist the authorities in discovering a mutiny, for which he was rewarded with his freedom.

Legends & Romances of Spain

At this stage we take our leave of the most consummate rogue in fiction ; but if Guzman de Alfarache is perhaps the most wily scoundrel in the records of romance, he is certainly one of the most original and amusing. It is noticeable, however, that his career, on the whole, was not a remunerative one, and that when he makes his farewell bow to us he is no better off than when we first encountered him. Perhaps the most amusing thing about his narrative is the sham propriety of tone in which it is couched—a style which was almost slavishly copied by Le Sage in his *Gil Blas*, who was not only obliged to this novel for its general atmosphere, but for many of the incidents which occur in his celebrated work.

Conclusion

We have trodden the ways of Spanish story, sublime, mock-heroic, and humorous. Perhaps no chapter in the world's literature is so rich in colour, or displays such a variety of mood and sentiment. Still the key-note is one of noble and dignified beauty, of chivalrous distinction, of exquisite propriety, courteous, immaculate, and un-spotted by vulgarity or sordid meanness. The wine-cup of Spanish romance is filled with the heart's blood of a nation august, knightly, imaginative, a people who have preferred ideals to gross realities, and the heights of national aristocracy to the deserts of false democracy "Poor Spain!" How often does the Anglo-Saxon utter the phrase in complacent self-assurance? With the solace of such a treasure-house of poetic and romantic wealth as she possesses, Spain may well rest in assured hope of the return of the brave days in praise of which her trovadores struck the lyre and her poets sang in stately

Conclusion

epic.   Poor Spain!   Nay, golden Spain—enchanted
cavern, glowing with the spoil of song, the rainbow
treasure of legend, and the gem-like radiance of immortal
romance!

> Her citizens, imperial spirits,
> Rule the present from the past ;
> On all this world of men inherits
> Their seal is set.